Intention and Interpretation

In the series
The Arts and Their Philosophies,
edited by
Joseph Margolis

Intention and
Interpretation

EDITED BY GARY ISEMINGER

Temple University Press

Philadelphia

Temple University Press
Philadelphia 19122
Copyright © 1992 by Temple University
All rights reserved
Published 1992
Printed in the United States of America

The paper used in this publication
meets the minimum requirements of
American National Standard for
Information Sciences—Permanence of
Paper for Printed Library Materials
ANSI Z39.48-1984 ∞

Library of Congress
Cataloging-in-Publication Data
Intention and interpretation / edited by
Gary Iseminger.
        p.   cm.—(The Arts and
    their philosophies)
    Includes bibliographical references
    and index.
    ISBN 0-87722-971-6
    I. Literature—Philosophy. 2. Intention
(Logic) in literature. 3. Criticism.
I. Iseminger, Gary. II. Series.
PN49.I66 1992
801'.95—dc20   92-1325

For *Andrea*,
for twenty-five years

Contents

Preface

WHAT IS THE CONNECTION, if any, between the author's intentions in (while) writing a work of literature and the truth (acceptability, validity) of interpretive statements about it? For the twenty years or so immediately following World War II, most of those who thought about the matter, reflecting the practice of the then New Criticism and echoing Wimsatt and Beardsley's seminal paper "The Intentional Fallacy" (1946), would have answered, without further ado, "None whatsoever!" Having been trained in that way at that time, I remember being somewhat taken aback when I first encountered the central text of what Beardsley has called the intentionalist "backlash," Hirsch's defense in *Validity in Interpretation* (1967) of "the sensible view that a text means what its author meant." I remember reading Hirsch's book and finding that he not only held this retrograde view but had an argument for it. I remember setting to work analyzing the argument to find out what was wrong with it, for I supposed that something *must* be wrong with it. But one of my principles of interpretation—of arguments at least, I will not say that it applies to works of literature—is a principle of charity: do the best you can by the text. And as I set to work on Hirsch's argument in this spirit, it seemed to me that I could do surprisingly well by it.

The argument as I eventually reconstructed it—perhaps it is not really Hirsch's argument finally, for such are the risks of charity—seemed neither to commit obvious blunders nor to depend on obviously false premises. The more I discussed it with various philosophers and literary theorists in various forums, the stronger it came to seem to me. At the least, what the reconstructed argument did was to identify very clearly just what needed to be assumed if an intentionalist position was to be secured in anything like Hirsch's way, and hence what the premises were, at least one of which must be challenged by anyone who wishes to avoid the intentionalist conclusion. And as I thought about what would have to be done to defend those premises, it seemed to me that almost immediately one got into very deep waters, not only in aesthetics, but in the philosophy of language, in the philosophy of mind, and even in ontology.

The idea then occurred to me of a larger project for which Hirsch's argument would serve as a starting point and the substance of which would consist of explorations of issues involving both the presuppositions of the argument and the consequences of accepting its conclusion. As I foraged through the literature with this project in mind, I discovered several discussions of Hirsch that seemed to identify the crucial points of contention admirably and to point out the directions one would have to take if one were to contest particular assumptions of the Hirschian argument. Thus Hirsch's argument was joined by discussions of it by Beardsley, Margolis, Knapp and Michaels, and Shusterman as central to my own reflections on these questions.

Finally, perhaps my own laziness and certainly my sense that others were better equipped to deal with these issues than I led me to conceive the project not as a monograph but as a collection, beginning with Hirsch's argument and the previously published critical discussions of his position just mentioned, edited to highlight the relevant alternatives, followed by my own attempt to identify and set out the issues and the alternative responses to them, and concluding with commissioned explorations of these alternatives by writers I knew to be interested in the subject and I hoped would articulate and defend the full range of possibilities. The result, I hoped, would be a volume more cooperatively written than collected and more unified than most anthologies.

I approached prospective contributors, some of whom I knew but many of whom I did not, on the basis of my knowledge of their work on this and related subjects. In the event, most of those whose work is included here are philosophers rather than literary theorists, and philosophers trained in the Anglo-American rather than the continental tradition. I do not think that the resulting bias, if such it be, means that the concerns of literary theorists or of philosophers in the continental tradition are slighted by the book. The one bias to which I admit is a bias in favor of the assessment of *arguments* as the most fruitful way to try to achieve some understanding on issues such as those discussed in this book. So literary critics such as Hirsch and Knapp and Michaels are included precisely because they have advanced their views by strikingly presented and eminently discussable arguments. And many of the "analytically" trained contributors not only discuss but are notably sympathetic to ideas, both continental and domestic, that currently challenge what were once perhaps matters of consensus among their mentors and peers.

I thank Carleton College, and especially Deans Peter Stanley and Roy Elveton, for two summer grants, under one of which a first draft of my contribution was written and under the other of which final editing was done; the Institute for Advanced Studies in the Humanities at Edinburgh University, and especially Assistant Director (now Director) Peter Jones, where I wrote a first draft of the Introduction; my fellow contributors, especially Richard Shusterman and Jerrold Levinson, for their cooperation and encouragement; Michael Hancher, for a helpful review and important suggestions; George Soule, for literary consultation; and Nikki Lamberty and Sharlet Johnson for help in preparing the manuscript.

Gary Iseminger

Introduction

I

"WHAT DOES THE LITERARY INTERPRETER do? He tells us what a literary work means." Thus says Monroe Beardsley,[1] who has written as thoughtfully and influentially on the subject as any philosopher in the past fifty years, and this is as good a place to start as any. Though there may well be ways of embodying interpretations that do not involve saying *what* something means (for example, reading a poem out loud), I shall follow Beardsley's lead and concentrate on what interpreters *say*, on *interpretive remarks*. Consider some putative examples:

1. Gerard Manley Hopkins's poem "Henry Purcell" refers to a famous English composer.

2. The poem "Henry Purcell" expresses the wish that Purcell shall have had good fortune.

3. "Henry Purcell" is a Roman Catholic poem.

Though none of these remarks is explicitly framed in terms of the notion of *meaning*, there seems to be no difficulty in regarding them as making claims about different aspects of the meaning of the works they mention. Now some might object to the inclusion of (1) on this list, on the grounds that for there to be an interpretation, there must be a *puzzle* to solve or a difficulty to overcome, and this one is just too easy. Others, perhaps somewhat similarly motivated, might not even be all that happy with (2), thinking of interpretations as more global pronouncements about the ideology of the work as a whole, more on the lines of (3). Without trying to legislate the proper use of "interpret," or claiming to analyze it, I want to focus attention primarily on remarks like (1) and (2), leaving remarks like (3) to take care of themselves. My reasons for this strategy are that the problems discussed in this book can, in general, be seen to arise most easily with simpler, more literal, more particularized and local cases, like (1) and (2), and, more important, that the discussion of these problems as they arise for examples more in the range of (3) is parasitic on discussion of the simpler cases. In general, questions about interpretation in the relatively banal sense suggested by Beardsley's characterization and exemplified by (1) and (2)—interpretation as, roughly, the attempt to understand reference and sense—will give us enough to be getting on with at first.

Interpretation, as exemplified by remarks like (1) and (2), is often usefully distinguished from *description* and from *evaluation*. Without necessarily endorsing this threefold distinction, and certainly without trying to explicate it or probe its boundaries, one might still provisionally suggest the extent of the domain of interpretation in this dimension by instancing clear cases of remarks about works of literature that fall outside that domain and in one of the others. A remark that seems to be paradigmatically *descriptive*, for example, is this:

4. The first line of "Henry Purcell" contains two occurrences of the word "have," two occurrences of the word "fallen," and three occurrences of the word "fair."

A remark that seems to be paradigmatically *evaluative* is this:

5. "Henry Purcell" is a great poem.

Much could be said about relations among these kinds of remarks. It seems plausible to suggest, for example, that description is logically prior to interpretation, which is, in turn, logically prior to evaluation. That is, what a literary work means is a function of, among other things, what words it contains (but not vice versa), while its value is a function of, among other things, what it means (but not vice versa). This is not to suggest that description is necessarily easy and unproblematic. Think of the difficulties of textual scholarship, which is just the attempt to establish what words occur how often and in what order in the work. Nor does the "order of knowing" necessarily replicate the logical order just suggested. It is not uncommon to conjecture that a text must go in a certain way on the grounds that it very likely had a certain meaning, and some have advocated making interpretive judgments on the grounds that a certain interpretation makes the work better. These issues deserve attention in themselves, but the focus of this book, insofar as possible, is mainly on the nature of interpretive remarks themselves, rather than on relations between them and other sorts of remarks.

II

We can get a further fix on our topic by observing that literature is, first, a *linguistic* phenomenon and, further, an *artistic* one—works of literature are linguistic works of art. The question of what it is to interpret a literary work may well be illuminated, then, by comparing that activity with others that come to the fore when one systematically varies the parameters of "linguisticality" and "artiness" in this description.

1. What can we learn about the interpretation of literary works by reflecting on the interpretation of nonlinguistic works of art, which comprises at least some of the activities of musical performers and conductors and the activities of critics of the visual arts. What, if anything, is special about interpreting works of *literary* art?

2. How is the interpretation of literary works of art to be compared with the interpretation of linguistic entities—texts or utterances—that make no claim to the status of art? How different is it in principle from the typically routine and everyday process of understanding what we read (newspapers, statutes, contracts, street signs, price tags) and hear (requests, greetings, promises, gossip)? What, if anything, is special about interpreting works of literary *art*?

3. What insights, if any, can we gain by reflecting on the interpretation of things that are neither works of art nor linguistic entities (diagrams, road signs, body language, dreams, clothing, cultural institutions and practices, archeological remains, geological formations)? Where does the interpretation of literary works of art fit into interpretation generally, even of nonlinguistic nonworks of art?

If one pursues the first line, stressing the connections among notions of interpretation spanning the various arts, one may be inclined to emphasize those aspects of literary interpretation that go beyond the mere unfolding of verbal meaning; one will perhaps see interpretation as having essentially to do with works of art in their "artiness," and so understanding a poem by Wordsworth, performing a concerto by Mozart, and "reading" a painting by Brueghel can come to seem to have more in common with one another than any of these, even the first, has in common with reading the morning newspaper.

Those who pursue the second comparison, in contrast, may be more inclined to see the issues primarily as issues in the philosophy of language, issues that arise about the ways in which we understand in general what people mean by what they say. They will perhaps not be especially impressed by the "literariness" of literature as a key to grasping what fundamentally goes on when we try to understand a poem, which is not to say that they must deny any important distinction between "A slumber did my spirit seal" and the day's report on hog futures.

Finally, to the extent that one stresses the connections between literary interpretation and the understanding of the nonlinguistic and nonartistic, one will see it as but a small corner of an endeavor with wider scope even than the philosophy of language or the philosophy of art—a general theory of symbol systems, perhaps, or of semiosis.

III

Although these wider frameworks within which reflections on the interpretation of literature may be set (whether profitably or not) concern many of the writers who have contributed to this volume, what I would like to do here is to consider another philosophical context for these questions, a context that is, so to speak, orthogonal to the frameworks just outlined. This is a context that can only be described as metaphysical, for the arguments and rejoinders in the essays that follow inevitably entail or presuppose answers to fundamental questions in "first philosophy," not just in the philosophy of language or the philosophy of art. I pose these questions in such a way that in general each question presupposes an answer to its predecessor. In this way it is possible to see some of the ways in which the questions interact, but I do not undertake to defend the answers presupposed, nor do I mean to suggest that later questions could not be reformulated to take account of different answers to the earlier questions than the answers I shall presuppose. (Yet, some of the disputes between the authors represented in this book are precisely over whether a particular answer to one of these questions does or does not entail a particular answer to another one.)

As I proceed through the questions, I try to situate the views of the authors of the previously published essays reprinted in the first part of the book—Hirsch, Beardsley, Margolis, Knapp and Michaels, and Shusterman—in the "space" thus provided. In this way the stage is set for the ensuing new essays by me, Carroll, Lyas, Krausz, Shusterman, Nathan, and Hermerén, and for Levinson's concluding essay, which responds to these new essays as well as advancing the argument in its own right.

Can there be good reasons for interpretive remarks like (1) and (2) at the start of this essay? Not everything that people say is subject to assessment by the standards of rationality; sometimes to ask people what their *reason* is for making a remark, as opposed to what *caused* them to make it, is inept. (I shall let the reader supply his or her own favorite example.) But (1) and (2) do not seem to be in this sense irrational remarks; it is natural to imagine either one of them as part of a conversation in which someone, on being asked what reason he or she had for the remark, would feel obliged to make a serious reply. All of our primary authors seem to agree on this point.

Are interpretive remarks like (1) and (2) statements with truth-values? Standards of rationality, though doubtless most often conceived of in terms of the rationality of *believing* some statement or proposition to be *true*, need not only be so conceived. Actions, requests, projects, hopes—these and many more may all be judged rational or irrational. If one finds such a "nonpropositional" construal of interpretive remarks attractive, a plausible alternative might involve thinking of them as *recommendations*—"Try reading the poem this way," rather than "This is what the poem in fact means." So a yes answer to the first question still leaves this new question open.

Margolis denies that interpretive remarks are straightforwardly true or false, but he argues that "truth-like" values (e.g., plausibility) attach to them.[2] It remains for Shusterman to insist that Margolis concedes too much to the (as he thinks) bankrupt idea of "an essential core of fixed, determinate, descriptive properties that constitute the work of art and are to be represented (even if augmented or extended) by valid interpretation"[3] and to stake out an austerely nonpropositional position, rejecting Margolis's contention that one should not infer from the fact that interpretive remarks are not straightforwardly true or false that they "lack a propositional form."[4]

Are the truth-values of interpretive statements like (1) and (2) determined solely by the state of the literary work they are about, or are they determined by relations between the work and something else? Supposing that we do not take the nonpropositional line and thus do attribute truth-values to interpretive remarks, one might still ask whether the states of affairs that would make these remarks true are relational or not. It is, of course, not always evident when a statement expresses a "relational fact." When we say that someone is intelligent (at first sight a property rather than a relation), for example, we may really be saying that she or he is more intelligent than most of her or his peers (a complex relation). Philosophers who have defended "ideal observer" theories (of ethical properties, say, or of perceptual qualities) argue, in effect, that what appear to be properties of objects are really relations between them and observers. Those who, like Hirsch, insist that the author's intention is determinative of the meaning of a literary work may be seen as claiming that the "fact" of meaning is relational in this way. On their view, one might say, the meaning that the interpreter seeks to grasp is a function of two variables, a text and an author. At least that is how Beardsley seems to interpret Hirsch when, in rejecting Hirsch's intentionalism, he invokes as one of his axioms what he calls the "Principle of Autonomy": "literary works are self-sufficient entities, whose properties are decisive in checking interpretations."[5]

Do interpretive statements like (1) and (2) have "bivalent" truth-values, that is, must they be either true or false? Is it so, for each one, that it is definitely true or false, whichever the case may be, and apart from how hard it may be for anyone to come to know which it is? Is it so that for any interpretive judgment and its direct denial (say, " 'Henry Purcell' expresses the wish that Purcell shall have had good fortune" and " 'Henry Purcell' does not express the wish that Purcell shall have had good fortune"), one of them is true and the other false?

One way in which the answer might be no would be if meaning were not only relational in the sense just considered but were "relative" in an individualistic (or cultural) sense. Not only is the "quality" of deliciousness, for example, evidently relational, but there seems in addition to be no "standard" relation (e.g., of the object to an ideal observer) that grounds it. Deliciousness is neither a quality of an "autonomous" object nor a relation between a (heteronomous?) object and an ideal observer; it is, to speak loosely, a relation between an object and a varying observer.[6] If interpretive remarks fit this model, of course, there would be no question of their having bivalent truth-values simpliciter. A literary work might have a certain meaning for me and not for you; the remark that it has (or does not have) that meaning (like the remark that someone is taller) would be neither true nor false until the other term of the relation were specified.

It is Margolis among our primary authors who is most insistent that interpretive remarks do not have bivalent truth-values, but it is not clear that his reasons are of the sort just adumbrated. His "Robust Relativism" seems rather to involve the more interesting claim that works of literature are "ontologically peculiar" in that they are of their very nature indeterminate, and that is why interpretive remarks about them need be neither true nor false. He argues that, like persons, artworks, words and sentences, and actions, they are "culturally emergent" entities, a status implying that their interpretation supports a "tolerance of alternative and seemingly contrary hypotheses." In defending his view, furthermore, he insists that the rationality of interpretation can be preserved without determinateness ("to be 'indeterminate' with respect to truth and falsity is not to be epistemically indeterminate");[7] a yes answer to our first question need not force our hand here, any more than it did with respect to the second and third questions.

The question whether or not a literary work is a "determinate" entity in this sense is one of the central questions of this volume, for the determinacy of meaning is one of the crucial premises of the Hirschian argument around which it revolves. That meaning is determinate (perhaps even that the notion of an entity of *any* sort that is *not* determinate is incoherent)[8] is supposed by Hirsch and Beardsley both, and it is the chief point at which Margolis parts company with them.[9]

Determinateness, though, means more for Hirsch than what has so far been suggested. "Verbal meaning, then, is what it is and not something else, and it is always the same. That is what I mean by determinacy."[10] Beardsley is equally clear that texts have "determinate meanings,"[11] though the defense of the *changelessness* of meaning is no part of his project, for one of his arguments against Hirsch depends on the assumption that the meaning of a text can change, and it may well be that what *he* calls determinate would be stigmatized by Hirsch as really only an indeterminate set of "possibilities."[12]

Whether there is agreement between Hirsch and Beardsley sufficient to allay the suspicion that the crucial differences between them are located here, then, is not easy to say. It is important to note, though, that they would agree that the sort of determinateness for which they both contend is fully compatible with the possibility of ambiguity. A literary work that is in fact ambiguous has determinately *both* meanings in question. The interpretive statement saying it has them both is true, and the interpretive statement denying that it has both is false. The interpretive statement saying it has only one is false; the interpretive statement denying that it has only one is true. The interpretive statement saying it has at least one is true; the interpretive statement denying that it has at least one is false. And so on.

Do the bivalent truth-values of interpretive statements like (1) and (2) depend at least in part on the truth-values of statements about the intentions of the authors of the works those statements are about? Suppose we accept the determinacy of works of literature, then Hirsch's argument, summarized in the following passage, is that this determinacy entails intentionalism.

> A determinate verbal meaning requires a determining will. Meaning is not made determinate simply by virtue of its being represented by a determinate sequence of words. Obviously, any brief word sequence could represent quite different complexes of verbal meaning, and the same is true of long word sequences, though it is less

obvious. If that were not so, competent and intelligent speakers of a language would not disagree as they do about the meaning of texts. But if a determinate word sequence does not in itself necessarily represent one, particular, self-identical, unchanging complex of meaning, then the determinacy of its verbal meaning must be accounted for by some other discriminating force which causes the meaning to be *this* instead of *that* or *that* or *that*, all of which it could be. That discriminating force must involve an act of will, since unless one particular complex of meaning is *willed* (no matter how "rich" and "various" it might be), there would be no distinction between what an author does mean by a word sequence and what he could mean by it. Determinacy of verbal meaning requires an act of will.[13]

Beardsley, of course, committed to at least some part of Hirsch's determinacy thesis but firmly opposed to intentionalism, must insist that at least that part of determinacy he accepts does *not* have the intentionalist consequences Hirsch claims to discern in it.

Supposing that the inference from determinateness to intentionalism is at all plausible, however, then anyone tempted by it has to be careful to recognize that a yes answer to our question is still compatible with the admission that there may well be fallacious appeals to intention in interpretation—for example, the supposition that the work should be judged according to what the author intended as opposed to what he or she achieved or that the author, being an authority on his or her own intentions, is therefore necessarily correct about the truth or falsity of any interpretive statements about his or her work.

Furthermore, the defender of intentionalism undertakes a responsibility to the vast recent philosophical literature on intention that finds inspiration in the work of Wittgenstein. If it often seems that some objections to the invocation of intention in criticism depend on views of intentions as private mental events that might not survive Wittgensteinian criticism, it may also seem that the Hirschian invocation of intention is equally susceptible to this kind of objection.

Do the truth-values of interpretive statements like (1) *and* (2) *depend only on the truth-value of statements about the intentions of the authors of the works they are about?* Hirsch's intentionalism recognizes the constraining power of language with respect to intention. It does not suppose with Humpty-Dumpty that when an author uses a word it means whatever he or she wants it to mean, and it thus aims to evade the force of a negative answer to Wittgenstein's rhetorical question

"Can I say 'bububu' and mean 'If it doesn't rain I shall go for a walk'?"[14] It sees the meaning of a literary work as a function of (at least) the capacities of the language in which it is written and the intentions of the author, a blending of convention and intention. It remains to Knapp and Michaels to argue against there being in *any* sense "a moment of interpretation"[15] prior to intention and thus to defend an intentionalist position with respect to the meaning of works of literature even more extreme than Hirsch's. What they say, that "the meaning of a text is simply identical to the author's intended meaning,"[16] does not sound very much different from what Hirsch says, that "a text means what its author meant," but they really *mean* it!

The pursuit of these questions leads inevitably to some of the most difficult and disputed territory in philosophy. While avoiding the temptation to declare intellectual bankruptcy, we do well to remember William Gass's remark that "in philosophy, you settle one bill only by neglecting another, a strategy which must eventually be seen to fail since all of them fall due at the same time."[17]

Gary Iseminger

NOTES

1. See Chapter 2, pp. 24–25.
2. See Chapter 3, p. 44.
3. See Chapter 5, p. 72.
4. See Chapter 5, p. 69.
5. See Chapter 2, p. 24.
6. I am reminded of Bertrand Russell's claim that the phrase "'a man' denotes not many men, but an ambiguous man." See Bertrand Russell, "On Denoting," in *Readings in Philosophical Analysis*, ed. Herbert Feigl and Wilfrid Sellars (New York: Appleton-Century-Crofts, 1949), p. 103.
7. See Chapter 3, p. 48.
8. For an argument to this effect, see Gareth Evans, "Can There Be Vague Objects?" *Analysis* 38 (1978).
9. Interestingly enough, Margolis, while certainly not endorsing this point, recognizes the force of something very much like it. "The idea that something is both actual *and* indeterminate in structurally important respects (not concerned with vague boundaries or the like) verges on the incoherent or the ontologically monstrous." See Joseph Margolis, "Aesthetic Interests and Aesthetic Qualities,"

introduction to pt. 1 of *Philosophy Looks at the Arts: Contemporary Readings in Aesthetics*, 3d ed. (Philadelphia: Temple University Press, 1987), p. 9.

10. See Chapter 1, p. 16.

11. See Chapter 2, pp. 31–32.

12. See Chapter 1, p. 15.

13. See Chapter 1, p. 16.

14. Ludwig Wittgenstein, *Philosophical Investigations* (New York: Macmillan, 1953), p. 18.

15. See Chapter 4, p. 53.

16. See Chapter 4, p. 51.

17. William Gass, *On Being Blue: A Philosophical Inquiry* (Boston: Godine, 1976), p. 65.

In Defense of the Author

1

E. D. HIRSCH, JR.

I

IT IS A TASK FOR the historian of culture to ex-
plain why there has been in the past four decades a heavy and largely victorious assault on the sensible belief that a text means what its author meant. In
the earliest and most decisive wave of the attack (launched by Eliot, Pound,
and their associates) the battleground was literary: the proposition that textual meaning is independent of the author's control was associated with the
literary doctrine that the best poetry is impersonal, objective, and autonomous; that it leads an afterlife of its own, totally cut off from the life of its
author.[1] This programmatic notion of what poetry should be became subtly
identified with a notion of what all poetry and indeed all forms of literature necessarily must be. It was not simply desirable that literature should
detach itself from the subjective realm of the author's personal thoughts and
feelings; it was, rather, an indubitable fact that all written language remains independent of that subjective realm. At a slightly later period, and for different
reasons, this same notion of semantic autonomy was advanced by Heidegger
and his followers.[2] The idea also has been advocated by writers who believe
with Jung that individual expressions may quite unwittingly express arche-
typal, communal meanings. In some branches of linguistics, particularly in
so-called information theory, the semantic autonomy of language has been a
working assumption. The theory has found another home in the work of non-
Jungians who have interested themselves (as Eliot did earlier) in symbolism,

though Cassirer, whose name is sometimes invoked by such writers, did not believe in the semantic autonomy of language.[3] As I said, it is the job of the cultural historian to explain why this doctrine should have gained currency in recent times, but it is the theorist's job to determine how far the theory of semantic autonomy deserves acceptance.

Literary scholars have often contended that the theory of authorial irrelevance was entirely beneficial to literary criticism and scholarship because it shifted the focus of discussion from the author to his work. Made confident by the theory, the modern critic has faithfully and closely examined the text to ferret out its independent meaning instead of its supposed significance to the author's life. That this shift toward exegesis has been desirable most critics would agree, whether or not they adhere to the theory of semantic autonomy. But the theory accompanied the exegetical movement for historical not logical reasons, since no logical necessity compels a critic to banish an author in order to analyze his text. Nevertheless, through its historical association with close exegesis, the theory has liberated much subtlety and intelligence. Unfortunately, it has also frequently encouraged willful arbitrariness and extravagance in academic criticism and has been one very important cause of the prevailing skepticism which calls into doubt the possibility of objectively valid interpretation. These disadvantages would be tolerable, of course, if the theory were true. In intellectual affairs skepticism is preferable to illusion.

The disadvantages of the theory could not have been easily predicted in the exciting days when the old order of academic criticism was being overthrown. At that time such naivetés as the positivistic biases of literary history, the casting about for influences and other causal patterns, and the postromantic fascination with the habits, feelings, and experiences surrounding the act of composition were very justly brought under attack. It became increasingly obvious that the theoretical foundations of the old criticism were weak and inadequate. It cannot be said, therefore, that the theory of authorial irrelevance was inferior to the theories or quasi-theories it replaced, nor can it be doubted that the immediate effect of banishing the author was wholly beneficial and invigorating. Now, at a distance of several decades, the difficulties that attend the theory of semantic autonomy have clearly emerged and are responsible for that uneasiness which persists in the academies, although the theory has long been victorious.

That this state of academic skepticism and disarray results largely from the theory of authorial irrelevance is, I think, a fact of our recent intellectual history. For, once the author had been ruthlessly banished as the determiner of his text's meaning, it very gradually appeared that no adequate principle existed for judging the validity of an interpretation. By an inner necessity the study of "what a text says" became the study of what it says to an individual critic. It became fashionable to talk about a critic's "reading" of a text, and this word began to appear in the titles of scholarly works. The word seemed to imply that if the author had been banished, the critic still remained, and his new, original, urbane, ingenious, or relevant "reading" carried its own interest.

What had not been noticed in the earliest enthusiasm for going back to "what the text says" was that the text had to represent *somebody's* meaning— if not the author's, then the critic's. It is true that a theory was erected under which the meaning of the text was equated with everything it could plausibly be taken to mean. (I have described in Appendix I the fallacies of this and other descriptions of meaning that were contrived to escape the difficulties of authorial irrelevance.)[4] The theory of semantic autonomy forced itself into such unsatisfactory, ad hoc formulations because in its zeal to banish the author it ignored the fact that meaning is an affair of consciousness not of words. Almost any word sequence can, under the conventions of language, legitimately represent more than one complex of meaning.[5] A word sequence means nothing in particular until somebody either means something by it or understands something from it. There is no magic land of meanings outside human consciousness. Whenever meaning is connected to words, a person is making the connection, and the particular meanings he lends to them are never the only legitimate ones under the norms and conventions of his language.

One proof that the conventions of language can sponsor different meanings from the same sequence of words resides in the fact that interpreters can and do disagree. When these disagreements occur, how are they to be resolved? Under the theory of semantic autonomy they cannot be resolved, since the meaning is not what the author meant, but "what the poem means to different sensitive readers."[6] One interpretation is as valid as another, so long as it is "sensitive" or "plausible." Yet the teacher of literature who adheres to Eliot's theory is also by profession the preserver of a heritage and the conveyor of knowledge. On what ground does he claim that his "reading" is more valid than that of any pupil? On no very firm ground. This impasse is a principal cause of the loss of bearings sometimes felt though not often confessed by academic critics.

One ad hoc theory that has been advanced to circumvent this chaotic democracy of "readings" deserves special mention here because it involves the problem of value, a problem that preoccupies some modern literary theorists. The most valid reading of a text is the "best" reading.[7] But even if we assumed that a critic did have access to the divine criteria by which he could determine the best reading, he would still be left with two equally compelling normative ideals—the best meaning and the author's meaning. Moreover, if the best meaning were not the author's, then it would have to be the critic's— in which case the critic would be the author of the best meaning. Whenever meaning is attached to a sequence of words it is impossible to escape an author.

Thus, when critics deliberately banished the original author, they themselves usurped his place, and this led unerringly to some of our present-day theoretical confusions. Where before there had been but one author, there now arose a multiplicity of them, each carrying as much authority as the next. To banish the original author as the determiner of meaning was to reject the only compelling normative principle that could lend validity to an interpretation. On the other hand, it might be the case that there does not really exist a viable normative ideal that governs the interpretation of texts. This would follow if any of the various arguments brought against the author were to hold. For if the meaning of a text is not the author's, then no interpretation can possibly correspond to the meaning of the text, since the text can have no determinate or determinable meaning. My demonstration of this point will be found [in the following section].

II

Reproducibility is a quality of verbal meaning that makes interpretation possible: if meaning were not reproducible, it could not be actualized by someone else and therefore could not be understood or interpreted. Determinacy, on the other hand, is a quality of meaning required in order that there be something to reproduce. Determinacy is a necessary attribute of any sharable meaning, since an indeterminacy cannot be shared: if a meaning were indeterminate, it would have no boundaries, no self-identity, and therefore could have no identity with a meaning entertained by someone else. But determinacy does not mean definiteness or precision. Undoubtedly, most verbal meanings are imprecise and ambiguous, and to call them such is to acknowledge their determinacy: they are what they are—namely, ambiguous and imprecise—and they are not univocal and precise. This is another way of saying that an ambiguous meaning has a boundary like any other verbal meaning, and that one of the frontiers on this boundary is that between ambiguity and univocality. Some parts of the boundary might, of course, be thick; that is, there might at some points be a good many submeanings that belonged equally to the meaning and not to it—borderline meanings. However, such ambiguities would, on another level, simply serve to define the character of the meaning so that any overly imprecise construing of it would constitute a misunderstanding. Determinacy, then, first of all means self-identity. This is the minimum requirement for sharability. Without it neither communication nor validity in interpretation would be possible.

But by determinacy I also mean something more. Verbal meaning would be determinate in one sense even if it were merely a locus of possibilities— as some theorists have considered it. However, this is a kind of determinacy that cannot be shared in any act of understanding or interpretation. An array of *possible* meanings is no doubt a determinate entity in the sense that it is not an array of *actual* meanings; thus, it too has a boundary. But the human mind cannot entertain a possible meaning; as soon as the meaning is entertained it is actual. "In that case, then," the proponent of such a view might argue, "let us consider the text to represent an array of different, *actual* meanings, corresponding to different actual interpretations." But this escape from the frying pan leads right into the amorphous fire of indeterminacy. Such a conception really denies the self-identity of verbal meaning by suggesting that the meaning of the text can be one thing and also another, different thing, and also another; and this conception (which has nothing to do with the ambiguity of meaning) is simply a denial that the text means anything in particular. I have already shown that such an indeterminate meaning is not sharable. Whatever it may be, it is not verbal meaning nor anything that could be validly interpreted.

"Then," says the advocate of rich variousness, "let us be more precise. What I really mean is that verbal meaning is historical or temporal. It is something in particular for a span of time, but it is something different in a different period of time." Certainly the proponent of such a view cannot be reproached with the accusation that he makes verbal meaning indeterminate. On the contrary, he insists on the self-identity of meaning at any moment of time. But . . . this remarkable, quantum-leap theory of meaning has no foundation in the nature of linguistic acts nor does it provide any criterion of validity in interpretation. If a meaning can change its identity and in fact does, then we have no norm for judging whether we are encountering the real meaning in a changed form or some spurious meaning that is pretending to be the one we seek. Once it is admitted that a meaning can change its characteristics, then there is no way of finding the true Cinderella among all the contenders. There is no dependable glass slipper we can use as a test, since the old slipper will no longer fit the new Cinderella. To the interpreter this lack of a stable normative principle is equivalent to the indeterminacy of meaning. As far as his interests go, the meaning could have been defined as indeterminate from the start, and his predicament would have been precisely the same.

When, therefore, I say that a verbal meaning is determinate, I mean that it is an entity which is self-identical. Furthermore, I also mean that it is an entity which always remains the same from one moment to the next—that it is changeless. Indeed, these criteria were already implied in the requirement that verbal meaning be reproducible, that it be always the same in different acts of construing. Verbal meaning, then, is what it is and not something else, and it is always the same. That is what I mean by determinacy.

A determinate verbal meaning requires a determining will. Meaning is not made determinate simply by virtue of its being represented by a determinate sequence of words. Obviously, any brief word sequence could represent quite different complexes of verbal meaning, and the same is true of long word sequences, though it is less obvious. If that were not so, competent and intelligent speakers of a language would not disagree as they do about the meaning of texts. But if a determinate word sequence does not in itself necessarily represent one, particular, self-identical, unchanging complex of meaning, then the determinacy of its verbal meaning must be accounted for by some other discriminating force which causes the meaning to be this instead of that or that or that, all of which it could be. That discriminating force must involve an act of will, since unless one particular complex of meaning is willed (no matter how "rich" and "various" it might be), there would be no distinction between what an author does mean by a word sequence and what he could mean by it. Determinacy of verbal meaning requires an act of will.

It is sometimes said that "meaning is determined by context," but this is a very loose way of speaking. It is true that the surrounding text or the situation in which a problematical word sequence is found tends to narrow the meaning probabilities for that particular word sequence; otherwise, interpretation would be hopeless. And it is a measure of stylistic excellence in an author that he should have managed to formulate a decisive context for any particular word sequence within his text. But this is certainly not to say that context determines verbal meaning. At best a context determines the guess of an interpreter (though his construction of the context may be wrong, and his guess correspondingly so). To speak of context as a determinant is to confuse an exigency of interpretation with an author's determining acts. An author's verbal meaning is limited by linguistic possibilities but is determined by his actualizing and specifying some of those possibilities. Correspondingly, the verbal meaning that an interpreter construes is determined by his act of will, limited by those same possibilities. The fact that a particular context has led the interpreter to a particular choice does not change the fact that the determination is a choice, even when it is unthinking and automatic. Furthermore, a context is something that has itself been determined—first by an author and then, through a construction, by an interpreter. It is not something that is simply there without anybody having to make any determinations. . . .

III

I [have] defined textual meaning as the verbal intention of the author, and this argues implicitly that hermeneutics must stress a reconstruction of the author's aims and attitudes in order to evolve guides and norms for construing the meaning of his text. It is frequently argued, however, that textual meaning has nothing to do with the author's mind but only with his verbal achievement, that the object of interpretation is not the author but his text. This plausible argument assumes, of course, that the text automatically has a meaning simply because it represents an unalterable sequence of words. It assumes that the meaning of a word sequence is directly imposed by the public norms of language, that the text as a "piece of language" is a public object whose character is defined by public norms.[8] This view is in one respect sound, since textual meaning must conform to public norms if it is in any sense to be verbal (i.e., sharable) meaning; on no account may the interpreter permit his probing into the author's mind to raise private associations (experience) to the level of public implications (content).

However, this basically sound argument remains one-sided, for even though verbal meaning must conform to public linguistic norms (these are highly tolerant, of course), no mere sequence of words can represent an actual verbal meaning with reference to public norms alone. Referred to these alone, the text's meaning remains indeterminate. This is true even of the simplest declarative sentence like "My car ran out of gas" (did my Pullman dash from a cloud of Argon?). The fact that no one would radically misinterpret such a sentence simply indicates that its frequency is high enough to give its usual meaning the apparent status of an immediate given. But this apparent immediacy obscures a complex process of adjudications among meaning possibilities. Under the public norms of language alone no such adjudications can occur, since the array of possibilities presents a face of blank indifference. The array of possibilities only begins to become a more selective system of *probabilities* when, instead of confronting merely a word sequence, we also posit a speaker who very likely means something. Then and only then does the most usual sense of the word sequence become the most probable or "obvious" sense. The point holds true a fortiori, of course, when we confront less obvious word sequences like those found in poetry. A careful exposition of this point may be found in the first volume of Cassirer's *Philosophy of Symbolic Forms*, which is largely devoted to a demonstration that verbal meaning arises from the "reciprocal determination" of public linguistic possibilities and subjective specifications of those possibilities.[9] Just as language constitutes and colors subjectivity, so does subjectivity color language. The author's or speaker's subjective act is formally necessary to verbal meaning, and any theory which tries to dispense with the author as specifier of meaning by asserting that textual meaning is purely objectively determined finds itself chasing will-o'-the-wisps. The burden of this section is, then, an attack on the view that a text is a "piece of language" and a defense of the notion that a text represents the determinate verbal meaning of an author.

One of the consequences arising from the view that a text is a piece of language—a purely public object—is the impossibility of defining in principle the nature of a correct interpretation. This is the same impasse which results from the theory that a text leads a life of its own, and, indeed, the two notions are corollaries, since any "piece of language" must have a changing meaning when the changing public norms of language are viewed as the only ones which determine the sense of the text. It is therefore not surprising to find that Wellek subscribes implicitly to the text-as-language theory. The text is viewed as representing not a determinate meaning, but rather a system of meaning potentials specified not by a meaner but by the vital potency of language itself. Wellek acutely perceives the danger of the view:

> Thus the system of norms is growing and changing and will remain, in some sense, always incompletely and imperfectly realized. But this dynamic conception does not mean mere subjectivism and relativism. All the different points of view are by no means equally right. It will always be possible to determine which point of view grasps the subject most thoroughly and deeply. A hierarchy of viewpoints, a criticism of the grasp of norms, is implied in the concept of the adequacy of interpretation.[10]

The danger of the view is, of course, precisely that it opens the door to subjectivism and relativism, since linguistic norms may be invoked to support any verbally possible meaning. Furthermore, it is not clear how one may criticize a grasp of norms which will not stand still.

Wellek's brief comment on the problem involved in defining and testing correctness in interpretation is representative of a widespread conviction among literary critics that the most correct interpretation is the most "inclusive" one. Indeed, the view is so widely accepted that Wellek did not need to defend his version of it (which he calls "Perspectivism") at length. The notion behind the theory is reflected by such phrases as "always incompletely and imperfectly realized" and "grasps the subject most thoroughly." This notion is simply that no single interpretation can exhaust the rich system of meaning potentialities represented by the text. Hence, every plausible reading which remains within public linguistic norms is a correct reading so far as it goes, but each reading is inevitably partial since it cannot realize all the potentialities of the text. The guiding principle in criticism, therefore, is that of the inclusive interpretation. The most "adequate" construction is the one which gives the fullest coherent account of all the text's potential meanings.[11]

Inclusivism is desirable as a position which induces a readiness to consider the results of others, but, aside from promoting an estimable tolerance, it has little theoretical value. Although its aim is to reconcile different plausible readings in an ideal, comprehensive interpretation, it cannot, in fact, either reconcile different readings or choose between them. As a normative ideal, or principle of correctness, it is useless. This point may be illustrated by citing two expert readings of a well-known poem by Wordsworth. I shall first quote the poem and then quote excerpts from two published exegeses to demonstrate the kind of impasses which inclusivism always provokes when it attempts to reconcile interpretations and, incidentally, to demonstrate the very kind of interpretive problem which calls for a guiding principle:

> A slumber did my spirit seal;
>   I had no human fears:
> She seemed a thing that could not feel
>   The touch of earthly years.
>
> No motion has she now, no force;
>   She neither hears nor sees,
> Rolled round in earth's diurnal course
>   With rocks, and stones, and trees.

Here are excerpts from two commentaries on the final lines of the poem; the first is by Cleanth Brooks, the second is by F. W. Bateson:

> [The poet] attempts to suggest something of the lover's agonized shock at the loved one's present lack of motion—of his response to her utter and horrible inertness. . . . Part of the effect, of course, resides in the fact that a dead lifelessness is suggested more sharply by

an object's being whirled about by something else than by an image of the object in repose. But there are other matters which are at work here: the sense of the girl's falling back into the clutter of things, companioned by things chained like a tree to one particular spot, or by things completely inanimate like rocks and stones. . . . [She] is caught up helplessly into the empty whirl of the earth which measures and makes time. She is touched by and held by earthly time in its most powerful and horrible image.

The final impression the poem leaves is not of two contrasting moods, but of a single mood mounting to a climax in the pantheistic magnificence of the last two lines. . . . The vague living-Lucy of this poem is opposed to the grander dead-Lucy who has become involved in the sublime processes of nature. We put the poem down satisfied, because its last two lines succeed in effecting a reconciliation between the two philosophies or social attitudes. Lucy is actually more alive now that she is dead, because she is now a part of the life of Nature and not just a human "thing."[12]

If we grant, as I think we must, that both the cited interpretations are permitted by the text, the problem for the inclusivist is to reconcile the two readings.

Three modes of reconciliation are available to the inclusivist:

1. Brooks's reading includes Bateson's; it shows that any affirmative suggestions in the poem are negated by the bitterly ironical portrayal of the inert girl being whirled around by what Bateson calls the "sublime processes of Nature."
2. Bateson's reading includes Brooks's; the ironic contrast between the active, seemingly immortal girl and the passive, inert, dead girl is overcome by a final unqualified affirmation of immortality.
3. Each of the readings is partially right, but they must be fused to supplement one another.

The very fact that the critics differ suggests that the meaning is essentially ambiguous. The emotion expressed is ambivalent and comprises both bitter regret and affirmation. The third mode of reconciliation is the one most often employed and is probably, in this case, the most satisfactory. A fourth type of resolution, which would insist that Brooks is right and Bateson wrong (or vice versa), is not available to the inclusivist, since the text, as language, renders both readings plausible.

Close examination, however, reveals that none of the three modes of argument manages to reconcile or fuse the two different readings. Mode 1, for example, insists that Brooks's reading comprehends Bateson's, but although it is conceivable that Brooks implies all the meanings which Bateson has perceived, Brooks also implies a pattern of emphasis which cannot be reconciled with Bateson's reading. While Bateson construes a primary emphasis on life and affirmation, Brooks emphasizes deadness and inertness. No amount of manipulation can reconcile these divergent emphases, since one pattern of emphasis irrevocably excludes other patterns, and, since emphasis is always crucial to meaning, the two constructions of meaning rigorously exclude one another. Precisely the same strictures hold, of course, for the argument that Bateson's reading comprehends that of Brooks. Nor can mode 3 escape with impunity. Although it seems to preserve a stress both on negation and on affirmation, thereby coalescing the two readings, it actually excludes both readings and labels them not simply partial, but wrong. For if the poem gives equal stress to bitter irony and to affirmation, then any construction which places a primary stress on either meaning is simply incorrect.

The general principle implied by my analysis is very simple. The submeanings of a text are not blocks which can be brought together additively. Since verbal (and any other) meaning is a *structure* of component meanings, interpretation has not done its job when it simply enumerates what the component meanings are. The interpreter must also determine their probable structure and particularly their structure of emphases. Relative emphasis is not only crucial to meaning (perhaps it is the most crucial and problematical element of all), it is also highly restrictive; it excludes alternatives. It may be asserted as a general rule that whenever a reader confronts two interpretations which impose different emphases on similar meaning components, at least one of the interpretations must be wrong. They cannot be reconciled.

By insisting that verbal meaning always exhibits a determinate structure of emphases, I do not, however, imply that a poem or any other text must be unambiguous. It is perfectly possible, for example, that Wordsworth's poem ambiguously implies both bitter irony and positive affirmation. Such complex emotions are commonly expressed in poetry, but if that is the kind of meaning the text represents, Brooks and Bateson would be wrong to emphasize one emotion at the expense of the other. Ambiguity or, for that matter, vagueness is not the same as indeterminateness. This is the crux of the issue. To say that verbal meaning is determinate is not to exclude complexities of meaning but only to insist that a text's meaning is what it is and not a hundred other things. Taken in this sense, a vague or ambiguous text is just as determinate as a logical proposition; it means what it means and nothing else. This is true even if one argues that a text could display shifting emphases like those magic squares which first seem to jut out and then to jut in. With texts of this character (if any exist), one need only say that the emphases shift and must not, therefore, be construed statically. Any static construction would simply be wrong. The fundamental flaw in the "theory of the most inclusive interpretation" is that it overlooks the problem of emphasis. Since different patterns of emphasis exclude one another, inclusivism is neither a genuine norm nor an adequate guiding principle for establishing an interpretation.

NOTES

1. The classic statement is in T. S. Eliot, "Tradition and the Individual Talent," *Selected Essays* (New York: Harcourt, Brace, 1932).

2. See, for example, Martin Heidegger, *Unterwegs zur Sprache* (Pfullingen: Neske, 1959).

3. See Ernst Cassirer, *The Philosophy of Symbolic Forms*; vol. 1, *Language*, trans. Ralph Manheim (New Haven: Yale University Press, 1953), particularly pp. 69, 178, 213, 249–50, and passim.

4. [Part of this appendix is included as the final section of this chapter—Ed.]

5. The random example that I use later in the book is the sentence "I am going to town today." Different sense can be lent to the sentence by the simple device of placing a strong emphasis on any of the six different words.

6. The phrase is from T. S. Eliot, *On Poetry and Poets* (New York: Farrar, Strauss and Cudahy, 1957), p. 126.

7. It would be invidious to name any individual critic as the begetter of this widespread and imprecise notion. By the "best" reading, of course, some critics mean the most valid reading, but the idea of bestness is widely used to embrace indiscriminately both the idea of validity and of such aesthetic values as richness, inclusiveness, tension, or complexity—as though validity and aesthetic excellence must somehow be identical.

8. The phrase "piece of language" comes from the first paragraph of William Empson's *Seven Types of Ambiguity* (New York: Meridian, 1955). It is typical of the critical school Empson founded.

9. Cassirer, *Philosophy of Symbolic Forms*, vol. 1, *Language*. It is ironic that Cassirer's work should be used to support the notion that a text speaks for itself. The realm of language is autonomous for Cassirer only in the sense that it follows an indepen-

dent development which is reciprocally determined by objective and subjective factors. See pp. 69, 178, 213, 249–50, and passim.

10. Rene Wellek and Austin Warren, *Theory of Literature* (New York: Harcourt, Brace, 1956), p. 144.

11. Every interpretation is necessarily incomplete in the sense that it fails to explicate all a text's implications. But this kind of incomplete interpretation may still carry an absolutely correct system of emphases and an accurate sense of the whole meaning. This kind of incompleteness is radically different from that postulated by the inclusivists, for whom a sense of the whole means a grasp of the various possible meanings on which a text can plausibly represent.

12. Cleanth Brooks, "Irony as a Principle of Structure," in *Literary Opinion in America*, ed. M.D. Zabel, 2d ed. (New York: Harper, 1951), p. 736; F.W. Bateson, *English Poetry: A Critical Introduction* (London: Longmans, Green, 1950), pp. 33, 80–81.

The Authority of the Text

2

MONROE C. BEARDSLEY

I

THE FIRST THING REQUIRED to make criticism possible is an object to be criticized—something for the critic to interpret and to judge, with its own properties against which interpretations and judgments can be checked. The Principle of Independence, as it might be called, is that literary works exist as individuals and can be distinguished from other things, though it is another question whether they enjoy some special mode of existence, as has been held. I think everyone must agree on this first postulate—here rather roughly stated. But there is another postulate that is logically complementary to the first: that literary works are self-sufficient entities, whose properties are decisive in checking interpretations and judgments. This is sometimes called the Principle of Autonomy, and it is of course the subject of much dispute.

Much of the dispute has raged around that special critical maneuver which William Wimsatt and I once named "The Intentional Fallacy." Is it really a fallacy? Or is it sound procedure (when properly understood, of course)? After some initial discussions, there was a period when our doctrine seemed secure, though needing corrections and precisions; however, I have the impression that in recent years there has been an Intentionalist Backlash. I do not propose to meet it head-on in these lectures. But the whole issue is so central to criticism and critical theory that it can hardly be avoided or ignored.

What does the literary interpreter do? He tells us what a literary work

Reprinted from *The Possibility of Criticism*, by Monroe C. Beardsley, pp. 16–21, 24–37, 42–44, by permission of the Wayne State University Press. Copyright © 1970 by Wayne State University Press.

means. And whatever else it is, a literary work is first of all a text, a piece of language. So what the interpreter reveals is the meaning of a text. But what is that?

This question will lead us into some fairly fundamental discussion when we later pursue it further. But as a start, let us dispose once and for all, if we can, of a theory that is consciously accepted by many critics and unconsciously followed by many others. It is clearly stated at the very beginning of a recent and significant work on the theory of interpretation—or "hermeneutics"—by E. D. Hirsch, whose views I shall have more to say about shortly. He writes:

> It is a task for the historian of culture to explain why there has been in the past four decades a heavy and largely victorious assault on the sensible belief that a text means what its author meant.[1]

I think there is no need to consult the historian of culture when the logician can give us the explanation so much more quickly and simply. For unfortunately the belief that a text means what its author meant is not sensible.

Let us call the Hirsch thesis—a common and familiar one—the Identity Thesis: that what a literary work means is identical to what its author meant in composing it.

The question is not whether textual meaning and authorial meaning can coincide—that is, be very similar. Certainly they can. The question is not whether textual meaning is often adequate evidence of authorial meaning. Certainly it often is. The question is whether they are one and the same thing. If they are, it follows, as Hirsch argues, that when the literary interpreter interprets a text, he is really discovering what the author meant in composing it. And from that proposition follow various consequences about the kinds of evidence that are relevant to interpretation and decisive in validating (i.e., confirming) an interpretation.

The Identity Thesis can be conclusively refuted by the following three arguments.

1. Some texts that have been formed without the agency of an author, and hence, without authorial meaning, nevertheless have a meaning and can be interpreted, for example, certain kinds of verbal mistake. The following comes from the *Portland Oregonian* by way of the *New Yorker*:

> "It showed that there is at least one officer on the Portland police force who had not seen Officer Olsen drunk," Apley quietly observed.

In contrast to Apley, Jensen argued like a man filled with righteous indigestion.

The final phrase is inadvertent, yet it is very intelligible. When Hart Crane wrote "Thy Nazarene and tender eyes," a printer's error transformed it into "Thy Nazarene and tinder eyes"; but Crane let the accidental version stand. Then there are poems composed by computers:

> While life reached evilly through empty faces
> While space flowed slowly o'er idle bodies
> And stars flowed evilly on vast men
> No passion smiled.[2]

Here one might claim that there is something like a hovering "authorial will," expressed in the instructions of the programmer, but the instructions were general, and the poem is a particular new composition of words. It has meaning, but nothing was meant by anyone.

Refut. #1

There are textual meanings without authorial meanings. Therefore textual meaning is not identical to authorial meaning.

Refut. #2

2. The meaning of a text can change after its author has died. But the author cannot change his meaning after he has died. Therefore, the textual meaning is not identical to the authorial meaning.

The OED furnishes abundant evidence that individual words and idioms acquire new meanings and lose old meanings as time passes; these changes can in turn produce changes of meaning in sentences in which the words appear. I cite these lines from Mark Akenside, *The Pleasures of Imagination* (II, 311–13), referring to "the Sovereign Spirit of the world":

> Yet, by immense benignity inclin'd
> To spread about him that primeval joy
> Which fill'd himself, he rais'd his plastic arm.

"Plastic arm" has acquired a new meaning in the twentieth century, and this is now its dominant one (though the older one has not disappeared). Consequently the line in which it occurs has also acquired a new meaning.

We are forced, then, to distinguish between what this line meant in 1744 and what it means in 1968. Of course we can inquire into both meanings, if we will; but these are two distinct inquiries. And if today's textual meaning of the line cannot be identified with any authorial meaning, it follows that textual meanings are not the same thing as authorial meanings.

Refut. #3

3. A text can have meanings that its author is not aware of. Therefore, it

can have meanings that its author did not intend. Therefore, textual meaning is not identical to authorial meaning.

It is not necessary to give examples to support my first premise, since Hirsch concedes that it is true. He himself gives the example[3] of a critic pointing out to an author that in his work he had suggested a similarity by parallel syntax. "What this example illustrates," he says, "is that there are usually components of an author's intended meaning that he is not conscious of." Thus it is my second proposition that he denies:

> It is not possible to mean what one does not mean, though it is very possible to mean what one is not conscious of meaning. That is the entire issue in the argument based on authorial ignorance. That a man may not be conscious of all that he means is no more remarkable than that he may not be conscious of all that he does.[4]

This analogy gives the case away. If the psychological act of "meaning" something (supposing that there is such a psychological act) were like the overt physical act of *doing* something, then it would be possible to mean unconsciously. But the only way one can mean something unconsciously is to say something that (textually) means something one is not aware of.

Consider Hirsch's discussion of the "implications" of texts. What can he do about the suggestions and intimations that a text may have, quite independently of what its author has (in Hirsch's words) "willed to convey" by it? Consider Senator Dodd's remark to the senators investigating the tax-free personal funds he obtained from four "testimonial dinners" that were advertised as political fund-raising events. He said: "If there is anything more common to Connecticut than nutmeg it is testimonial affairs, and they go on there every week." He certainly did not will to suggest that his testimonial dinners were as phony as the celebrated wooden nutmegs sold by the old Yankee peddlers, who thus gave Connecticut its nickname. But that is what he did suggest. Hirsch's solution of the problem is not the sensible one of admitting that textual meaning can go beyond authorial meaning; instead, he tries to stretch the concept of will far enough so that whatever the text does mean can be said to be "willed" by the author—however unwittingly.

"It is possible," says Hirsch, "to will an et cetera, without in the least being aware of all the individual members that belong to it."[5] True enough. But what does it prove? I can ask someone to bring me all the books on the top shelf, without knowing the names of any of the books. But then I have not asked for any particular book. Suppose *Huckleberry Finn* is on the top shelf and is brought to me—it does not follow that I asked for *Huckleberry Finn*. Similarly, a poet can agree to stand behind all of the implications of his poem, without knowing what the implications are. But if the poem turns out to have a particular implication that he was not aware of, it does not follow that he willed that particular implication. Whatever is unwitting is unwilled. . . .

II

Though I think we must reject [Hirsch's] . . . argument in the end, both the argument itself and the objections to it are instructive; they help us to a better understanding of what interpretation is and how it is successfully done.

Hirsch's main argument can be stated in a classic *reductio-ad-absurdum* form: If textual meaning is not identical to authorial meaning, then there is no "determinate" textual meaning at all. But this is absurd; therefore, textual meaning is identical to authorial meaning.

The steps in the argument are these:

> Almost any word sequence can, under the conventions of language, legitimately represent more than one complex of meaning. A word sequence means nothing in particular until somebody either means something by it or understands something from it.[6]

> A determinate verbal meaning requires a determining will. Meaning is not made determinate simply by virtue of its being represented by a determinate sequence of words. Obviously, any brief word sequence could represent quite different complexes of verbal meaning, and the same is true of long word sequences, though it is less obvious. . . . Unless one particular complex of meanings is *willed* (no matter how "rich" or "various" it might be), there would be no distinction between what an author does mean by a word sequence and what he could mean by it. Determinacy of verbal meaning requires an act of will.[7]

Hence Hirsch's "provisional" definition of "verbal meaning" (i.e., the meaning of a text):

> Verbal meaning is whatever someone has willed to convey by a particular sequence of linguistic signs and which can be conveyed (shared) by means of those linguistic signs.[8]

The statement that "almost any word sequence can, under the conventions of language, legitimately represent more than one complex of meaning" is Hirsch's postulate of the "indeterminacy" of possible meaning. This is a considerable exaggeration.[9]

Consider an old campaign button found in the street. It reads "Vote for Senator Kennedy." Shorn of any larger context, this text provides no way of determining which of the two senators it refers to. It has two possible referents, but no actual one. A great many comparatively short and colloquial texts and utterances may be indeterminate in one respect or another—though none of them can be indeterminate in *all* respects, and therefore every one of them can at least be partially interpreted without any information about its authorial meaning. But surely we can find plenty of counterexamples in the indeterminacy postulate. Take one of Hirsch's own examples: "Nothing pleases me so much as the Third Symphony of Beethoven."[10] No doubt we can think of a lot of questions that this single utterance does not answer. But what is indeterminate about it? Hirsch suggests that it is indeterminate because the speaker's friend can reply, "Does it please you more than a swim in the sea on a hot day?" Of course, the friend is interested in discovering what the man was trying to say, or thought he was saying; whether he was mentally comparing the symphony with other musical compositions, other works of art, or pleasures in general. But clearly the friend is not asking for a removal of any indeterminacy in the original remark. (Indeed, the remark must be pretty determinate, or we would not be able to see that it is flatly self-contradictory—since something must please the speaker as much as the *Eroica*, namely the *Eroica* itself.) The friend is in fact asking for further information about the speaker's attitude. The original remark is less informative than if the speaker had said, "No other symphony pleases me as much as Beethoven's Third," but it is no less determinate.

There is, of course, the phenomenon of ambiguity—a term I use in a strictly logical sense, not for multiplicity of meaning but for indecisiveness of meaning. It is not hard to find or invent a short sentence that is simply ambiguous. But the more complex the text, the more difficult it is (in general) to devise two incompatible readings that are equally faithful to it. Hirsch's prime example, which originally appeared in his *PMLA* article reprinted as Appendix I of his book, is Wordsworth's Lucy poem "A Slumber Did My Spirit Seal."

> A slumber did my spirit seal;
>   I had no human fears:
> She seemed a thing that could not feel
>   The touch of earthly years.

No motion has she now, no force;
    She neither hears nor sees,
Rolled round in earth's diurnal course
    With rocks, and stones, and trees.

Hirsch brings together two sharply opposed interpretations of this poem, in order to argue that unless we introduce considerations of the poet's will and thought, the poem cannot be decisively interpreted. The first interpretation is by Cleanth Brooks:

> [Wordsworth] attempts to suggest something of the lover's agonized shock at the loved one's present lack of motion—of his response to her utter and horrible inertness. . . . He chooses to suggest it . . . by imagining her in violent motion. . . . Part of the effect, of course, resides in the fact that a dead lifelessness is suggested more sharply by an object's being whirled about by something else than by an image of the object in repose. But there are other matters which are at work here: the sense of the girl's falling back into the clutter of things, companioned by things chained like a tree to one particular spot, or by things completely inanimate, like rocks and stones. . . . She is touched by and held by earthly time in its most powerful and horrible image.[11]

The second interpretation is by F. W. Bateson:

> But the final impression the poem leaves is not of two contrasting moods, but of a single mood mounting to a climax in the pantheistic magnificence of the last two lines. . . . The vague living-Lucy of this poem is opposed to the grander dead-Lucy who has become involved in the sublime processes of nature. . . . Lucy is actually more alive now that she is dead, because she is now a part of the life of Nature and not just a human "thing."[12]

This is an ingeniously chosen example—a plainer conflict between well-qualified readers could hardly be found. As Hirsch insists, the two interpretations cannot be reconciled; at least one must be false. But he also insists that they do equal justice to the text, that from internal evidence alone—that is, by anything that can be appealed to in the meanings of the words and phrases in the poem—there is no way to decide between them. He concludes that in order for the poem to have a "determinate" textual meaning, "authorial will" must determine it:

Only, then, in relation to an established context, can we judge that one reading is more coherent than another. Ultimately, therefore, we have to posit the probable horizon for the text, and it is possible to do this only if we posit the author's typical outlook, the typical associations and expectations which form in part the context of his utterance. . . . The poet is not an *hommes moyen sensuel*; his characteristic attitudes are somewhat pantheistic. Instead of regarding rocks and stones and trees merely as inert objects, he probably regarded them in 1799 as deeply alive, as part of the immortal life of nature. Physical death he felt to be a return to the source of life, a new kind of participation in nature's "revolving immortality." From everything we know of Wordsworth's typical attitudes during the period in which he composed the poem, inconsolability and bitter irony do not belong in its horizon.[13]

Now if in fact the two interpretations were equally supported by the text, we would simply have to conclude that the poem is radically ambiguous. But this is surely not the case. Brooks's reading is (uncharacteristically) distorted. Lucy is not "whirled"; she is "rolled." She does not fall back into a "clutter of things," but is placed among trees, which do not really suggest "dead lifelessness." An orderly "diurnal course" is not "violent motion." Brooks has simply substituted words with connotations quite absent from the poem, and built his own "horrible image" out of them. We do not need to appeal to the poet's biography to know that Brooks's bitter reading will not do. But if Hirsch cannot make his postulate of (practically) universal indeterminacy stick in this chosen case, it seems fair to conclude that examples of radically indeterminate poems are not all that easy to come by.

Even if they were, as I have said, it would not help to turn to the poet and investigate his "typical attitudes" at the time of writing. An ambiguous text does not become any less ambiguous because its author wills one of the possible meanings. Will as he will, he cannot will away ambiguity. There is something odd about the notion of "willing" a meaning. It is as though we ordered someone, "Say 'cat' and mean dog." Can one do that? How does one do it?[14] True I can say, "Vote for Senator Kennedy!" and think of Edward Kennedy. Do I thereby make the word "Kennedy" in that utterance mean *Edward Kennedy*? This is quite impossible.

The fundamental error, as I see it, in Hirsch's account of verbal meaning is summed up in his statement, quoted above: "A determinate verbal meaning requires a determining will." My position is, rather, that texts acquire determinate meaning through the interactions of their words without the intervention of an authorial will. When possible meanings are transformed into an actual meaning, this transformation is generated by the possibilities (the Leibnizian compossibilities) themselves.

possible vs. actual meaning; determining

If this were not the case, I do not believe we could give a really determinate sense to Hirsch's "indeterminacy." For what does it mean to say that the noun "line" is "indeterminate"? Only, so far as I can see, that it is capable of acquiring different *determinate* meanings when placed in varied contexts: "dropping someone a line," "a line of type," "throwing the drowning man a line," "the manufacturer's current line," etc. If the meanings in these contexts were not fairly determinate, it would not make sense to call the single word "indeterminate," because we would not have a clear concept of what it is that the word lacks, by itself. It would be beside the point to reply that "line" in "a line of type" is also indeterminate, because it does not specify how long the line is. The limitation is *indefiniteness*, which is a quite different thing from "indeterminacy," and is removed (when it is removed) in a quite different way—not by enlarging the controlling verbal context but by supplying further information.

What worries Hirsch is that unless textual meaning is taken as identical to authorial meaning, there may be no standards of validity in interpretation.

> For, once the author had been ruthlessly banished as the determiner of his text's meaning, it very gradually appeared that no adequate principle existed for judging the validity of an interpretation. By an inner necessity the study of "what a text says" became the study of what it says to an individual critic.[15]

> To banish the original author as the determiner of meaning was to reject the only compelling normative principle that could lend validity to an interpretation.[16]

I hold that there is no such "inner necessity" and that we are not limited to Hirsch's dilemma. . . .

Textual meaning is not reducible to authorial meaning. But does it take precedence over it? We have not yet established the full authority of the text. For if the two meanings are not identical, then there are two possible interpretation-tasks or inquiries: (1) to discover the textual meaning, and (2) to discover the authorial meaning. Though admittedly progress in either of these inquiries may be of some assistance in the other, they remain distinct. But which of them is the proper function of the literary interpreter?

No one can deny that there are many practical occasions on which our task is precisely to try to discover authorial meaning, or intention: what the speaker or writer had in mind and wanted us to understand. When there is a difficulty in reading a will or a love letter, or in grasping an oral promise or instruction, our primary concern is with authorial meaning. If there is ambiguity or the possibility of misspeaking, we want to correct it. To do this, we may avail ourselves of such evidence as fuller explanations by the author himself, if we can find him, and information about his actions (as when the testator's intention about a particular beneficiary is not plain, but his probable intention may be supported by information about his previous behavior toward that person.) [17]

All this seems beyond dispute. But I hold that the case is different when we turn to *literary* interpretation. The proper task of the literary interpreter is to interpret textual meaning. I support this claim by two arguments, one drawn from logical, the other from aesthetic, considerations.

The first argument is an old one: it involves the well-known dispute about the "availability" of the author. It is nicely pointed up by Cleanth Brooks in a passage from one of his finest essays:

> Was this, then, the attitude of Andrew Marvell . . . toward Oliver Cromwell in the summer of 1650? The honest answer must be: I do not know. I have tried to read the poem, the "Horatian Ode," not Andrew Marvell's mind. That seems sensible to me in view of the fact that we have the poem, whereas the attitude held by Marvell at any particular time must be a matter of inference—even though I grant that the poem may be put in as part of the evidence from which we draw inferences. [18]

The only thing in this passage to which I would take exception is the (non-logical) implication that our reading of the poem is not "a matter of inference." In a way it is not, but in a way it is. The important point is Brooks's statement that he is a poem-reader, not a mind-reader. Nor does he merely say this; throughout essay after essay he exhibits an unfailing sense of this distinction, which is so crucial, so obvious, and yet so often lost sight of.

There is a special and important sense in which the authors of many literary works are not available: they cannot be appealed to independently of the text in order to settle disputes about interpretation. Consider the case of the *Eroica*-admirer mentioned above. His friend can say to him, "You're talking loosely. Surely you don't want to say what you've just said, so explain yourself further." Such words cannot now be addressed to Marvell or Wordsworth. If two interpreters come up with different interpretations of a poem, they can compare their interpretations and test them against the poem. But they can seldom compare their interpretations with the author's own interpretation of his work, since few such authorial interpretations exist. It is in this sense that literary authorial meaning is often inaccessible. Not always, of course; living poets can still be appealed to, and many reply; Romantic poets have left behind evidence of their feelings and attitudes on divers subjects, and this can legitimately be used to support inferences about *authorial* meaning in disputed cases—for example, in the Wordsworth case. But for authorial meaning in the usual case, no evidence besides the work itself can be forthcoming. That is one reason I conclude that the *general* and *essential* task of the literary interpreter cannot be the discovery of authorial meaning.

The foregoing argument is not conclusive, of course. One could still maintain that even where there is no independent evidence of authorial meaning— no recourse but the text itself—the literary interpreter is properly concerned with the textual meaning not for its own sake but only for the authorial meaning it discloses. With or without independent evidence of it, authorial meaning would remain the proper object of literary interpretation. I hope my second (and more fundamental) argument will dispose of this view.

What is the primary purpose of literary interpretation? It is, I would say, to help readers approach literary works from the aesthetic point of view, that is, with an interest in actualizing their (artistic) goodness. The work is an object, capable (presumably) of affording aesthetic satisfaction. The problem is to know what is there to be responded to: and the literary interpreter helps us to discern what is there so that we can enjoy it more fully.

Now the goodness in which we take an interest (when our interest is aesthetic) is something that arises out of the ingredients of the poem itself: the ways its verbal parts—its structure and texture—combine and cooperate to make something fresh and novel emerge. The words have to work on us. They work by manipulating our understanding of parts to make us experience a whole that contains something not in the parts. Heterogeneous works, improbably yoked, make suddenly a metaphor, and something is meant there that was never meant before. The names and verbs strung together concresce into a story, with dramatic tensions and resolutions. Regional qualities play on the surface—wit, or tenderness, or elation.[19] Themes and theses rear up to be contemplated.

It is in its language that the poem happens. That is why the language is

[margin annotations: "if no evidence still meaning strictly authorial"]

[margin annotation: "2nd argument aesthetics"]

the object of our attention and of our study when its meaning is difficult to understand. It is not the interpreter's proper task, then (I argue), to draw our attention off to the psychological states of the author—as would be suitable if we were approaching the work from a historical point of view. His task is to keep our eye on the textual meaning.

This second argument is somewhat condensed and no doubt takes for granted quite a few assumptions about art and aesthetics (some of which I have defended elsewhere).[20] But even if this argument, too, is inconclusive, I hope it points in the right direction. Mainly, I want to show that if we once pose the question, Which of the two meanings is the proper object of literary interpretation? it can be satisfactorily answered only by considering the function of literary interpretation, the nature of literature, and the nature of artistic goodness.

I confess to qualms about the stiffness and formality of my purported demonstration. Why can we not, it might be asked, supplement textual meaning with touches of authorial meaning when the latter enriches the former? Sometimes a fact about the author, of which the text itself gives not the slightest hint, adds something aesthetically valuable to the work, if we are permitted to take it as part of the work. Why not, then, admit it?

An interesting recent example is provided in a review by William Jay Smith of Marianne Moore's *Complete Poems*. In this volume, Miss Moore has omitted all but the first few lines of her famous poem on "Poetry," and has modified the remaining ones slightly. The reviewer refers to the words

<blockquote>
one discovers in
it, after all, a place for the genuine.
</blockquote>

and writes:

> It may be that she wishes these lines to stand as a kind of coda, an ironic footnote to this complete volume; "after all," set off as it is now by commas, takes on a new emphasis and significance at the time of her eightieth birthday (*New Republic*, February 24, 1968).

The proposal is to identify the speaker of this (new) poem with the author. Since the speaker thus becomes eighty years old, the phrase "after all" now means "after all these many years of writing poetry," or something of the sort. And the question I am raising is whether the critical maneuver is thoroughly legitimate. Is there any harm in treating the speaker as an octogenarian? Would not some advantage be gained for the poem by doing so?

I suppose that in many cases (I have doubts about this one) there might be no harm, and the importation might be allowable. But I insist that it is (clearly) an importation. The text of the poem does not supply an eighty-year-old speaker, nor, I think, does it require one to make poetic sense. We would not really be interpreting the poem, but treating the act of writing the poem, for the moment, as a biographical event. A poem, if reasonably tight, can take a certain amount of this kind of treatment without serious harm. And, after all, the boundaries of textual meaning . . . are not all that sharp. Some things are definitely said in the poem and cannot be overlooked; others are suggested, as we find on careful reading; others are gently hinted, and whatever methods of literary interpretation we use, we can never establish them decisively as "in" or "out." Therefore whatever comes from without, but yet can be taken as an interesting extension of what is surely in, may be admissible. It merely makes a larger whole.

But this concession will not justify extensive borrowings from biography. Suppose we read a dull poem, and then its author tells us that he means it to be ironic. We can try to read it as ironic—try to import the irony from authorial meaning into textual meaning. And no doubt, as Hirsch would say, our willingness to cooperate may lead us to find clues to irony in the text itself. But if the alleged irony remains unsupported by the text, even after further analysis, then it cannot be experienced as a quality of the poem. It is as if the poem merely told us it was ironic, but did not succeed in being ironic. We would still not be enjoying irony aesthetically—any more than we would be enjoying drama aesthetically if we watched two actors sit quietly on a stage holding up placards stating that they hate each other.

The literary text, in the final analysis, is the determiner of its meaning. It has a will, or at least a way, of its own. The sense it makes—along with the sound it makes—is what it offers for our aesthetic contemplation. If that contemplation is rewarding, there is no need for an author to hover about like a nervous cook, waiting to supply some condiment that was left out of the soup. And if that contemplation is not rewarding, there is nothing the author can do about it, except rewrite—that is, give us another poem. . . .

III

Margolis says that an interpretation can be "reasonable," but not "simply true or false."[21] I find this position puzzling. For I do not see how an interpretation could be reasonable unless reasons can be given to show its superiority to some alternatives; and I do not see how the reasons could count unless they are reasons for thinking it true. But Margolis's main thesis is that

> the philosophically most interesting feature of critical interpretation is its tolerance of alternative and seemingly contrary hypotheses. . . . Given the goal of interpretation, we do not understand that an admissible account necessarily precludes all others incompatible with it.[22]

Margolis points me out as one of those who has espoused the old-fashioned view that if two proposed interpretations of an aesthetic object are logically incompatible, then at least one of them must be rejected. It is, he says, a mistake to think that "there is some ideal object of criticism toward which all relevant experiences of a given work converge. . . . If we simply examine the practice of critics, I think we shall find no warrant at all for the claim."

My own examination of the practice of critics has led me to question this sweeping statement. I find the critic Samuel Hynes, for example, contrasting the opinions of Clark Emery and Hugh Kenner on the *Cantos* and adding: "Obviously they cannot both be right; if the passage describes an earthly paradise, then it cannot be a perversion of nature."[23] I find E. D. Hirsch remarking: "No doubt Coleridge understood *Hamlet* rather differently from Professor Kittredge. The fact is reflected in their disparate interpretations. . . . Both of them would have agreed that at least one of them must be wrong."[24] I find Frank Kermode commenting in a similar vein on the line between "liberty" and "license" in interpretation.[25]

We do not discover, according to Margolis's view, that interpretations are true or false, but only that they are "plausible"—and though two incompatible statements cannot both be true, they can both be plausible. But plausibility is at least an appearance of truth based upon relevant evidence, and any statement that is plausible must be in principle capable of being shown to be true or false. Margolis does not deal with any of the sorts of real-life dispute over interpretation that exercise critics most—for example, Wordsworth's Lucy poem discussed [earlier]. . . . It seems that when he is talking about interpretations he has in mind a Freudian or Marxist or Christian "interpretation." This is bringing to bear on the work an "admissible myth,"[26] or looking at the work through the eyes of some such grand system. If that is the kind of thing which is in question, then I have no quarrel with his principle of tolerance. The story of "Jack and the Beanstalk," for example, can no doubt be taken as Freudian symbolism, as a Marxist fable, or as a Christian allegory. I emphasize the phrase "can be taken as." It is true that "readings" such as these need not exclude each other. But the reason is surely that they do not bring out of the work something that lies momentarily hidden in it; they are rather ways of using the work to illustrate a pre-existent system of thought. Though they are sometimes called "interpretations" (since this word is extremely obliging), they merit a distinct label, like *superimpositions*.

[margin note: Margolis] The issue between Margolis and myself, then, can be stated in this way: he holds that all interpretations have what he calls a "logical weakness," that is, they tolerate each other even when they are incompatible. In contradiction to this view, I hold that there are a great many interpretations that obey what *[margin note: Beardsley]* might be called the principle of "the Intolerance of Incompatibles," that is, if two of them are logically incompatible, they cannot both be true. Indeed, I hold that *all* of the literary interpretations that deserve the name obey his principle. But of course I do not wish to deny that there are cases of ambi- *[margin note: reconciliation? where draw a line betw. ambiguity and clarity?]* guity where no interpretation can be established over its rivals; nor do I wish to deny that there are many cases where we cannot be sure that we have the correct interpretation.

NOTES

1. E. D. Hirsch, *Validity in Interpretation* (New Haven: Yale University Press, 1967), p. 1 [Chapter 1, p. 11]. Hirsch has replied to some of his critics in *Genre* 2 (March 1969): 57–62.

2. Wilbur Cross, "Machine Miltons," *New York Times Magazine*, December 4, 1966, p. 59.

3. Hirsch, *Validity in Interpretation*, p. 21.

4. Ibid., p. 22.

5. Ibid., p. 49.

6. Ibid., p. 4 [Chapter 1, p. 13].

7. Ibid., pp. 46–47 [Chapter 1, p. 16]; cf. pp. 3 [Chapter 1, p. 13], 68.

8. Ibid., p. 31.

9. George Dickie, in his review of Hirsch's book in the *Journal of Aesthetics and Art Criticism* 26 (Summer 1968): 551–52, suggests that Hirsch is in danger of an infinite regress. For if (nearly) every text is indeterminate, and its indeterminacy can be removed only by another text (say, a statement by the author), which is in turn indeterminate, etc., then how is interpretation possible? But if interpretation must in the end rest on some "semantically autonomous" utterance, why can that not be the poem itself?

10. Hirsch, *Validity in Interpretation*, p. 48.

11. Cleanth Brooks, "Irony as a Principle of Structure," in *Literary Opinion in America*, ed. M. D. Zabel, 2d ed. (New York: Harper, 1951), p. 736.

12. F. W. Bateson, *English Poetry: A Critical Introduction* (London: Longmans, Green, 1950), pp. 33, 80–81.

13. Hirsch, *Validity in Interpretation*, Appendix I, pp. 238–39. I thank my colleague Samuel Hynes for help in understanding the subtleties in this poem and in these interpretations. I also owe to him the Hart Crane example.

Since giving this lecture, I have read a judicious discussion of the poem and Hirsch's treatment of it, by Don Geiger, *The Dramatic Impulse in Modern Poetics* (Baton Rouge: Louisiana State University Press, 1967), pp. 132–45. Geiger questions whether we can appeal to a fixed "typical outlook" of Wordsworth at this period of his life (see especially pp. 144–45). He has also called my attention to some interesting remarks by John Oliver Perry, in the introduction to his *Approaches to the Poem* (San Francisco: Chandler, 1965), pp. 13–16. Perry tries to reconcile Brooks and Bateson by discerning, behind the "overt speaker," an "implicit speaker" in the poem.

14. Cf. Ludwig Wittgenstein, *Philosophical Investigations* (New York: Macmillan, 1953), 1:510: "Make the following experiment: *say* 'It's cold here' and *mean* 'It's warm here.' Can you do it?—And what are you doing as you do it?"

15. Hirsch, *Validity in Interpretation*, p. 3 [Chapter 1, pp. 12–13].

16. Ibid., p. 15.

17. There is another kind of activity that is loosely called "interpretation" but should be kept distinct, I believe, from the discovery of either authorial meaning or textual meaning: it is more of a constructive or ampliative process. Augustine's rule for "figurative" reading of Scripture (*De doctrina christiana* 3.10.14; 3.15.23) is to find a reading that will promote the reign of charity; and some judicial constructions of the Constitution (as when "searches and seizures" is taken to include electronic eavesdropping and wiretapping) are surely extensions of the original doctrine. I think it is a mistake to try to assimilate literary criticism to these activities, as Hirsch seems to do in his book (chap. 5); see Stuart Hampshire's demonstration of the variety of activities that go under this name ("Types of Interpretation," in *Art and Philosophy*, ed. Sidney Hook [New York: New York University Press, 1966], pp. 101–8; cf. F. E. Sparshott, *The Concept of Criticism* [Oxford: Clarendon Press, 1967], sec. 21).

18. Cleanth Brooks, "Literary Criticism: Marvell's 'Horatian Ode'" (1946), in *Explication as Criticism*, ed. W. K. Wimsatt, Jr. (New York: Columbia University Press, 1963), p. 125.

19. For an interesting discussion of the status of such qualities (and also of the

distinction between authorial and textual meaning), see Guy Sircello, "Expressive Qualities of Ordinary Language," *Mind* 76 (1967): 548–55.

20. Monroe C. Beardsley, *Aesthetics* (New York: Harcourt, Brace and World, 1958); and Monroe C. Beardsley, "On the Creation of Art," in *Aesthetic Inquiry*, ed. Monroe C. Beardsley and Herbert M. Schueller (Belmont, Calif.: Dickenson, 1967).

21. Joseph Margolis, *The Language of Art and Art Criticism* (Detroit: Wayne State University Press, 1965), p. 76.

22. Ibid., pp. 91–92. [See Chapter 3, p. 41, for a later and slightly revised version of this claim.]

23. Samuel Hynes, "Whitman, Pound, and the Prose Tradition," in *The Presence of Walt Whitman*, English Institute Papers, ed. R.W.B. Lewis (New York: Columbia University Press, 1962), pp. 129–30.

24. Hirsch, *Validity in Interpretation*, p. 137.

25. *New York Review of Books*, September 24, 1964, apropos Jan Kott's *Shakespeare*.

26. Margolis, *Language of Art*, p. 93.

3

Robust Relativism

JOSEPH MARGOLIS

I

PHILOSOPHICALLY, THE MOST interesting feature of critical interpretation is its tolerance of alternative and seemingly contrary hypotheses. We should not allow incompatible descriptions of any physical object to stand: at least one would require correction, else we should find the disparities due to the different purposes the descriptions were to serve or the different circumstances under which they were rendered. But given the goal of interpretation—the imputation of a coherent design under conditions descriptively insufficient for that purpose—we do not understand that an admissible account necessarily precludes all others incompatible with itself. (Stephen Pepper, however, has always insisted that there is some ideal object of criticism toward which all relevant experience of a given work converge.)[1] Advancing a view similar to that of Monroe Beardsley, more recent writers—Hirsch, Olsen, Reichert—in a variety of ways, also favored exclusively correct and comprehensive interpretations;[2] but no one has shown why nonconverging interpretations cannot be legitimately defended. Olsen inadvertently provides a useful clue about this lacuna. "To deal with a text as a literary work," he says, "the reader need not attribute any further intentions to the author, for example intentions concerning the 'meaning' of a work. It is one of the rules of the game that the literary work is autonomous in the sense that the understanding of it is independent of the author's interpreta-

Joseph Margolis, *Art and Philosophy: Conceptual Issues in Aesthetics* (Atlantic Highlands, N.J.: Humanities Press, 1980), pp. 156–64. Reprinted by permission of the author. Notes supplied by the editor on the basis of references originally included in the text.

tion of his own production. The author's literary intentions are expressed in the work." Nevertheless, (1) rather in the manner of Wimsatt's concession previously considered,[3] Olsen is bound to admit that the author's interpretation is relevant if it may be construed as already expressed in the work; (2) there is no satisfactory way, as we have seen in examining Hirsch's strong claims,[4] of fixing authorial intent within a work so as to exclude the relevance of changing interpretive schemata; (3) there is no logical reason why, even if authorial intent may be validly ascribed, a work may not support plural, nonconverging interpretations consistently with such intent; and (4) there is, as against Wellek and Wimsatt,[5] no operative sense in which a work is "autonomous," like a "monument" or physical object, so that what is internal and external to, or descriptive and interpretive of, a particular work may, for all ascriptions, be formally distinguished. Essentially, the issue is a conceptual one. There is no doubt that individual critics tend to favor their own interpretations as exclusively correct; they also seem to believe that canons could be formulated, acceptable to the profession, that would vindicate some exclusively correct interpretation. But the collective practice of critics shows a distributed tolerance for competing canons—without any loss of rigor.

I should like to suggest an analogue of this curious tolerance in the physical sciences. One sometimes asks, "How was our solar system created?" "How was the moon formed?" "How did life originate?" "Are all the races of man descended from a common stock?" At the present stage of our researches, these questions must be adjusted. For "How was our solar system created?" we substitute "How could it have been created?" For "Are all the races of man descended from a common stock?" we substitute "Is it conceivable that they originated from different evolutionary lines, or, alternatively, from the same evolutionary line?" Questions of this sort do not involve contrary-to-fact conditions. The answers afforded are such that the consequent of our conditional is true (the facts about the present solar system); and the antecedent is meaningful but, under present circumstances, incapable of being verified. We imagine a set of initial conditions, compatible with known laws of nature and operating in accord with selected suitable laws, by means of which we explain certain features of our present world. Some such accounts, like Buffon's hypothesis or the Kant–Laplace hypothesis, may be demonstrably false; the correct account may be unavailable; and in its absence, alternative hypotheses may be entertained in accord with alternatively preferred causal models, without violating any relevant facts. Peirce has characterized the process as "abduction."[6] The important point is that interpretive judgments applied where, in principle, we cannot say with certainty what is or is not "in" a given work cannot be confirmed in the strong sense in which, normally, causal claims can be. We are restricted there to appraisals of reasonableness or plausibility, which, though relevant as well to a distinct scientific interest (to, say, how to confine research to the most promising lines of inquiry),[7] do not represent the strongest logical claims that science can relevantly make.

Now, disregarding the possibility of verifying, at some future time, a given hypothesis about the origin of the solar system, we are in a position, at present, to assess the *plausibility* of such a hypothesis; it is even possible to gauge to some extent the degree of plausibility of alternative hypotheses. We have, then, a procedure for determining the plausibility of causal hypotheses that is logically distinct from that of determining their truth. Not altogether dissimilarly, we are able to assign probabilities to contrary propositions, without contradiction; all that we need remember is that, in epistemic contexts, we cannot detach such probabilized propositions from the evidence relative to which they are said to be probable.[8] In aesthetic criticism, correspondingly, we may determine the truth of statements entering into our description of an artwork and we may determine the plausibility of interpretive statements. Just as a hypothesis about the origin of the solar system must accord with known laws and facts of the system, would-be interpretations must accord with the description of a given work and with admissible myths or schemes of imagination. It is emphatically not necessary to hold, for instance with Monroe Beardsley,[9] that if relevant supporting reasons can justify a judgment, that judgment must be such that it "can be true or false." Beardsley concedes as much, though he does not pursue the matter, for he notes that "there might be reasons for making a certain judgment that are not reasons for saying it is true, if it should be the case that judgments cannot be true or false." He mentions P. H. Nowell-Smith's account, purporting to show that even verdictives, such as estimates, though not usually said to be true or false, nevertheless "surely involve a claim to truth, which may be allowed or disallowed."[10] But he considers no other possibilities. Beardsley's own conviction, obviously, is that interpretations and evaluations must be true or false, but he does not show why this must be so. If one insists that all cognitive claims "involve a claim to truth," we actually do meet that condition by conceding that interpretive claims must be compatible with what is (minimally) descriptively true of a given work. That every judgment—taken distributively—must be true or false is an unfounded superstition that Austin for one (whom Beardsley professes to follow) has effectively exploded. A trim way of pressing the point is this: falsity is opposed not only to truth but to plausibility; there is an epistemic asymmetry in assessing claims of truth and falsity.

The following provide the principal distinctions between the "true" and the "plausible."

1. We invoke plausibility only when we cannot actually determine truth.
2. No plausible account may be incompatible with an admittedly true statement.
3. Neither true nor false statements may be viewed as merely plausible or implausible, and neither plausible nor implausible statements are logically precluded from being judged true or false.
4. Where the statements "P is true" and "Q is true" are contraries, the statements "P is plausible" and "Q is plausible" are not contraries.
5. Statements are judged plausible or implausible in virtue of their use of preferred explanatory models in any given domain.

Where such models may be weighted for preferability, and the features of what is to be accounted for also weighted for priority and importance in explanation, the plausibility of the corresponding statements may also be graded. In science, for example, we may be asked to account plausibly for the origin of the moon without assuming the gravitational activity of any body outside our present solar system, but in accord with the density, size, and composition of the moon itself. Correspondingly, in criticism, we may be asked to interpret an artwork in accord with some well-defined myth in a way that gives due prominence to preferred features of the work itself. For example, an interpretation of Hamlet must provide an account of Hamlet's "indecision" and must be pitted, dialectically, against the corpus of accumulated interpretations that are themselves considered relatively plausible. Needless to say, explanation in interpretive contexts is normally not construed in causal terms.

Though they are always marginal to the main effort of science, considerations of plausibility are more nearly central to aesthetic criticism. In fact, scientific speculations of the sort illustrated are treated in terms of plausibility only because of a technical inability to gain the desired information; critical interpretations, on the other hand, are logically weak in principle. It is this weakness, probably, that gives the appearance of lack of rigor to critical pronouncements. But to construe the logical weakness of judgments as a lack of rigor in a given discipline is, at the very least, to be unsympathetic to the special interests of that discipline. Furthermore, the reason these judgments are weak depends, as we have argued,[11] on the very nature of an artwork and on the impossibility of providing a principle for demarcating what is and what is not in a particular work. If one concedes the point, it becomes quite impossible to show that interpretive judgments *can* be true.

This tolerance does not entail that any artwork can convincingly support plural, nonconverging interpretations. It means only that we cannot logically preclude the eligibility of such accounts. In practice, it may well be that only works of certain sorts will support divergent interpretations: possibly T.S. Eliot's poetry can and Ezra Pound's cannot. At any rate, we cannot ask for more precision than the subject will allow.

Critical interpretations, then, are noticeably weaker than statements of fact. But they are weaker logically, not methodologically. There is absolutely no difference in conceptual rigor in defending divergent interpretations and in confirming exclusive physical facts. What is more important, the methods and procedures associated with deciding the latter are flatly inadequate in resolving questions about the former. There is no reason why, granting that criticism proceeds in an orderly way, practices cannot be sustained in which aesthetic designs are rigorously imputed to particular works when they cannot be determinately found in them. Also, if they may be imputed rather than found, there is no reason why incompatible designs cannot be jointly defended.

II

It takes little imagination to see that admitting that judgments which are incompatible on the model of assigned truth-values (true and false) may be jointly defended in terms of the assignment of other values is tantamount to the adoption of a form of relativism. The entailment is indifferent to context; hence, if defensible, relativism may be extended in every domain of inquiry. For example, it may be extended to evaluative disputes. More ambitiously, it may be extended to moral and ontological disputes, to the interpretation of human history itself, or to theories of explanatory adequacy. It is important to appreciate the generality of the issue, even though the argument is couched here in terms of the special concerns of aesthetic appreciation.

But relativism is a suspect doctrine.[12] There seems, in fact, to be a simple way to refute it. Construe it as a conservative thesis: that, for some set of judgments, it is not the case that no judgments of that set can in principle be valid (skepticism), or that judgments can be validly defended on one principle only (what Richard Henson has recently termed "universalism"). Assign truth-values, then, to judgments on relativistic grounds and assume that, in relevantly significant disputes, the correct assignment of incompatible truth-values depends on the use of competing (relativistic) "principles." There is no need to attempt to individuate such principles. The point of the exercise is that, on the hypothesis, relativism leads to contradiction, since judgments would then be able to be validly shown to be both true and false.

The argument is impeccable but indecisive—for an elementary reason. Grant only that a putatively relativistic set of judgments lacks truth-values (true and false) but takes values of other sorts, or takes "truth-values" other than true and false. This, of course, is precisely the maneuver we have adopted. It is also possible to hold that judgments are relativized in the sense that every validating "principle" is said to subtend its own sector of judgments and that no two principles have intersecting sectors. This, roughly, is the theme of conventionalism and of subjectivism in values. I. C. Jarvie treats relativism as entailed by subjectivism, but he does not consider other forms of relativism—though he does distinguish "diversity of evaluation" from "failure to settle disputes," and though he resists inferring subjectivism from such "diversity."[13] But, although conventionalism is a possible strategy, it is quite uninteresting. It fails to admit a range of *competing* claims, by not admitting minimal grounds justifying the joint application of competing principles. It fails, therefore, to admit not only incompatible judgments relative to a particular principle but also "incongruent" judgments—judgments that, construed in terms of truth and falsity, would be incompatible, that are actually not incompatible, and that involve the use of predicates jointly accessible to competing principles. The weaker or conventionalist form of relativism is uninteresting whether truth itself be thought to be relativized to a particular language,[14] or whether a restricted range of judgments be thought to be defensible only in terms of some particular convention or "implicit agreement."[15] I suggest that what we want instead is a form of moderate or "robust" relativism. Actually, the requirements of the coherence of interlinguistic communication entail the inadequacy of relativized accounts of truth. Even if ascriptions of "truth" were relativized, we would require a conception of truth that is not language-relative even if what is true can only be formulated in a way subject to the local features of particular languages, and even if the system of beliefs of a society (including its beliefs about the meanings of what may be said) changes diachronically. Radical relativism regarding truth, meaning, consistency, and knowledge cannot but be incoherent;[16] for, wherever alternative doctrines, theories, claims, or judgments are construed as debatable, we implicitly commit ourselves to their joint intelligibility and testability. In this sense, we cannot relativize meaning and truth, even if our actual criteria and procedures for determining particular meanings and particular truths are open to revision. But the indefensibility of radical relativism does not entail the indefensibility of all forms of relativism; and the denial that a particular kind of judgment (for instance, interpretive judgments) can be flatly true or false, or reliably known to be true or false, does not at all entail radical relativism.[17] On the contrary, interpretive (also: appreciative, evaluative, ideological) judgments are conceptually dependent on a range of considerations that cannot be relativized in the same way.

The distinction of a robust relativism, then, includes the following necessary constraints: (1) the rejection of skepticism and universalism for a given set of judgments; (2) the provision that such a set of judgments takes values other than truth and falsity and includes incongruent judgments; (3) the rejection of cognitivism—entailed by (2) in any case—that we possess a matching cognitive faculty (perception or intuition, for instance) the normal exercise of which enables us to make veridical discriminations of the presence or absence of the properties designated;[18] (4) the admission of the joint relevance of competing principles in validating the ascriptions or appraisals in question, that is, the admission of some theory explaining such tolerance—entailed by (2). On reflection, these four conditions appear to be sufficient as well as necessary. They are, in any case, jointly compatible and undercut what may fairly be taken to be the least specialized attack on relativism. Of course, it is not entailed by the above that all judgments (taken collectively) be defensibly construed as behaving relativistically. That would require construing truth relativistically and would be tantamount to retreating to a radical version of the weaker sense of relativism. But it may be insisted that a further condition (5) should be appended, namely, that relativistic sets of judgments presuppose some range of nonrelativistic judgments, or that relativistic judgments are dependent on there being some viable range of nonrelativistic judgments. I take (5) to be entailed by (1); still, the provision precludes the possible embarrassment of conceding that we may say that it is true that relativistic judgments ("incongruent" in the sense supplied) do have the values (other than true and false) that they are said to have. It may also be claimed that genuinely relativistic theories should be distinguished sharply from theories that merely admit that the validity of any range of judgments is relative to the supporting evidence, or to the supporting considerations on which that is said to depend. So a further condition (6) may be required, namely, that a set of judgments is relativistic if their validation is determined by considerations bearing on the sensibilities or epistemic states of those who relevantly judge. (This may in fact be the fair sense of the relativistic interpretation of Protagoras's dictum.) But (6) appears to be entailed by (2). Hence, a robust relativism need not reduce to subjectivism, since not only can supporting

non-subjective

essential

reasons be supplied and demanded, but also the validity of relevant judgments may actually be confirmed. I am, therefore, proposing a middle ground between skepticism, conventionalism, and subjectivism, on the one hand, and universalism, cognitivism, and absolutism, on the other.[19] What I am calling a robust relativism entails that there be certain minimal constraints—in terms of what is simply true and false—that relativistic judgments must accommodate. To put the issue this way shows that it is quite insufficient to say merely that interpretation is "indeterminate" (as not being true or false). The fact is that epistemic values of some sort can be assigned interpretations. It is true that interpretive judgments exhibit, as Robert Matthews argues, "epistemic weakness";[20] but to be "indeterminate" with respect to truth and falsity is not to be epistemically indeterminate. On the contrary, it is in virtue of our theory of artworks that we disallow ascriptions of truth and falsity of particular claims and require that interpretations meet criteria of critical plausibility—which entail (1) compatibility with the describable features of given artworks and (2) conformability with relativized canons of interpretation that themselves fall within the tolerance of an historically continuous tradition of interpretation.

A final word about "incompatible" and "plausible" may be in order. Incompatibles cannot be jointly true. There is, however, nothing logically odd about admitting, relative to a certain body of evidence, that "in six months, Nixon will be president" and "in six months, Nixon won't be president" are both plausible, though they cannot both be true. In context, this means that the states of affairs that would make either true cannot jointly obtain, though the evidence or supporting reasons available for each (which is the only relevant consideration bearing on plausibility—or probability) validates the judgment. Considerations of plausibility and probability, then, concern epistemic constraints on propositions; considerations of truth do not. Here, incidentally, is a strong reason for not treating the statement "in six months, Nixon will be president" as equivalent either to "it is true that, in six months, Nixon will be president" or to "it is plausible that, in six months, Nixon will be president." Though the plausibility of each of the pair of statements about Nixon may be affected by the plausibility of the other, they may be jointly plausible—though it is obviously not plausible (it is impossible) to maintain the conjunction of those statements. Our proposal, therefore, does not violate any of the usual logical constraints. Thus, musical interpretations A and B of Brahms's Fourth Symphony or literary interpretations A and B of Hamlet are incompatible in the straightforward sense that there is no interpretation C in which A and B can be combined. But that is not to say that A and B cannot both be plausible. (The equivocation on "A" and "B" is benign enough.) When, therefore, I say that "we allow seemingly incompatible accounts of a given work . . . to stand as confirmed," I mean to draw attention to the fact that the accounts in question would be incompatible construed in terms of a model of truth and falsity, but are not incompatible construed in terms of plausibility.[21] We have, then, succeeded in showing the coherence of a critical practice that tolerates the joint defensibility of interpretive judgments that, on a model of truth and falsity, would be incompatibles. And we have shown both that such a model is favored by independent considerations regarding the very nature of artworks[22] and that there are no compelling counterproposals among its best-known opponents.

NOTES

1. See Stephen Pepper, The Work of Art (Bloomington: Indiana University Press, 1955). See also Donald Henze, "Is the Work of Art a Construct?" Journal of Philosophy 52 (1955), and "The Work of Art," Journal of Philosophy 54 (1957).

2. See Monroe Beardsley, Aesthetics (New York: Harcourt, Brace and World, 1958); E. D. Hirsch, Jr., Validity in Interpretation (New Haven: Yale University Press, 1967 [see Chapter 1]); Stein Haugom Olsen, The Structure of Literary Understanding (Cambridge: Cambridge University Press, 1978); and John Reichert, Making Sense of Literature (Chicago: University of Chicago Press, 1978).

3. See W. K. Wimsatt, Jr., The Verbal Icon (Lexington: University Press of Kentucky, 1954). [Wimsatt's concession is discussed in a passage not reprinted here. — Ed.]

4. See Hirsch, Validity in Interpretation. [Margolis's examination of Hirsch's claim occurs in a passage not reprinted here—Ed.]

5. See Rene Wellek, Concepts of Criticism (New Haven: Yale University Press, 1965); and Wimsatt, Verbal Icon.

6. See Charles Sanders Peirce, "Abduction and Induction," in The Philosophy of Peirce: Selected Writings, ed. Justus Buchler (New York: Harcourt, Brace, 1940).

7. See Michael Polanyi, Personal Knowledge (Chicago: University of Chicago Press, 1962).

8. See Carl Hempel, Aspects of Scientific Explanation (New York: Free Press, 1965).

9. See Monroe C. Beardsley, The Possibility of Criticism (Detroit: Wayne State University Press, 1970). [See Chapter 2, p. 37.]

10. See P. H. Nowell-Smith, "Acts and Locutions," in Art, Mind, and Religion, ed. W. H. Capitan and D. D. Merrill (Pittsburgh: University of Pittsburgh Press, 1965).

The term "verdictive" is used by Nowell-Smith in the sense of J. L. Austin, *How to Do Things with Words* (Oxford: Oxford University Press, 1962).

11. [This argument is given in a passage not reprinted here—Ed.]

12. See E. D. Hirsch, Jr., *The Aims of Interpretation* (Chicago: University of Chicago Press, 1976).

13. See I. C. Jarvie, "The Objectivity of Criticism in the Arts," *Ratio* 9 (1967).

14. See Alfred Tarski, "The Semantic Conception of Truth and the Foundation of Semantics," *Philosophy and Phenomenological Research* 4 (1944); Willard Van Orman Quine, *Word and Object* (Cambridge, Mass.: Harvard University Press, 1960); and Donald Davidson, "Truth and Meaning," *Synthese* 17 (1967).

15. See Gilbert Harman, "Moral Relativism Defended," *Philosophical Review* 84 (1975). Compare Roger Trigg, *Reason and Commitment* (Cambridge: Cambridge University Press, 1973).

16. *Contra* Paul Feyerabend, *Against Method* (London: NLB; Atlantic Highlands, N.J.: Humanities Press, 1975). Compare Stephen Lukes, "Relativism: Cognitive and Moral," *Proceedings of the Aristotelian Society*, supplementary vol. 48 (1974).

17. *Contra* Hirsch, *Aims of Interpretation*.

18. See Joseph Margolis, "Moral Cognitivism," *Ethics* 85 (1975).

19. Compare Peter Winch, "Understanding and Explanation in Sociology and Anthropology," and I. C. Jarvie, "Understanding and Explanation in Sociology and Social Anthropology," both in Robert Borger and Frank Cioffi, eds., *Explanation in the Behavioural Sciences* (Cambridge: Cambridge University Press, 1970).

20. See Robert J. Matthews, "Describing and Interpreting Works of Art," *Journal of Aesthetics and Art Criticism* 36 (1977). Compare Denis Dutton, "Plausibility and Aesthetic Interpretation," *Canadian Journal of Philosophy* 7 (1977).

21. *Contra* Annette Barnes, "Half an Hour before Breakfast," *Journal of Aesthetics and Art Criticism* 34 (1976).

22. [The author's discussion of the nature of art and its bearing on the logical status of interpretive judgments occurs in a passage not reprinted here—Ed.]

The Impossibility of Intentionless Meaning

4

STEVEN KNAPP AND
WALTER BENN MICHAELS

I

THE CLEAREST EXAMPLE OF the tendency to gen-
erate theoretical problems by splitting apart terms that are in fact inseparable
is the persistent debate over the relation between authorial intention and the
meaning of texts. Some theorists have claimed that valid interpretations can
only be obtained through an appeal to authorial intentions. This assumption
is shared by theorists who, denying the possibility of recovering authorial
intentions, also deny the possibility of valid interpretations. But once it is
seen that the meaning of a text is simply identical to the author's intended
meaning, the project of grounding meaning in intention becomes incoherent.
Since the project itself is incoherent, it can neither succeed nor fail; hence
both theoretical attitudes toward intention are irrelevant. The mistake made
by theorists has been to imagine the possibility or desirability of moving from
one term (the author's intended meaning) to a second term (the text's meaning), when actually the two terms are the same. One can neither succeed nor
fail in deriving one term from the other, since to have one is already to have
them both. . . .

The fact that what a text means is what its author intends is clearly stated

Steven Knapp and Walter Benn Michaels, "Against Theory," in *Against Theory: Literary
Studies and the New Pragmatism*, edited by W.J.T. Mitchell (Chicago: University of Chicago
Press, 1985), pp. 12–18, © 1982, 1983, 1984, 1985 by The University of Chicago; and Steven
Knapp and Walter Benn Michaels, "Against Theory 2: Hermeneutics and Deconstruc-
tion," *Critical Inquiry* 14 (1987): 49–58, © 1987 by The University of Chicago. Reprinted
by permission of the authors and publisher.

by E. D. Hirsch when he writes that the meaning of a text "is, and can be, nothing other than the author's meaning" and "is determined once and for all by the character of the speaker's intention."[1] Having defined meaning as the author's intended meaning, Hirsch goes on to argue that all literary interpretation "must stress a reconstruction of the author's aims and attitudes in order to evolve guides and norms for construing the meaning of his text." Although these guides and norms cannot guarantee the correctness of any particular reading—nothing can—they nevertheless constitute, he claims, a "fundamentally sound" and "objective" method of interpretation (pp. 224, 240).

What seems odd about Hirsch's formulation is the transition from definition to method. He begins by defining textual meaning as the author's intended meaning and then suggests that the best way to find textual meaning is to look for authorial intention. But if meaning and intended meaning are already the same, it's hard to see how looking for one provides an objective method—or any sort of method—for looking for the other; looking for one just is looking for the other. The recognition that what a text means and what its author intends it to mean are identical should entail the further recognition that any appeal from one to the other is useless. And yet, as we have already begun to see, Hirsch thinks the opposite; he believes that identifying meaning with the expression of intention has the supreme theoretical usefulness of providing an objective method of choosing among alternative interpretations.

Hirsch, however, has failed to understand the force of his own formulation. In one moment he identifies meaning and intended meaning; in the next moment he splits them apart. This mistake is clearly visible in his polemic against formalist critics who deny the importance of intention altogether. His argument against these critics ends up invoking their account of meaning at the expense of his own. Formalists, in Hirsch's summary, conceive the text as a "piece of language," a "public object whose character is defined by public norms." The problem with this account, according to Hirsch, is that "no mere sequence of words can represent an actual verbal meaning with reference to public norms alone. Referred to these alone, the text's meaning remains indeterminate." Hirsch's example, "My car ran out of gas," is, as he notes, susceptible to an indeterminate range of interpretations. There are no public norms which will help us decide whether the sentence means that my automobile lacks fuel or "my Pullman dash[ed] from a cloud of Argon." Only by assigning a particular intention to the words "My car ran out of gas" does one arrive at a determinate interpretation. Or, as Hirsch himself puts it, "The

array of possibilities only begins to become a more selective system of *probabilities* when, instead of confronting merely a word sequence, we also posit a
speaker who very likely means something" (p. 225 [see Chapter 1, p. 17]).[2]

This argument seems consistent with Hirsch's equation of meaning and
intended meaning, until one realizes that Hirsch is imagining a moment of
interpretation before intention is present. This is the moment at which the
text's meaning "remains indeterminate," before such indeterminacy is cleared
up by the *addition* of authorial intention. But if meaning and intention really
are inseparable, then it makes no sense to think of intention as an ingredient
that needs to be added; it must be present from the start. The issue of determinacy or indeterminacy is irrelevant. Hirsch thinks it's relevant because he
thinks, correctly, that the movement from indeterminacy to determinacy involves the addition of information, but he also thinks, incorrectly, that adding
information amounts to adding intention. Since intention is already present,
the only thing added, in the movement from indeterminacy to determinacy,
is information *about* the intention, not the intention itself. For a sentence like
"My car ran out of gas" even to be recognizable as a sentence, we must already
have posited a speaker and hence an intention. Pinning down an interpretation of the sentence will not involve adding a speaker but deciding among a
range of possible speakers. Knowing that the speaker inhabits a planet with
an atmosphere of inert gases and on which the primary means of transporta-
tion is railroad will give one interpretation; knowing that the speaker is an
earthling who owns a Ford will give another. But even if we have none of
this information, as soon as we attempt to interpret at all we are already committed to a characterization of the speaker as a speaker of language. We know,
in other words, that the speaker intends to speak; otherwise we wouldn't be
interpreting. In this latter case, we have less information about the speaker
than in the other two (where we at least knew the speaker's planetary origin),
but the relative lack of information has nothing to do with the presence or
absence of intention.

This mistake no doubt accounts for Hirsch's peculiar habit of calling the
proper object of interpretation the "author's meaning" and, in later writings,
distinguishing between it and the "reader's meaning."[3] The choice between
these two kinds of meaning becomes, for Hirsch, an ethical imperative as well
as an "operational" necessity. But if all meaning is always the author's meaning, the alternative is an empty one, and there is no choice, ethical or operational, to be made. Since theory is designed to help us make such choices, all
theoretical arguments on the issue of authorial intention must at some point
accept the premises of anti-intentionalist accounts of meaning. In debates

about intention, the moment of imagining intentionless meaning constitutes the theoretical moment itself. From the standpoint of an argument against critical theory, then, the only important question about intention is whether there can in fact be intentionless meanings. If our argument against theory is to succeed, the answer to this question must be no.

The claim that all meanings are intentional is not, of course, an unfamiliar one in contemporary philosophy of language. John Searle, for example, asserts that "there is no getting away from intentionality," and he and others have advanced arguments to support this claim.[4] Our purpose here is not to add another such argument but to show how radically counterintuitive the alternative would be. We can begin to get a sense of this simply by noticing how difficult it is to imagine a case of intentionless meaning.

Suppose that you are walking along a beach and you come upon a curious sequence of squiggles in the sand. You step back a few paces and notice that they spell out the following words:

> A slumber did my spirit seal;
> I had no human fears:
> She seemed a thing that could not feel
> The touch of earthly years.[5]

This would seem to be a good case of intentionless meaning: you recognize the writing as writing, you understand what the words mean, you may even identify them as constituting a rhymed poetic stanza—and all this without knowing anything about the author and indeed without needing to connect the words to any notion of an author at all. You can do all these things without thinking of anyone's intention. But now suppose that, as you stand gazing at this pattern in the sand, a wave washes up and recedes, leaving in its wake (written below what you now realize was only the first stanza) the following words:

> No motion has she now, no force;
> She neither hears nor sees,
> Rolled round in earth's diurnal course
> With rocks, and stones, and trees.

One might ask whether the question of intention still seems as irrelevant as it did seconds before. You will now, we suspect, feel compelled to explain what you have just seen. Are these marks mere accidents, produced by the mechanical operation of the waves on the sand (through some subtle and unprecedented process of erosion, percolation, etc.)? Or is the sea alive and striving to express its pantheistic faith? Or has Wordsworth, since his death, become a sort of genius of the shore who inhabits the waves and periodically inscribes on the sand his elegiac sentiments? You might go on extending the list of explanations indefinitely, but you would find, we think, that all explanations fall into two categories. You will either be ascribing these marks to some agent capable of intentions (the living sea, the haunting Wordsworth, etc.) or you will count them as nonintentional effects of mechanical processes (erosion, percolation, etc.). But in the second case—where the marks now seem to be accidents—will they still seem to be words?

Clearly not. They will merely seem to *resemble* words. You will be amazed, perhaps, that such an astonishing coincidence could occur. Of course, you would have been no less amazed had you decided that the sea or the ghost of Wordsworth was responsible. But it is essential to recognize that in the two cases your amazement would have two entirely different sources. In one case, you would be amazed by the identity of the author—who would have thought that the sea can write poetry? In the other case, however, in which you accept the hypothesis of natural accident, you're amazed to discover that what you thought was poetry turns out not to be poetry at all. It isn't poetry because it isn't language; that's what it means to call it an accident. As long as you thought the marks were poetry, you were assuming their intentional character. You had no idea who the author was, and this may have tricked you into thinking that positing an author was irrelevant to your ability to read the stanza. But in fact you had, without realizing it, already posited an author. It was only with the mysterious arrival of the second stanza that your tacit assumption (e.g., someone writing with a stick) was challenged and you realized that you had made one. Only now, when positing an author seems impossible, do you genuinely imagine the marks as authorless. But to deprive them of an author is to convert them into accidental likenesses of language. They are not, after all, an example of intentionless meaning; as soon as they become intentionless they become meaningless as well.

The arrival of the second stanza made clear that what had seemed to be an example of intentionless language was either not intentionless or not language. The question was whether the marks counted as language; what determined the answer was a decision as to whether or not they were the product of an intentional agent. If our example has seemed farfetched, it is only because there is seldom occasion in our culture to wonder whether the *sea* is an intentional agent. But there *are* cases where the question of intentional agency might be an important and difficult one. Can computers speak? Arguments over this question reproduce exactly the terms of our example.

Since computers are machines, the issue of whether they can speak seems to hinge on the possibility of intentionless language. But our example shows that there is no such thing as intentionless language; the only real issue is whether computers are capable of intentions. However this issue may be decided—and our example offers no help in deciding it—the decision will not rest on a theory of meaning but on a judgment as to whether computers can be intentional agents. This is not to deny that a great deal—morally, legally, and politically—might depend on such judgments. But no degree of practical importance will give these judgments theoretical force.

The difference between theoretical principle and practical or empirical judgments can be clarified by one last glance at the case of the wave poem. Suppose, having seen the second stanza wash up on the beach, you have decided that the "poem" is really an accidental effect of erosion, percolation, and so on and therefore not language at all. What would it now take to change your mind? No theoretical argument will make a difference. But suppose you notice, rising out of the sea some distance from the shore, a small submarine, out of which clamber a half dozen figures in white lab coats. One of them trains his binoculars on the beach and shouts triumphantly, "It worked! It worked! Let's go down and try it again." Presumably, you will now once again change your mind, not because you have a new account of language, meaning, or intention but because you now have new evidence of an author. The question of authorship is and always was an empirical question; it has now received a new empirical answer. The theoretical temptation is to imagine that such empirical questions must, or should, have theoretical answers.

Even a philosopher as committed to the intentional status of language as Searle succumbs to this temptation to think that intention is a theoretical issue. After insisting, in the passage cited earlier, on the inescapability of intention, he goes on to say that "in serious literal speech the sentences are precisely the realizations of the intentions" and that "there need be no *gulf* at all between the illocutionary intention and its expression."[6] The point, however, is not that there *need* be no gulf between intention and the meaning of its expression but that there *can* be no gulf. Not only in serious literal speech but in *all* speech what is intended and what is meant are identical. In separating the two Searle imagines the possibility of expression without intention and so, like Hirsch, misses the point of his own claim that when it comes to language "there is no getting away from intentionality." . . .

II

The attempt to imagine that a text can mean something other than what its author intends is not restricted to writers interested in interpretive method. In fact, the denial that meaning is determined by intention is central to [a] project as indifferent to method as hermeneutics. For hermeneutics, a text means what its author intends but also necessarily means more, acquiring new meanings as readers apply it to new situations. . . . Since [hermeneutics is] . . . committed to the view that a text can mean something other than what its author intends, [it is] . . . also committed to the view that a text derives its identity from something other than authorial intention. The text is what it is, no matter what meaning is assigned to it by its author and no matter how that meaning is revised by its readers.

What gives a text its autonomous identity? On most accounts, the answer is linguistic conventions—the semantic and syntactic rules of the language in which the text is written. One of our aims in the present essay is to criticize the particular notion of textual identity advanced by hermeneutics . . . but our more general target is the notion that there can be any plausible criteria of textual identity that can function independent of authorial intention. . . .

According to Paul Ricoeur, "there is a problem of interpretation," a problem that arises from "the very nature of the verbal intention of the text." Because "the objective meaning is something other than the subjective intention of the author," a text "may be construed in various ways." But this problem, for Ricoeur and for hermeneutics generally, is also an opportunity, since the "surpassing of the intention by the meaning" frees interpretation from its dependence on the author's intention, which is "often unknown to us, sometimes redundant, sometimes useless, and sometimes even harmful as regards the interpretation of the verbal meaning of his work." Liberated from the author, we can now understand the text in the "nonpsychological and properly semantical space" that "the text has carved out by severing itself from the mental intention of its author."[7]

It is above all in writing, according to Ricoeur, that the "semantic autonomy" of language, "nascent and inchoate . . . in living speech," become fully manifest (IT, p. 25). In living speech, "the subjective intention of the speaker and the discourse's meaning overlap each other in such a way that it is the same thing to understand what the speaker means and what his discourse means." In writing, however, "the author's intention and the meaning of the text cease to coincide" (IT, p. 29). Because intention and meaning come apart, the "text's career escapes the finite horizon lived by its author. What the text means now matters more than what the author meant when he wrote it" (IT, p. 30). Or, as Hans-Georg Gadamer puts it, "What is fixed in writing has detached itself from the contingency of its origin and its author and made itself free for new relationships."[8] This step, the text's becoming available for new relationships, is what opens the possibility of hermeneutics. The text takes on a life of its own and henceforth can be understood "only if it is understood in a different way every time" (TM, p. 276). "The real meaning of a text," Gadamer writes, "does not depend on the contingencies of the author . . . for it is always partly determined also by the historical situation of the interpreter and hence by the totality of the objective course of history" (TM, p. 263). Nor is this merely the epistemological commonplace that understanding is always contextual; it is the ontological claim that a text's interpretive history is part of the meaning of the text itself.

For readers acquainted with American formalism, the claim that a text "has detached itself from the contingency of its origin" and therefore that its meaning always in principle goes beyond its author has a familiar ring. As long ago as 1946, W. K. Wimsatt and Monroe C. Beardsley argued in their essay "The Intentional Fallacy" that a poem "is detached from its author at birth and goes about the world beyond his power to intend about it or control it."[9] For Wimsatt and Beardsley, the meaning of a text was determined by "public" features of language such as "semantics and syntax."[10] But where for Wimsatt and Beardsley the meaning of the text itself, once detached from authorial intention, was permanent and unchanging, for Gadamer the detachment of meaning from intention shows, as we have noted, that "a text is understood only if it is understood in a different way every time." And this recognition defines "the task of historical hermeneutics," which is "to consider the tension that exists between the identity of the common object and the changing situation in which it must be understood" (TM, p. 276). In other words, for Gadamer, interpretation goes "beyond mere reconstruction" of the author's intention (TM, p. 337); the changing situation in which the text must be understood is itself part of the text's meaning. Thus the "fundamental hermeneutic problem" is inseparable from what Gadamer calls the "problem of application," how to "adapt the meaning of a text to the concrete situation" of the interpreter (TM, pp. 274, 275). . . .

What is required for the hermeneutic notion of application to work is a criterion of textual identity that will allow the text to remain the same while its meaning changes. As we noted earlier, hermeneutics finds this criterion in what Ricoeur calls the "verbal" or "objective" meaning of the text, which, because it is "something other than the subjective intention" of the author, may be "construed in various ways" (IT, p. 76). Although, for Ricoeur and for hermeneutics generally, it is in writing that the difference between verbal meaning and subjective intention fully emerges, there is no reason in principle why it cannot emerge in speech as well. In what circumstances might it seem plausible to say that the verbal meaning of a text or utterance transcends the author's intention?

Suppose someone says "go" in circumstances suggesting that he must mean something else. Perhaps the speaker is a passenger in a car that has just pulled up to a railroad crossing. He says "go," but the driver hesitates when she notices that the gate is down and a train is approaching. The problem she faces is the apparent discrepancy between the verbal meaning of "go"— what "go" means according to the rules of English—and what she takes to be the speaker's likely intention. But isn't her problem only a negative version of what we characterized earlier as the hermeneutic opportunity? If a text can have a conventional meaning different from its intended meaning, then its meaning is clearly not fixed once and for all by intention; it is, as Gadamer says, "free for new relationships."

But does this example show that a text or utterance can have a conventional meaning independent of authorial intention? Suppose the driver decides that the passenger is being ironic. Is irony a case where intention and meaning come apart? After all, the utterance only counts as ironic if the speaker's meaning is not simply the conventional one. At the same time, however, the utterance only counts as ironic if the speaker *intends* that both the conventional meaning and the departure from conventional meaning be recognized. Since both aspects of an ironic utterance are equally intentional, irony in no way frees the meaning of the utterance from the speaker's intention.

If irony is not a case where a text's verbal meaning transcends its author's intention, is there any case in which it does—any case in which the author's or speaker's intention really does seem, in Ricoeur's words, "useless . . . as regards the interpretation of the verbal meaning of his works?" Suppose the driver knows that when the passenger says "go," he simply means "stop"; nevertheless she insists on taking "go" to mean what it means according to the conventions of English, that is "go." There is no question this time of the speaker being ironic: he does not intend the conventional meaning to be taken ironically; he does not intend the conventional meaning at all. The driver, knowing what he intends, chooses to disregard it, preferring instead the conventional or "verbal" meaning. Such a response might seem odd in the context of this example, since disregarding the passenger's intended meaning could be suicidal. But perhaps the driver wants to commit suicide; in any event cases in which an author's intention is known but disregarded are (allegedly) typical in literary criticism. What might seem odd in all such cases is not the possibility of disregarding the author's intention but the possibility of knowing it in the first place. After all, the whole point of the example is that the passenger is not following the rules of English; so how does the driver know what he means? What does she know if she knows that the speaker means "stop" when he says "go"?

What she knows, presumably, is another set of conventions, a set of conventions that link the sound "go" with the meaning "stop." Insofar as these conventions are different from the conventions of English, and insofar as the identity of a language is determined by its conventions, the passenger isn't speaking English but some other language. What the driver knows is the other language; she knows that "go" in English means "go" but that "go" in the passenger's language means "stop." By choosing the English meaning over the passenger's meaning, she is not simply choosing one meaning over another, she is choosing one set of conventions over another—one language over another. But if the passenger and the driver are following different linguistic conventions, in what sense do "go" as he says it and "go" as she hears it have the same conventional or "verbal" meaning? And if the verbal meaning is not the same, how can verbal meaning provide the "common object" that, according to Gadamer, makes it possible for a single text to mean what its author intends and also something more?

Would this outcome (the disappearance of a common verbal meaning) be altered by a stipulation that the author and the interpreter share a single language? Suppose the driver disregards the passenger's intention not because he is speaking a different language but because she prefers a different meaning of the English word "go": he means "get out of the car" but she prefers "drive forward." Here, perhaps, it could be said that the verbal meaning of "go" (the meaning assigned to "go" by the conventions of English) includes both meanings; hence it might seem that the "go" he says and the "go" she prefers, despite their difference in meaning, amount to a single object. And this third version of the example does seem to yield the principle that, in our view, lies at the heart of hermeneutics: a single text can't mean just anything ("go," in English, can't nonironically mean "stop"), but a single text can mean anything the conventions of its language allow it to mean. Unlike the case of irony, where the author intends both the verbal meaning and some departure from it, and unlike the case of translation, where there is no common verbal meaning, in this case there is a common verbal meaning that includes both what the author intends and what the interpreter prefers. The work of application would thus consist of selecting the most appropriate meaning from the range of meanings made available by the language, a meaning that might or might not coincide with the meaning intended by the author.

If what hermeneutics needs is a criterion of textual identity such that a text can mean what its author means and also something more, then the stipulation that author and interpreter share the same language (so that the text means what its author means plus whatever else it can mean in that language) is indeed one way of satisfying that need. The trouble is that it is by no means the only way. For if there are other criteria that will serve equally well, the question arises, Why choose this one? Suppose one were to locate the identity of the text not in its verbal meaning but simply in the letters on the page. In that case, anything those letters might mean in any language would count as a valid interpretation of the same text. The same text—"go"—would mean what it meant in English and also what it meant in the passenger's language, as well as what it could be used to mean in any language, living, dead, or yet to be invented. Why, then, choose verbal meaning over letters? Presumably for the very reason that the criterion of verbal meaning limits the range of possible meanings (while still allowing more than one), whereas the criterion of letters would allow an infinite range of meanings. Allowing every meaning the letters would allow would be like playing poker with all cards wild. The interest of the game—the "tension that exists between the identity of the common object and the changing situation in which it must be understood"—can only be preserved if the range of possible interpretations is somehow limited.

But while this consideration justifies the choice of verbal meaning over letters, it won't explain why hermeneutics chooses verbal meaning over some other equally limiting criterion. Suppose we revise the rule that a text means what its author intends plus whatever else it can mean in a given language to read that a text means what its author intends plus whatever else it can mean in a given language—except for its verbs, which mean what the author intends plus the antonyms of whatever they can mean in the language.[11] An English sentence like "No vehicle shall be permitted in the park" could now be correctly interpreted to mean "No vehicle shall be excluded from the park." Why prefer the stipulation that verbs mean what they can mean in the language to the stipulation that verbs mean the opposite of what they can mean in the language? Obviously not because it limits the range of possible meanings; both stipulations accomplish that. The answer must be that the range of possible meanings provided by the language rule is somehow more appropriate than the range of possible meanings provided by the antonym rule. A judge who interpreted "No vehicle shall be permitted in the park" to prohibit baby carriages and a judge who interpreted it to allow them would still seem to be interpreting the same law. But would a judge who interpreted it to allow *all* vehicles—cars, trucks, tanks—still be interpreting the same law? How could there be a law (how would anyone *follow* a law) that could be correctly interpreted to have two contradictory meanings?

At this point, the apparent advantage of verbal meaning as a criterion of textual identity becomes clear. While the antonym rule allows interpretations directly opposed to the author's intentions, and while other imaginable rules would allow interpretations utterly irrelevant to the author's intention,[12] the verbal meaning rule limits interpreters to meanings that may go beyond the author's intention but nonetheless seem plausibly related to it. And this claim to establish some relation to the author's intention is what saves verbal meaning from being just one game among others. But is it true that limiting interpreters to the meanings allowed by the author's language guarantees any degree of proximity to the author's intention? Suppose the law excluding vehicles from the park was written after 1936, when I. A. Richards introduced the terms "tenor" and "vehicle" to name the two halves of a metaphor.[13] Is the judge who, following the verbal meaning rule, interprets the law to exclude poems any closer to the legislators' intention than a judge who, following some other rule, interprets the law to exclude cabbages? Indeed, one can imagine cases where following the verbal meaning rule will yield the same result as following the antonym rule: for example, in contemporary American English "bad" can mean "good." What such examples show is that there is no necessary relation between the meaning the author intends and any one of the meanings the author's words can have in the language—except for the one the author intends. And the relation is not one of relative proximity but of identity.

Since the rules of the language do not provide a range of meanings that are necessarily closer to the author's intention than the range of meanings provided by any other set of rules,[14] how are they relevant at all? They are relevant not because they provide a range of possible meanings but because they provide clues to the meaning the author intends. The dictionary definition of "vehicle" is useful not because it determines the range of possible meanings "vehicle" can have but because it provides clues to what an English-speaking author might mean by "vehicle." But if the interest of verbal meaning reduces to an interest in clues to what an author intends, what sense is there in appealing to the notion of verbal meaning as a way of going beyond authorial intention?

The hermeneutic choice of verbal meaning as a criterion of textual identity, then, turns out to be either arbitrary or incoherent. If what hermeneutics wants is only a criterion that will allow a text to mean what its author intends and also something more, then the choice of verbal meaning is arbitrary—other criteria (letters, antonyms, and so on) will do just as well. And if the choice of verbal meaning is not arbitrary—if it can be justified by regarding verbal meaning as evidence of authorial intention—then the notion that it gives the text an identity independent of authorial intention is incoherent. The "common object" that will allow a text to mean what its author meant and also something more thus disappears; either the common object is the product of an utterly arbitrary choice or there is no common object. In either case, there is no "tension" between the identity of a "common object" and the "changing situation in which it must be understood." If the choice of a criterion is arbitrary, there is no tension because the rules of the game can be adjusted to make the common object fit any situation. And if there is no common object, there is no tension because the interpreter who disregards the author's intention is not interpreting the same text but producing a new one. Because, in both cases, there can be no tension between the permanent identity of a text and the "changing situation" in which the text is understood, what Gadamer calls the "problem of application"—how to "adapt the meaning of a text to the concrete situation" of the interpreter—never arises. If, in Gadamer's view, the "fundamental hermeneutic problem" is the "problem of application," in our view, the problem of hermeneutics is that there is no fundamental hermeneutic problem.

NOTES

1. E. D. Hirsch, Jr. *Validity in Interpretation* (New Haven: Yale University Press, 1967), pp. 216, 219. Our remarks on Hirsch are in some ways parallel to criticisms offered by P. D. Juhl in the second chapter of his *Interpretation: An Essay in the Philosophy of Literary Criticism* (Princeton: Princeton University Press, 1980). . . . All further citations to [Hirsch's book] . . . will be included in the text.

2. The phrase "piece of language" goes back, Hirsch notes, to the opening paragraph of William Empson's *Seven Types of Ambiguity*, 3d ed. (New York: Meridian, 1955).

3. See E. D. Hirsch, Jr., *The Aims of Interpretation* (Chicago: University of Chicago Press, 1976), p. 8.

4. John R. Searle, "Reiterating the Differences: A Reply to Derrida," *Glyph* 1 (1977): 202.

5. Wordsworth's lyric has been a standard example in theoretical arguments since its adoption by Hirsch; see *Validity in Interpretation*, pp. 227–30 [see Chapter 1, pp. 19–20] and 238–40.

6. Searle, "Reiterating," p. 202.

7. Paul Ricoeur, *Interpretation Theory: Discourse and the Surplus of Meaning* (Fort Worth: Texas Christian University Press, 1976). All further references to this work, abbreviated *IT*, will be included in the text.

8. Hans-Georg Gadamer, *Truth and Method*, trans. and ed. Garrett Barden and John Cumming (New York: Continuum, 1975), p. 357. All further references to this work, abbreviated *TM*, will be included in the text.

9. W. K. Wimsatt, Jr., and Monroe C. Beardsley, "The Intentional Fallacy," in Wimsatt, *The Verbal Icon: Studies in the Meaning of Poetry* (Lexington: University Press of Kentucky, 1954), p. 5.

10. Ibid., p. 10.

11. It might be objected that the second rule is not quite *equally* limiting, since in allowing each verb to mean what the author intends plus the antonyms of what it can mean in the language, the rule adds one meaning for each verb. This objection could be met by a stipulation that the antonym of one possible meaning of each verb—say, the second meaning in some specified dictionary—be excluded.

12. For instance, the meaning of each word could include the meanings of all other words in the language with the same number of letters.

13. I. A. Richards, *The Philosophy of Rhetoric* (1936; reprinted, New York: Oxford University Press, 1965), p. 96.

14. Any other set of rules, that is, that allows the author's intended meaning as one possible meaning.

Interpretation, Intention, and Truth

5

RICHARD SHUSTERMAN

I

ONE OF THE MOST SALIENT and powerful trends in the last few decades of literary theory has been the attempt to discredit and displace the traditional project of intentionalist interpretation, the idea that the meaning of a text is to be identified with or found in the intention of its author. Intentionalism surely suffered a sharp and more than momentary blow with the rise of the New Criticism and its influential doctrine of the intentional fallacy, articulated by Wimsatt and Beardsley.[1] But more recent and perhaps still more devastating have been the poststructuralist doctrine of "the death of the Author," heralded by Barthes,[2] and the related rise of the poetics of reader response.

Yet despite the forceful onslaught of these influential doctrines, Anglo-American literary theory has been reluctant to abandon completely the idea that texts mean what they are intended to mean. Influential as it was, New Critical anti-intentionalism soon faced what Beardsley called the "intentionalist backlash."[3] It came not only from the phenomenologically based theory of E. D. Hirsch, but through various analytically motivated theories based on a Gricean (and ultimately Austinian) account of meaning in terms of speech acts. For we must remember that though Austin more famously defined the illocutionary act as "a conventional act," he also regarded it, qua act, as having an essential intentional aspect,[4] a point which escaped neither Strawson nor Derrida.[5] Indeed for all his anti-intentionalist zeal, Beardsley seems compelled by his Austinian speech-act theory of literature (that a "poem is an imitation

Reprinted from the *Journal of Aesthetics and Art Criticism* 46, no. 3 (1988): 399–403, by permission of the American Society for Aesthetics.

of a compound illocutionary act") to admit that at least one intention of the author must be recognized in literary interpretation, namely, his intention to produce a literary work of art rather than an ordinary speech act.[6]

The Austinian–Gricean line of intentionalist defense has been recently reformulated with a vengeance in Knapp and Michaels's powerful essay "Against Theory," which has provoked so much controversy and discussion as to generate a book about it.[7] Their defense of intentionalism is not explicitly directed against Beardsley and Wimsatt (whose New Critical program has already been superseded by more recent and fashionable theories) but primarily at today's prevailing anti-intentionalists—the poststructuralist textualists like de Man—who see literary texts as intentionless language rather than intended speech acts, which instead are what Knapp and Michaels maintain all language must always be.[8] Holding that "meanings are always intentional," they argue that therefore "what a text means and what its author intends it to mean are identical."[9]

With philosophy of language's growing recognition that sentence and utterance meaning cannot be fully explained in purely extensional terms, that language is in some (but not necessarily mentalistic) sense intrinsically and irreducibly intentional, it is hard not to sympathize with the rehabilitation of intention as an inescapably relevant factor in literary interpretation. However, to admit this does not commit us to denying the point of the intentional fallacy thesis and accepting the alternative of Knapp and Michaels. We must be careful not to confuse the seemingly incontrovertible assertion that all linguistic or textual meaning is intentional with the very challengeable assertion that the meaning of a text is identical with the author's intention or intended meaning.

This is precisely Knapp and Michaels's mistake. By simplistically conflating "meaning" with "authorially intended meaning" they thereby absurdly preclude the possibility of someone's speech or writing failing to mean what it was intended to mean, a possibility which is indeed a very frequent actuality. Rejecting this conflation, one can still grant the identification of meaning with intention or intended meaning in more than the holistic sense that there could be no linguistic meaning without a background of human intentionality, no "possibility of language prior to and independent of intention."[10] One can even hold that every individual linguistic text requires some particular intention for its meaning. A string of letters accidentally produced by a computer or by the movement of the tide on the sand would still depend for its meaning on an intentional act, here the intention of the reader to see the marks as a meaningful text, as language rather than simply marks. However, even if we deny with Knapp and Michaels that "there can in fact be intention-less meanings" and accept their premise that texts seen as "intentionless . . . become meaningless as well" and thus that in some sense "what is intended and what is meant are identical," it still does not follow that "the meaning of a text is simply identical to the author's intended meaning." [11] All that follows is that the meaning of a text is inseparable from some intention (or group of intentions) or another. But the necessary meaning-securing intentions could belong to readers of the text rather than to its original author. Thus Knapp and Michaels's argument fails to clinch the case for identifying the text's meaning with authorial intention, unless we are prepared to count any of its readers as the author. But such a drastic remedy would undermine their whole project of intentionalist, author-orientated criticism by dismantling the very notion of author.

Their failure, however, is very instructive in its unstated erroneous assumption that the only sort of intentions that matter for textual meaning and criticism are the author's. This assumption is symptomatic of theory's typical and mistaken neglect of readers' intentions and their variety and importance. . . .

II

Even without going into the details of any specific theory, we can easily see why academic theorists and critics would prefer to deal only with the intention of the author. For this provides, at least in theory, a single, determinate, unchanging focus and standard for all the different readings or interpretations of the work to converge upon and be judged by their fidelity to such intention. But, moreover, since this unique and fixed meaning is only available in theory, it also allows (if not encourages) a continuing diversity of interpretive efforts and approaches.

In short, the elusive notion of authorial intention paradoxically provides both the security of the possibility of achieving objective truth and convergence in literary interpretation (something that the academic industry requires for its legitimation as a scientific, positivist enterprise productive of formulatable, teachable truths) and also the security that this objective truth or meaning cannot be conclusively or once and for all demonstrated, thereby ensuring that the demand for continued interpretive efforts and new readings will not be extinguished.[12] This demand is perhaps even more crucial than truth to the academic industry, where the production of ever-new interpretations and critical perspectives is necessary for its own reproduction and advancement (as it is for the personal careers of its participants).

The implicit recognition that the value of continued demand and productivity outweighs that of legitimation through the ideas of determinacy and truth can explain why academic criticism has so enthusiastically embraced first the banishment of the author (already in New Criticism) and then the further banishment of the circumscribed, determinate work so as to exult in the productive freedom of pluralistic textuality (as expressed in Barthes and deconstruction). Understandably, those who oppose this free-wheeling, creative interpretive productivity express the fear that such practice will destroy the coherence of criticism as a scholarly cognitive discipline converging on the truth.[13]

Literary theorists of the more conservative Anglo-American tradition, so long preoccupied with the question of authorial intention as to ignore that of the reader, have characteristically assumed that the interpreting reader's intention is (or should be) essentially uniform and that it is (or should be) essentially cognitive. The case of Beardsley is instructive. In arguing (against Hirsch) for the logical (and possibly real) difference between a text's meaning and what its author intended it to mean, Beardsley initially recognizes that this difference permits at least two different interpretive projects: "to discover the textual meaning . . . and to discover the authorial meaning." But then he simply assumes monistically that there must be only one interpretive aim or practice that could be "proper." We are therefore compelled to choose from among the diverse "possible interpretive tasks or inquiries . . . which of them is the proper function of the literary interpreter," his "*general and essential* task"; and Beardsley of course recommends the choice of textual meaning because of its greater availability and allegedly richer aesthetic rewards.[14] However, once this choice is made the interpreter's aim is not aesthetic richness *per se*, but truth or correctness, where interpretations "must be in *principle* capable of being shown to be true or false."[15] For Beardsley, then, the only proper aim is discovery of the text's nonauthorially defined but determinate meaning (through public linguistic rules) which will not permit contradictory interpretive statements to be correct.

The Anglo-American theorists Beardsley attacks for opposing his view nevertheless share Beardsley's assumption that legitimate interpretation essentially aims at descriptive truth or some relativized cognitive analogue. Thus Hirsch is committed to the goal of "knowledge in interpretation," believing that literary study is and should be a form of "humanistic knowledge," an "empirical inquiry" and "cognitive discipline," where qualified interpreters, "working together or in competition, can add to the knowledge" of literature.[16] Indeed Hirsch's advocacy of authorial intention as the criterion of tex-

[margin notes: "Hirsch vs Beardsley." "Beard on textual meaning" "B's aim according to S."]

tual meaning is made only to secure the goal of objective interpretive knowledge, his argument being that only a text's determinacy of meaning will allow such knowledge and that only authorial intention can provide such determinacy. Thus, though aware that "authorial intention is not the only possible norm of interpretation," Hirsch holds "it is the only practical norm for a cognitive discipline of interpretation."[17] Without it there is simply too much freedom, indeterminacy, and instability in the public linguistic conventions governing meaning to secure convergence on a single interpretation with which the work's meaning (and thus the work itself as a meaningful entity) may be identified, thereby providing a stable object for literary study and criticism.

Margolis, Beardsley's other major target, might seem an exception to the assumption of cognitive monism in interpretive intentions, since he advocates a "robust relativism" which frees interpretive validity not only from authorial intention but also from strict determinacy of meaning, thereby allowing the possible validity of conflicting interpretations. Yet though he liberally accepts the plurality and nonconvergence of interpretive approaches (Marxist, Freudian, existentialist, etc.); though he eschews the idea of a single, exclusive, and exhaustive interpretive truth in order to advocate a plurality of interpretations whose validity may be affirmed and defended in relative terms of "plausibility"; and, finally, though he pluralistically divides the standard interpretive enterprise into two logically distinct (though hardly independent) activities or moments—"describing" and "interpreting," Margolis ultimately makes the same assumption of interpretive uniformity at the fundamental logical level. Critical interpretation, as contrasted with interpretive performance (to which it is in many ways quite similar) is essentially a cognitive enterprise aimed at generating true or "truthlike" propositions. Rejecting the prescriptivist and emotivist views which see interpretive statements as quasi-imperatival or affective rather than propositional, Margolis argues that their reasonable claim that interpretive judgments "do not take the values 'true' and 'false' does not entail that such judgments lack a propositional form or are unable to take substitute values of a suitable [truth-like or cognitive] kind"; and he indeed goes on to insist that "epistemic values of some sort can be assigned to interpretations."[18] His advocacy of the notions of plausibility and implausibility represents his attempt to provide such truthlike values or, as he puts it, " 'truth-values' other than true and false."[19] Likewise, his advocacy of relativism rests on the faith "that relativism is not in principle incompatible with a cognitive conception of interpretation; . . . that the defense of plural, nonconverging interpretations is not, on cognitive grounds, incoherent."[20]

Indeed, far from rejecting the factor of propositional truth from interpretation, Margolis contends that any plausible interpretation of a work must be based on descriptions of the work that are (and are determinably) true rather than merely relativistically plausible: "interpretative claims must be compatible with what is (minimally) descriptively true of a given work. . . . No plausible account may be incompatible with an admittedly true statement."[21] It is what Margolis calls "description," as distinguished from interpretation but as the necessary substratum for it, which provides the true statements on which any plausible interpretation must be based. Descriptions, unlike interpretations, are simply true or false of the literary work independent of relativizing critical context. They display the intolerance of incompatibles (which Beardsley and Hirsch ascribe to interpretations): either "an object . . . *has* or *has not* the properties . . . described."[22]

On Margolis's model, true descriptions are to plausible interpretations what facts are to scientific theories whose truth cannot be decisively demonstrated. Facts or descriptions both provide the evidential basis for the explanatory theory or interpretation and also constitute what that (scientific or interpretive) theory is supposed to explain. Moreover, though both interpretations and scientific theories go beyond the descriptively true or factually given (and thus allow the plausibility of conflicting accounts), they surely rest on the true.[23] However, though both go beyond true statements, they seem to differ importantly in the fact (noted by Margolis) that aesthetic interpretation, unlike scientific theory, helps significantly to constitute the reality it treats, developing the meaning of the work it interprets. " 'Interpreting' . . . suggests a touch of virtuosity, an element of performance, a shift from a stable object whose properties are enumerable to an object whose properties pose something of a puzzle or challenge—with emphasis . . . on some inventive use of the materials present, on the added contribution of the interpreter, and on a certain openness toward possible alternative interpretations," beyond the borders of what is descriptively true of the work.[24]

Margolis here cleverly tries to satisfy and balance the fundamentally conflicting demands of continued productivity and truth, as indeed Beardsley and Hirsch also tried to in their own implicit and unknowing manner. If for Hirsch the author's intention satisfied the claim of truth, its elusiveness promised the claim of continuing interpretation. If for Beardsley truth could be secured through public conventions of meaning, continued productivity of interpretation was assured through the fact that these conventions were continually changing. For Margolis, truth is given in description's account of the work of art's hard and undeniable properties, while interpretation's creative

contribution toward extending the work beyond those core descriptive properties allows for a continued, never-ending interpretive productivity, based
on and constrained by truth but not confined to it.

Margolis's account of interpretive logic seems clearly superior to Hirsch's
and Beardsley's, not only because it more accurately reflects the dominant
trend in actual practice but because it can positively allow for, explain, and
even encourage the contemporaneous production of different plausible ways
of interpreting a work, and yet maintain all the while that interpretation contains and presents truth about the work, through the descriptive truths on
which it is based. His strategy of distinguishing the moments of description
and interpretation (with its consequent division of labor into truth and productivity) would be an ideal solution were it not for the fact that the distinction cannot be maintained in a firm, principled, more-than-pragmatic way.

First of all, we must remember that every description of a work of art
involves an interpretation of it, since it involves a selection of what to describe, what aspects of the work are important as to be worth describing.
No description describes everything, egalitarianly reflecting all that can be
said truly about a work. But what more acutely undermines the idea of any
firm and definite distinction between descriptive truth (presenting the work's
core of incontrovertible properties) and interpretive elaboration is that what
is taken as descriptively true (the so-called hard facts on which interpretation
is based) will often shamelessly depend on which interpretation of the work
we come to adopt.[25] For example, Hamlet's love for his father (which he both
declares and might seem to express in his mourning, melancholy behavior)
has been taken as a descriptive "hard fact" of the play. But if we come to adopt
the very plausible Freudian interpretation of Hamlet's mood, delay, and behavior toward his mother, this apparent firm fact evaporates into Hamlet's
self-deluding rationalization.[26] More generally, we can be led from what we
originally see as simple facts about the work to reach an interpretation of the
work which dislodges or recasts the facts by showing the work in such a way
that the original descriptions no longer ring true or adequate. (Indeed, narrative art and the enjoyable surprises in reading are often based on this sort of
phenomenon.)

Thus, any distinction between describing and interpreting (as between
understanding and interpreting) can only be relative and formal. It must be
a pragmatic, shifting, heuristic distinction, not an unchanging one which
would provide a firm and incorruptible core of determinate truth for simple
and final description. In other words, it is not that we all agree how to describe
the facts and differ only in what interpretations we elaborate from them. It

is rather that the descriptive facts are simply whatever we all strongly agree upon, while interpretations are simply what commands less consensus and displays (and tolerates) wider divergence.

The idea of an essential core of fixed, determinate, descriptive properties which constitute the work of art and are to be represented (even if augmented or extended) by valid interpretation cannot be successfully maintained; and its untenability undermines theories like Margolis's (and Beardsley's and Hirsch's) which rest on it. . . .

NOTES

1. Wimsatt and Beardsley's attack on intentionalism began as early as 1943 with an entry in J. T. Shipley's *Dictionary of World Literature*, predating their classic paper "The Intentional Fallacy," which first appeared in 1946 in the *Sewanee Review* and has since been reprinted in W. K. Wimsatt, Jr., *The Verbal Icon* (Lexington: University Press of Kentucky, 1954) and in numerous anthologies.

2. See R. Barthes, "The Death of the Author," in *Image, Music, Text* (New York, 1977), pp. 142–48.

3. See Monroe C. Beardsley, *The Possibility of Criticism* (Detroit: Wayne State University Press, 1970), p. 17. [See Chapter 2, p. 24.]

4. See J. L. Austin, *How to Do Things with Words* (Oxford: Oxford University Press, 1962), pp. 105, 106, 110, and 146, where Austin says that we need to know "the specific way in which they are intended, first to be in order or not in order, and second to be 'right' or 'wrong.'"

5. See P. F. Strawson, "Intention and Convention in Speech Acts," *Philosophical Review* 73 (1964): 439–60. See also Jacques Derrida, "Signature Event Context," in *Glyph* 1 (1977); 172–97 (reprinted in his *Margins of Philosophy* [Chicago: University of Chicago, 1982]).

6. Beardsley, *Possibility of Criticism*, pp. 58–61.

7. See Steven Knapp and Walter Benn Michaels, "Against Theory," in *Against Theory*, ed. W.J.T. Mitchell (Chicago: University of Chicago Press, 1985), pp. 11–30. [See Chapter 4.]

8. In a recent sequel entitled "Against Theory 2: Hermeneutics and Deconstruction" (*Critical Inquiry* 14 [1987]: 49–69), Knapp and Michaels extend their intentionalist critique to the hermeneutic theories of Gadamer and Ricoeur [see Chapter 4], the semiotic conventionalism of Goodman and Elgin, and the deconstructionist textualism of Derrida. However, their basic line of argument does not change: There is just no way "that a text can mean something other than what its

author intended" nor can there be "any plausible criteria of textual identity (e.g., in terms of syntax, linguistic conventions, or traditions of identification) that can function independent of authorial intention" (p. 50), simply because without some determining intention texts could neither mean nor be identified as such. Knapp and Michaels's argument thus remains vulnerable to the critique I offer below of confusing the notion of "authorial intention to mean" with that of "intentional meaning" *tout court*.

I should also note that Knapp and Michaels misrepresent Beardsley's anti-intentionalism as holding the view that textual meaning is "permanent and unchanging" (pp. 51, 68). On the contrary, the apparent fact that a text's meaning can change (through the changes in its words' meanings) long after an author is dead and thus unable to change his meaning is one of Beardsley's central arguments to prove that textual meaning is not logically identical to authorial meaning. See Beardsley, *Possibility of Criticism*, p. 19.

9. Knapp and Michaels, "Against Theory," pp. 19, 24. Indeed, because of their firm premise that language necessarily "has intention already built into it" so that we can never "separate language and intention," Knapp and Michaels see the attempts of intentionalist theorists like Hirsch and Juhl to ground the connection between textual meaning and authorial intention as being otiose and misguided. In thus challenging the theoretical efforts of intentionalists and anti-intentionalists alike, their radical position is appropriately entitled "Against Theory."

10. Ibid., p. 19.

11. Ibid., pp. 15, 16, 17, 12. [See Chapter 4.]

12. How elusive and spectral this notion is can be seen in the evasive formulation of its most forthright exponent, E. D. Hirsch. On the one hand, he tries to suggest its pragmatic value as a definite criterion or touchstone which would rule out interpretations inconsistent with what the empirical, historical author could have intended. But, afraid of psychologism and aware that literary (if not all) intentions can be too complex to be mechanically deduced from the known historical and biographical facts alone and are anyway somehow socially informed, Hirsch retreats from locating the requisite authorial intention in an empirical author and instead turns the author into an imaginative construct, "the speaking subject" which "is not . . . identical with the subjectivity of the author as an actual historical person." And this authorial-subject abstraction rather than providing a clear factual touchstone for interpretation needs to be interpretively constructed itself in terms of the text. See E. D. Hirsch, Jr., *Validity in Interpretation* (New Haven: Yale University Press, 1967), pp. 242–44.

13. See, for example, E. D. Hirsch, Jr., *The Aims of Interpretation* (Chicago, 1987), pp. 12–13. It is very revealing, however, that in defending literary study as con-

trolled and constrained by the aim of knowledge, Hirsch feels the need to guarantee its future productivity by expansionist measures of enlarging the scope and canon of literary studies.

"The recent over-emphasis on aesthetic values in literature has had a restrictive and inhibiting effect on literary criticism and literary study. The aesthetic conception of literature has too rigidly limited the canon of literature and has too narrowly confined the scope of literary study, *leaving present-day scholars with little to do that is at once 'legitimate' and important*. I argue for the legitimacy of several important parts of inquiry which have recently been excluded from 'literary' study; and I argue for the expansion of the literary canon" (p. 12, my emphasis).

Marxist theorists might note that such expansionism goes with Hirsch's capitalist image of criticism "as a corporate enterprise" and a "professional practice." See Hirsch, *Validity in Interpretation*, p. 109; and E. D. Hirsch, Jr., "On Justifying Interpretive Norms," *Journal of Aesthetics and Art Criticism* 43, no. 1 (1984): 91.

14. Beardsley, *Possibility of Criticism*, pp. 31, 34 (Beardsley's emphasis). [See Chapter 2, pp. 32, 34.]

15. Ibid., pp. 41–43. [See Chapter 2, pp. 36–38.]

16. Hirsch, *Aims of Interpretation*, pp. 1, 12, and Hirsch, "On Justifying Interpretive Norms," p. 91.

17. Hirsch, *Aims of Interpretation*, p. 7.

18. Joseph Margolis, *Art and Philosophy* (Atlantic Highlands, N.J.: Humanities Press, 1980), pp. 11, 153–54, 163. [See Chapter 3, p. 48.]

19. Ibid., p. 161. [See Chapter 3, p. 46.]

20. Ibid., p. 150.

21. Ibid., p. 159. [See Chapter 3, p. 44.]

22. Ibid., p. 111.

23. For Margolis's comparison of interpretations to scientific hypotheses, see ibid., pp. 157–60. [See Chapter 3, pp. 42–45.]

24. Ibid., p. 111.

25. This problem of the circular interdependence of description and interpretation is a manifestation of the perhaps more basic circular interdependence of work-identity and interpretation, where accuracy of interpretation is measured against the work's identity, but where the latter can only be determined through the former. I discuss this problem at some length in "Four Problems in Aesthetics," *International Philosophical Quarterly* 22 (1982): 21–33, and in *The Object of Literary Criticism* (Atlantic Highlands, N.J.: Humanities Press, 1984), pp. 50–64. This circularity is somewhat related to the hermeneutic circle's problem of understanding, fore-understanding, and interpretation. On this problem, see my *T. S. Eliot and the Philosophy of Criticism* (New York: Columbia University Press, 1988), pp. 124–33.

26. I take this example from Richard Wollheim, *Art and Its Objects* (Harmondsworth, England, 1975), p. 107, where it is used to attack the interpretive theory of Morris Weitz. I have elsewhere shown that Weitz's and Margolis's theories share the very same logical structure and are open to the same nondescriptivist critique. See Richard Shusterman, "The Logic of Interpretation," *Philosophical Quarterly* 28 (1978): 310–24.

6

An Intentional Demonstration?

GARY ISEMINGER

I

WHAT IS THE CONNECTION, if any, between the author's intentions in writing a work of literature and the truth (acceptability, validity) of interpretive statements about it? E. D. Hirsch has argued for a close connection in his vigorous defense of what he calls "the sensible belief that a text means what its author meant."[1] Here is his argument:

> A determinate verbal meaning requires a determining will. Meaning is not made determinate simply by virtue of its being represented by a determinate sequence of words. Obviously, any brief word sequence could represent quite different sequences of verbal meaning, and the same is true of long word sequences, though it is less obvious. . . . But if a determinate word sequence does not necessarily represent one, particular, self-identical, unchanging complex of meaning, then the determinateness of its verbal meaning must be accounted for by some other discriminating force which causes the meaning to be *this* instead of *that* or *that* or *that*, all of which it could be. This discriminating force must be an act of will, since unless one particular complex of meaning is *willed* . . . there would be no distinction between what an author does mean by a word sequence and what he could mean by it. Determinacy of verbal meaning requires an act of will.[2]

What I propose to do in this essay is to present and evaluate not so much an interpretation of this passage as an argument inspired by it. (Hirsch can claim it if he wants it, but I won't try to foist it on him if he doesn't.) It will help, I think, to confine the argument initially to a single case and worry later about the extent of its applicability. For this purpose, let me take the

76

beginning of Gerard Manley Hopkins's poem "Henry Purcell," which I shall label Text 1, and two imagined interpretive statements about it, which I shall identify as 1A and 1B.

> Text 1
>
> Have fair fallen, O fair, fair have fallen,
> > so dear
> To me, so arch-especial a spirit as heaves
> > in Henry Purcell,
> An age is now since passed, since parted;
> > with the reversal
> Of the outward sentence low lays him,
> > listed to a heresy, here.[3]

1A. The poem "Henry Purcell" expresses the wish that Henry Purcell shall have had good fortune.

1B. The poem "Henry Purcell" does not express the wish that Henry Purcell shall have had good fortune.

With this example in hand, I shall simply present the argument as it applies to it in a "regimented" form; the remainder of my essay, then, will be devoted to trying to figure out what, if anything, the argument shows.

1. Text 1 is compatible with interpretive statement 1A about the poem "Henry Purcell," and Text 1 is compatible with interpretive statement 1B about the poem "Henry Purcell."
2. Exactly one of the two interpretive statements 1A and 1B is a true interpretive statement about the poem "Henry Purcell."
3. If exactly one of two interpretive statements about a poem, each of which is compatible with its text, is true, then the true one is the one that applies to the meaning intended by the author.

Therefore,

4. Of the two interpretive statements 1A and 1B about the poem "Henry Purcell," the true one is the one that applies to the meaning intended by the author.

Now this argument is certainly a valid one; the interesting issues, therefore, are what can be said on behalf of the premises and what it would matter if the conclusion should indeed turn out to be true.

II

The plausibility of the first premise hinges on relatively simple facts about ambiguity in English words and constructions, though these facts are not always easy to discern in this somewhat cryptic and convoluted poem. Hopkins himself offers the following paraphrase in correspondence with Robert Bridges:

> The first lines mean: May Purcell, O may he have died a good death and that soul which I love so much and which breathes or stirs so unmistakeably in his works have parted from the body and passed away, centuries since though I frame this wish, in peace with God! so that the heavy condemnation under which he outwardly or nominally lay for being out of the true Church may in consequence of his good intentions have been reserved.[4]

But Hopkins is disturbed by the possibility of a different reading:

> One thing disquiets me: I meant "fair fall" to mean fair (fortune be)fall; it has since struck me that perhaps "fair" is an adjective proper and in the predicate and can only be used in cases like "fair fall the day," that is, may the day fall, turn out, fair. My line will yield a sense that way indeed, but I never meant it so. Do you know any passage decisive on this?[5]

The issue, it seems, is whether the wish being expressed is that good things shall have happened to (fair fortune shall have befallen) Purcell or rather that he shall have become a good person or done good things (shall have fallen, turned out, fair). These are clearly distinct wishes, and what premise 1 of my Hirschian argument claims is that these words in this order can be used to express either one (which is not to exclude the possibility that they might be used to express both at once.)[6]

Bridges was evidently able to reassure Hopkins by quoting from Love's Labour's Lost, Act II, scene i, line 124, "Now fair befall your mask!—fair fall the face it covers!" Responds Hopkins,

> The quotation from L.L.L. is decisive. "Fair befall your mask" must have the same construction as "Fair fall the face beneath it." Now "fair befall" certainly means "Fair fortune, all that is fair, nothing but what is fair/befall" and "fair" is there a substantive and governs the verb. So therefore it is and does in "Fair fall," which is what I wanted.[7]

If the reassurance afforded by this passage from Shakespeare is accepted, the claim that there are (at least) two alternative readings of the text, according to one of which it expresses a certain wish and according to the other of which it does not—the claim, that is, made by premise 1—seems very plausible indeed.

It is important, I think, to see what is *not* being invoked in this defense of premise 1. In particular, the claim there advanced does *not* depend on any confusion between public "meaning" and private "associations"; nor does it require that we endorse the Humpty-Dumpty Theory of Language, according to which a text can mean anything anyone wants it to mean. (Hopkins's worry is precisely whether the text *can* mean, among other things, what he *wants* it to mean.) The compatibility of the two different interpretive statements with the one text need not be purchased cheaply (if illegitimately) by finding something ("associations," say, or Hirsch's "significance,"[8]) for interpretation to be about, which is *bound* to vary from individual, or by talking as if the text settles *nothing* by itself and hence is compatible with *anything.*

Another way to put the point is that the notion of a text is here being taken as a relatively rich notion—not just an inscription but a type in some language, capable of being used to say some things and not others; and the notion of an interpretation is being taken as a relatively impoverished one—involving merely the choice among alternative dictionary definitions. And the point of premise 1 is that, even with the gap between text and interpretation thus narrowed as much as it can be, that gap still remains. The text supports more than one interpretation.

It is appropriate here to consider the possible generalization of premise 1 to other texts and to other kinds of interpretive statements. On the latter point first, is it so clear that statements 1A and 1B deserve to be called interpretive statements at all? It has to be admitted that at best they are pretty low-level ones, though of a sort of which Hirsch himself often gives examples. ("My car ran out of gas [did my Pullman dash from a cloud of argon?]")[9] But the sort of interpretive dispute Hirsch considers in some detail, for instance, that between Brooks and Bateson about Wordsworth's "A Slumber Did My Spirit Steal," has to do rather with the general tone of the poem: is it affirmative or rather pessimistic? And "interpretation" also sometimes suggests the attempt to understand a work in terms of some larger (ideological?) scheme, as when we speak of a Christian, Freudian, or Marxist interpretation of a work.

I don't think that anything in the argument in fact hinges on the claim that statements 1A and 1B are themselves interpretive statements. For surely the acceptability of these more exciting kinds of interpretive statements will be limited and controlled by the correctness of statements like 1A and 1B in much the same way that the acceptability of statements like 1A and 1B is limited and controlled by facts about the language in which the text is written. (It is perhaps not too fanciful to suggest, for example, that a specifically Roman Catholic interpretation of the poem would be made much more plausible by 1A's being correct; this wish of good fortune, as Hopkins explains it in his gloss, is a wish that only a Roman Catholic would make.) If, as our conclusion has it, the truth of statements like 1A and 1B is internally connected with facts about the author's intentions, then so will be the acceptability of our more glamorous interpretations. So even if someone should object, on the grounds that 1A and 1B are not interpretive statements, to my Hirschian argument as given, if it can be shown that, whatever status those statements themselves have, which one of them is true is internally connected with the author's intentions, the same will follow concerning more glamorous interpretive statements. (Notice that my argument here does not entail that of two "full-fledged" interpretations, say, Christian and Marxist, one and only one will be correct or that of two such interpretations of that sort, the better is the one the author intended it to have. This will be clearer after I have discussed the second premise; for now the point is that interpretations in that sense may differ without being contradictory. My argument is about interpretive statements that have been specifically chosen as contradictories.)

What about the extension of the point to other *texts*? Note, first, that nothing in the argument hinges on the "literariness" of the text. Certainly, the difficulties of understanding it are increased by the use of the "singular imperative (or optative if you like) of the past" tense of "have" [10] and by the fact that in neither reading is "fair fall" exactly current idiomatic English (nor, I surmise, was it a hundred years ago). But suppose the latter problem solved by the consultation of a dictionary and the former abstracted from by considering a cry, somewhat on the lines of "Long live the Queen!" of "Fair fall Henry Purcell!" The problem of which wish we are wishing is still there and in exactly the same form. Hirsch explicitly says that his point applies to "any brief word sequence," [11] so even though it is not a specifically "literary" phenomenon, it is presumably applicable to the "brief word sequences" that are the texts of, say, sonnets.

What about *length*? Hirsch also says that "the same is true of long word sequences, though it is less obvious." [12] To this, Beardsley has replied: "It is not hard to find or invent a short sentence that is simply ambiguous. But the more complex the text, the more difficult it is (in general) to devise two incompatible readings that are equally faithful to it." [13] The point about length, presumably, is that, as the sentences succeed one another, even if each individual sentence is ambiguous, one is typically led by the context to resolve ambiguities one way rather than another. It may be, for example, that someone who was unsure how to read the first two lines of "Henry Purcell" would be moved by reading the next two to some such reflection as this: "Purcell's problem, according to the poem, is that he was a Protestant, is damned for it, and having died in that state, couldn't have done anything himself to repair the situation; if that's so, it makes more sense to wish that something good shall have happened to him than that he shall have done something good." Having so reflected, then, he would be inclined to accept statement 1A and might perhaps even deny the second conjunct of premise 1.

But the point is not that either reading of the first two lines will ground an equally satisfying reading of the poem; it is only that, *considered as a text,* Text 1 rules out neither statement 1A nor statement 1B, and this would be so no matter how much the surrounding text might talk about the impossibility of Purcell having done anything for himself after his death and about the necessity of grace having been freely bestowed on him if he is not to be damned. The thoughts and wishes thus taken to be expressed by the poem might indeed be in some sense incoherent and unsatisfying, but they would seem to be expressible thoughts and wishes, and there seems to be no way to tell from *the text considered as a text* that they are not there being expressed. This is all that premise 1 claims, and the fact that, as interpreters, we routinely and usually correctly pick our way through mine fields of ambiguities all day everyday on the basis of cues from the larger contexts, both linguistic and "existential," in which ambiguous sentences occur, is not to the point.

My final comment on premise 1 is that it makes explicit the claim that *the text is not the poem.* Premise 1 distinguishes text 1 from (the first part of) the poem "Henry Purcell." I will not dwell on this point now, but I think it is crucial for the argument. This distinction between text and poem no doubt raises difficulties that will have to be faced, as well as not being particularly harmonious with a place where Hirsch says it is a matter of choice, not ontology, that we take the author's will as "normative" in interpretation.[14] Hirsch has been praised precisely for refusing to frame the issue in ontological terms by Meiland, who also argues, however, that, when the question is so construed, Hirsch's reasons simply do not justify this particular choice of a "normative" principle as opposed to some other possible one.[15] For just this very reason, it seems to me that the argument I have given, based on but distinct from Hirsch's, will require a defense of an "ontology" of the literary work, at least to the extent that it is claimed to be not identical to a text.

I conclude that, with the proviso that the distinction between text and poem remains to be explicated and defended, premise 1 seems very plausible indeed, and it seems, further, that a similar claim would be true of most written texts in natural languages.

III

The second premise is simply the application of the laws of excluded middle and noncontradiction to statements 1A and 1B. They are contradictories, so, by the first law, at least one of them is true and, by the second, at most one of them is.

It is crucial to recognize that they *are* contradictory, not just different. No advocacy of "rich variousness" in interpretation, no celebration of ambiguity and multiplicity of meaning is to the point. No doubt there is a great deal more, even in this part of the poem, than the mere wish to Purcell that he shall have had good fortune; perhaps the ambiguities are being deliberately "foregrounded" and we are meant to understand both wishes as simultaneously expressed. (Of course, Hopkins tells us this is not so, but suppose for the moment that it is, or think of other poems where, in similar situations, such a supposition would be plausible.) But then 1A is true and 1B is false. If, instead of 1A and 1B, we had either the pair

> 1A. The poem "Henry Purcell" expresses the wish that Henry Purcell shall have had good fortune.
> and
> 1B′. The poem "Henry Purcell" expresses the wish that Henry Purcell shall have done good things.

or the pair

> 1A′. The poem "Henry Purcell" does not express the wish that Henry Purcell shall have done good things.
> and
> 1B. The poem "Henry Purcell" does not express the wish that Henry Purcell shall have had good fortune.

then the situation would be different; nothing makes it logically impossible for both 1A and 1B′ to be true or for both 1A′ and 1B to be false, for example.

For purposes of the present argument, premise 2, I think, is what Hirsch's talk about the "determinateness of verbal meaning" comes to. The poem has at least one and at most one of two complementary properties. Hirsch himself often seems to mean more than this by determinateness,[16] but this relatively straightforward and uncontroversial claim seems to me to be all that he *needs* to mean here.

Could we plausibly *deny* that poems are determinate even in this minimal sense?[17] Can we make plausible a restriction on the scope of the law of excluded middle (or, less likely, the law of non-contradiction)? I think that more needs to be said about this, but all I want to argue here is that some such relatively high price will have to be paid if one wants to deny premise 2 and that asserting 2 does *not* fly in the face of claims about ambiguity and richness as characteristic of literature. To defend premise 2 is not necessarily to advocate interpretive intolerance and reveal a prosaic mind unfit to respond to the subtleties of art. (Notice, by the way, that no claim is here being made that a work of literature cannot *contain* or *express* contradictory propositions, in whatever way literary works contain or express propositions.)

There might appear to be ways of challenging premise 2 less drastic than challenging evidently fundamental logical laws, and although these are certainly possible in the abstract, they do not seem to be very attractive options here. For instance, one might try to evade the force of the law of excluded middle in a given case by suggesting that, for "categorial" reasons, *neither* a predicate *nor* its complement applies to a thing. Whatever the merits of this strategy in general, there seems to be little initial plausibility to the suggestion specifically that it is a "category mistake" to think of poems as either expressing or not expressing wishes.

Another possibility would be to suggest that statements 1A and 1B are only apparently contradictory because the expression "expresses the wish that Henry Purcell shall have had good fortune" is not used in the same sense in the two sentences; hence, the two properties attributed in 1A and 1B are not really complementary. Again, where there is ambiguity there is always this possibility, but I think we can just *specify* that the interpreters who, we are supposing, made claims 1A and 1B are both using this expression in the same sense (and are both referring to the same poem, etc.).

A slightly more promising version of this strategy is to suggest that 1A and 1B are not, as they appear to be, straightforward, one-place predications about the poem but should rather be parsed as *relational* statements about Text 1 and varying interpretations. Thus, it might be urged, statement 1A should really be expanded into

> 1A''. The text "Henry Purcell," *under interpretation A*, expresses the wish that Henry Purcell shall have had good fortune.

Statement 1B should be read as

1B''. The text "Henry Purcell," *under interpretation B*, does not express the wish that Henry Purcell shall have had good fortune.

Now, of course, there is nothing to prevent them from both being true.

Once again, what becomes crucial is the ontological claim that there *are* poems and that they are not identical with their texts. All I want to say about that here is that there does seem to me to be a presumption in favor of the view that there are poems, and reflection suggests reasons of the sort that are summarized in the first two premises for refusing to identify them with their texts. At the least, the kind of relational reparsing of statements 1A and 1B just suggested would, I should think, have to be motivated by something more than the bare desire to deny premise 2 and thus avoid the intentionalist conclusion. (In particular, it will *not* do to suggest that such a reparsing is required to protect some sort of "critical pluralism," in any sense in which such a view can legitimately be thought of as the only sane alternative to some kind of totalitarian, monomaniacal, fascistic "one-best-way-"ism.)

If statements 1A and 1B are, as they appear to be, attributions of complementary predicates to the same thing, and if that thing is appropriately "determinate" in the sense that it satisfies the laws of noncontradiction and excluded middle, then premise 2 is plainly true.

IV

Premises 1 and 2 tell us that exactly one of two statements about a poem is true and that the text by itself is insufficient to determine which one it is. Premise 3 aims to provide us with the necessary further principle. Once again, what principle appears plausible will depend on our conception of the nature of the object in question, in this case, our notion of the "ontology" of the literary work.

Here again, I think, Hirsch tries to make the notion of determinacy do more of the work by itself than it can. He says, "A determinate verbal meaning requires a determining will," but this just seems wrong. Indeterminacy *could* be resolved under circumstances such as these by a random process; what is wrong with that is that there does not seem to be any reason to suppose that in so doing we would get the *right* answer about the meaning of the *poem* except by chance. It seems to me, therefore, that one must think of the poem as in part *constituted* by something like *willed* or *intended* meanings from among those compatible with the text in order to defend such a principle as premise 3.

A notable omission from the argument at this point, as Hirsch gives it, is the specification of *whose* will is crucial. Here again, reflections on the ontology of the poem are required and not just appeal to determinacy. *Anybody's will* would suffice to resolve indeterminacy—a casual reader's, a critic's, the poet's brother-in-law's.[18] But, under the natural supposition that the poem, though not identical to the text, is created by the writer of the text (and, typically, in writing it), it is not much of a jump to argue that it is the author's will rather than anyone else's that resolves the indeterminacy. This is perhaps a short way with those who think of the critic or reader as a kind of partner in a joint venture with the poet. Once again, however, except as colorful *facons de parler*, such thoughts do not seem very impressive as *premises* when stacked up against the intuition that poets make poems (which is not to say, of course, that one could not be argued out of that intuition).

It is important to recognize that premise 3 is an ontological principle rather than an epistemological one. It is not, except indirectly, advice on how one is likely to find *out* which of the two contradictory statements about the poem is true; instead, it claims to tell us what *makes* the true one true. (This point renders Beardsley's Principle of Autonomy, "that literary works are self-sufficient entities, whose properties are decisive in checking interpretations and judgments,"[19] impotent against the kind of intentionalism here being advanced.) In the example I have chosen we have the author's retrospective statement that he intended to wish good fortune to Purcell rather than to wish that he shall have done well, and I am prepared to take his word. The crucial point, though, is not what Hopkins said later about the poem, but what he intended when he wrote it. What he said later is important only because in this case he happens to have said later just what it was that he did intend when he wrote it. This gives us, presumably, a certain epistemic advantage and makes this a useful example to work with. But it must not be supposed that I am suggesting that we are powerless to interpret without the author's having told us what he or she meant or that the author is privileged as a critic of his or her own work. What *determines* which of the two contradictory statements is true of the poem is a combination of what the powers of the text are and which of those powers the author intended to activate. How *we* "determine" which is true is a different matter, and, of course, only rarely do we have evidence of the sort that Hopkins has given us.

It is perhaps necessary to say something about the free bandying about of words like "will" and "intend." Does a principle like that embodied in premise 3 involve a commitment to a mentalistic view of the sort that no self-respecting philosopher can any longer support? I do not think one who accepts premise 3 is necessarily committed to any particular theory of intentions, but a certain picture of language and thought and their relation is involved.

(What follows may well run counter to Wittgensteinian orthodoxy, but, since Wittgenstein himself eschewed theory, it may be possible to disagree with him without being committed to a theory.)

Sentence types can be used to say certain things rather than others, and where a given type can be used to say more than one thing, which one (or more) among the possibilities it is being used to say on a given occasion is a function of some fact about the user, a fact that, for want of a better word, we can describe as the intention of the user. Such a view does not imply the Humpty-Dumpty theory; nor does it necessarily imply any mysterious penumbra giving meaning to utterances. It does imply that context does not determine meaning, though it may be what we most often have to go on in trying to discover it. To elaborate on one of the examples from Hirsch cited earlier, imagine someone standing by a disabled automobile, holding a red can, flagging down a passing car, and saying to the person who has stopped to give assistance, "My car just ran out of gas." Might such a person be using that sentence on that occasion to say that his Pullman just dashed from a cloud of argon? It seems to me obvious that he might be, and that what would make it the case that he was, if he was, would be some fact about what that person's thoughts were at the time he uttered the sentence (together with the fact that the sentence can be so used, of course.)

Any attempt to deny this, I suspect, springs either from dogmatic adherence to a contextualist theory of meaning, from confusion of impossibility with (extreme) improbability, or from confusion between epistemological and ontological questions. (Furthermore, the fact that, when queried, he says that is what he meant does not entail that it is; he can, of course, lie to us.) If the only way to accommodate these intuitions about the relation between language and thought is through a mentalistic conception of intention, then that seems to me to be the best possible argument for mentalism. But, for present purposes, all that needs to be insisted on, I think, is what might be called anticontextualism, the view that it is some fact about the user of a sentence that makes it the case that, in using it, he is saying one (or more) of the things it can be used to say rather than some other or others.[20]

Along with this mentalistic account (if such it be) of disambiguation, one needs also to suppose (what might not be granted on all hands either) that the relation between thought and language is not different in this regard in literary contexts from what it is in ordinary communication. I will not pause to defend this view in detail, but I will say that I do not think that recognition of significant categorical distinctions, if such there be, between literary and other uses of language need imply that there is any difference in this regard.

If, in general, what is said on a given occasion is a function of what the sentences used *can* be used to say and what the user means to say from among those possibilities, and if the interpretation of literature is, in this respect, like the interpretation of utterances generally, then premise 3 seems very plausible.

V

At this point it will be useful to consider a fundamental challenge to the Hirschian argument I have presented (though not necessarily to its conclusion). The burden of this challenge is that Hirsch himself has not been sufficiently radical in identifying the meaning of the text with what the author intends. This is the claim of Steven Knapp and Walter Benn Michaels.[21] Now, of course, Hirsch does say that the meaning of a text "is, and can be, nothing other than the author's meaning."[22] Knapp and Michaels argue, however, that despite this remark and others like it, consideration of Hirsch's argument shows that he supposes that a text can have meaning prior to and independent of the author's intention; he is in fact "imagining a moment of interpretation before intention is present, . . . the moment at which the text's meaning 'remains indeterminate,' before such indeterminacy is cleared up by the addition of authorial intention."[23]

Now whether or not this is true of Hirsch, it seems to be true of the argument I have presented. Moreover, my explication and defense of that argument, especially of its first and third premises, makes fairly substantive assumptions about just what provides us with an interpretable "object" prior to the "addition of authorial intention." What does this is the language of the text, which, as determined by the conventions of that language, delimits the possible meanings among which authorial intention can specify one (or more). Knapp and Michaels identify this assumption as the principle that "a single text can't mean just anything . . . , but a single text can mean anything the conventions of its language allow it to mean."[24] Their attack on this picture of the relation between intention and convention is embodied in two very interesting examples. The first is that of the "wave-poem." Suppose you are walking on the beach and see squiggles in the sand that spell out the first stanza of "A Slumber Did My Spirit Steal." You seem to be able to interpret this without assumptions about any author or his or her intentions. But now suppose, as you are watching, a wave washes up and recedes, leaving behind the second stanza.

> As long as you thought the marks were poetry, you were assuming
> their intentional character. . . . It was only with the mysterious ar-

rival of the second stanza that your tacit assumption (e.g., someone writing with a stick) was challenged and you realized you had made one. . . . [The marks] are not, after all, an example of intentionless meaning; as soon as they become intentionless they become meaningless as well. The arrival of the second stanza made clear that what had seemed to be an example of intentionless language was either not intentionless or not language.[25]

What does this example show? Perhaps that the conventions that constitute certain types as items in a language are themselves inconceivable except as the product of intending beings. So in that sense here is no intentionless meaning. Perhaps even that *tokens* of these types are not to be thought of as meaningful and hence subject to interpretation except as produced by such beings, so that even in this somewhat stronger sense there is no intentionless meaning. But it does not show that there is no sense in which we can attach meaning to and thus interpret linguistic items (sentence types) independent of the *specific* meanings intended by the users of those items on the given occasion of their use. This is not "intentionless" meaning, a "moment of interpretation before intention is present," but it is interpretation *independent of the specific intention of the author to "mean this or that"* (as Hirsch puts it). Nothing in the wave-poem example shows that interpretation independent of intention in *this* sense is impossible, and it is only intentionless meaning in this sense that is presupposed in my defense of the Hirschian argument.[26] But of course the notion of meaning independent of intention even in this sense depends on telling some such story as that adumbrated earlier about the limitations on possible meaning imposed on authors by the conventions of the language in which they write. And Knapp and Michaels think that that story, which presupposes that there is such a thing as a text with a conventional "verbal meaning" independent of and transcending the author's intentions, is ultimately incoherent.[27]

Once again, an example makes the point, though here they consider and attempt to defuse an example that is supposed to illustrate this notion of independent meaning:

> In what circumstances might it seem plausible to say that the verbal meaning of a text or utterance transcends the author's intention?
>
> Suppose someone says "go" in circumstances suggesting that he must mean something else. Perhaps the speaker is a passenger in a car that has just pulled up to a railroad crossing. He says "go," but the driver hesitates when she notices that the gate is down and a train

is approaching. The problem she faces is the apparent discrepancy between the verbal meaning of "go"—what "go" means according to the rules of English—and what she takes to be the speaker's likely intention. . . .

Suppose [further that] the driver disregards the passenger's intention . . . because she prefers a different meaning of the English word "go": he means "get out of the car" but she prefers "drive forward." . . . This . . . version of the example does seem to yield the principle that . . . a single text cannot mean just anything ("go," in English, cannot nonironically mean "stop"), but a single text can mean anything the conventions of English allow it to mean. . . . In this case there is a common verbal meaning that includes both what the author intends and what the interpreter prefers.[28]

So why do Knapp and Michaels not endorse this invocation of meaning independent of the author's intention? Their argument is essentially this: on the picture presupposed in my defense of Hirsch, the picture they aim to refute, interpretation is ultimately to be thought of as the selection of the author's intended meaning from among the members of a larger set of possible meanings, and what is needed at the outset is some way to specify the set of possible meanings of which the author's intended meaning will be a member. The invocation of verbal meaning does this, but not uniquely. Why not, for example, let the set be specified as containing the author's intended meaning plus the verbal meaning constructed from the *antonyms* of the words constituting text or utterance? "At this point, the apparent advantage of verbal meaning . . . becomes clear. While the antonym rule allows interpretations directly opposed to the author's intentions, . . . the verbal meaning rule limits interpreters to meanings that may go beyond the author's intention but nonetheless seem plausibly related to it," which have some "degree of proximity" to it.[29]

But if this is the aim of the invocation of verbal meaning, Knapp and Michaels have no difficulty in showing that it is not achieved. The verbal meanings of the text *not* intended by the author are not in any obvious sense "closer" to the meaning he or she intends. (Interpreting "go" to mean "stand up" and acting accordingly will result in the driver coming closer to fulfilling the passenger's intention than interpreting it as referring to a Japanese game of strategy.) "There is no necessary relation between the meaning the author intends and any one of the meanings the author's words can have in the language—except for the one the author intends. And the relation there is not one of relative proximity but of identity."[30]

But why must the advantage of choosing the set of verbal meanings as the set among whose members to search for the author's intended meaning be explicated in terms of their supposed "proximity" to one another in the sense just illustrated? That they should be "plausibly related" to the author's intention is one thing; that this "plausible relation" should consist in "proximity" is another. Why should not this plausible relation consist precisely in the fact that they are all things that the author might mean *in the sense that they are all things that, given the conventions of the language, the text can be used to say*, as opposed to things that the author might mean in the sense that they are all things that someone in the author's situation is likely to be trying to convey? As far as I can see, Knapp and Michaels's attempt to reduce to absurdity the view that a text can mean anything the conventions of language allow it to mean simply begs the question at this point, by supposing that the "plausible relation" between members of the set of possible meanings must consist in their "proximity" to one another.

More needs to be done, of course, to defend the picture of language invoked in the Hirschian argument than simply finding a dubious step in an argument purporting to be a knock-down argument against it. If it is agreed that verbal meaning ought to be invocable in the attempt to discern the intentions of authors, we still need to compare different pictures of how this can take place. On Knapp and Michaels's view,

> Since the rules of language do not provide a range of meanings that are necessarily closer to the author's intention than the range of meanings provided by any other set of rules, . . . they are relevant not because they provide a range of possible meanings but because they provide clues to the meaning the author intends. The dictionary definition of "vehicle" is useful not because it determines the range of possible meanings "vehicle" can have but because it provides clues to what an English-speaking author might mean by "vehicle."[31]

I have in effect objected to the word "since" in this passage, arguing that it is a non sequitur to claim that the lack of "proximity" between different dictionary meanings of a word entails that these definitions do not specify different possible meanings available to a user of that word. But the competing views remain to be discussed. Just what does Knapp and Michaels's contrast between determining a "range of possible meanings" and providing "clues to what an . . . author might mean" amount to?

Consider the attempt to infer, while standing at a crossroads, where someone went, and compare it with the attempt to infer, while looking at some tools, what someone was trying to do with them. The defender of the Hirschian argument, it seems to me, would model the inference to the author's intention from verbal meaning on the former; Knapp and Michaels, on the latter. However one proceeds to settle on one member of a finite set of alternatives, it is certainly intelligible that the members of that set might themselves be determined by reflection on the possibilities in the sense in which the availability of roads in certain directions determines possibilities and does not merely offer a "clue" as to where someone might have gone. And these possibilities need not be especially "close" to one another. (The roads may go in opposite directions.) In the case of the tools, by contrast, we might ask ourselves, "What do people usually do with things like this?" and, presumably, the various things they usually do would have "some degree of proximity" to one another. (Driving spikes into wood is a lot like sinking posts in the ground.)

The analogy proposed here is, of course, imperfect. Any attempt to understand the way dictionary definitions limit the membership of the set among whose members we propose to look for the author's meaning on the model of the provision of alternative possibilities would have to recognize that the way in which the rules of language specify possibilities is very different from the way in which roads do.[32] But the contrast does seem clear between specifying a set of actions among whose members one proposes (by whatever means) to infer that one was done in terms of what actions were *possible* under the circumstances and specifying that set in terms of what actions are likely to be done in circumstances of that kind.

The issue, then, is which way to conceive the inference from dictionaries to speech-acts. There is, as Knapp and Michaels recognize, a long and distinguished tradition that conceives of the rules of language as specifying possibilities in just the way they reject. What is clear, I think, is that the issue needs to be faced head-on and that Knapp and Michael's short way with the picture of language presupposed in the Hirschian argument will not do. Given that their alternative is, in effect, an attempt to reinstate the Humpty-Dumpty Theory of Language, the temptation is irresistible to conclude this examination of their attempted knock-down argument against this picture of language with the exclamation, "There's *no* glory for you!"[33]

VI

Perhaps I can now sum up the ontological theses with which I have been trying to prop up my Hirschian argument by proposing a revision of the "sensible belief" with which Hirsch begins, the belief that "a text means what its author meant." Beardsley calls this the Identity Thesis, that "what a literary work means is identical to what its author meant in composing it."[34] Let me formulate the Identity Thesis as follows, in order to highlight the assumption, embodied in Beardsley's discussion of it, that *the work is a text*:

> *Identity Thesis.* A literary work is a text whose meaning is identical to what its author intended (meant) in composing it.

Let me now propose for discussion instead the following, less memorable, but also, I think, less objectionable principle, which I shall call the Revised Identity Thesis. To defend this thesis is, I think, to defend the crucial identity (between the meaning of the work and the meaning intended by the author) *without* defending the "identity" of the poem and the text. (I shall phrase it in such a way as to ease comparison between the two principles; if this makes the Revised Identity Thesis somewhat less than self-explanatory, explanation follows immediately.)

> *Revised Identity Thesis.* A (typical) literary work is a textually embodied conceptual structure, whose conceptual component is (identical to) the structure—compatible with its text—which its author intended (meant) in composing it.

Several remarks are in order concerning this proposal. Note, first, that I do *not* propose it as embodying a set of conditions severally necessary and jointly sufficient for something to deserve to be called a literary work of art. For one thing, it is clear that sufficient conditions are not in question; virtually any textually transmitted message, whether literary or not, meets these conditions. I *do* claim that typical or central cases exemplify these conditions; roughly speaking, they specify a genus of which literature is a species. (I take it also that this is as true of typical or central cases of very recent literature as it is of literature of previous eras, despite the fact that at least some contemporary literature, in common with contemporary art of other kinds, sets out consciously to subvert features which have been typical or central in traditional literature.) In any case, the issue as to whether what is being claimed necessarily holds for all literary works of art or is true only of typical and central cases cuts across the issue as to whether the Revised Identity Thesis is preferable to the Identity Thesis; either one could be formulated in either way.

Another point to note is that such devices as irony and metaphor, surely central to literature, though certainly not restricted to it, make the relation of "compatibility" with the text invoked in the Revised Identity Thesis a much more complex one than simply that of being expressible by the text interpreted literally.[35] I shall not attempt to spell out this relationship here, but two remarks are in order. One is that, however complex that relationship may become, it seems to me that it will be some function of that fundamental relation between a text and a conceptual structure such that the first, interpreted literally, is capable of expressing the second. The other is that this issue, again, is by no means restricted to literature, but arises for any theory that attempts to explain, in terms of the actualization of linguistic potential, how people mean what they mean by what they say.

The Revised Identity Thesis makes it quite clear that what is primarily at issue is a view about the "identity" of the literary work *itself*, an "ontology" of the literary work, rather than a view about the "identity" of two "meanings," the work's and the author's.

The claim is that a typical literary work is a member of a set of ordered pairs, the pairs in question being those whose first member is a text and whose second member is a conceptual structure (a "meaning"). The text is a structure of linguistic types in some language, typically produced by the author of the work; the conceptual structure is one that meets two conditions, that of being compatible with the text and that of being intended by the author.[36]

VII

A literary work is determinate with respect to properties with respect to which a text is indeterminate, and authors typically create literary works by writing texts and meaning something by them. These two intuitively plausible claims seem to me finally to be the foundation of the Hirschian argument. The first does not rule out "rich variousness," but it does support premises 1 and 2, and hence the distinction between poem and text; the second does not make it impossible for a literary work to have properties its author did not intend it to have, but it does make plausible the principle embodied in premise 3. If these views are acceptable, then so is the conclusion that the truth conditions of interpretive statements about a typical literary work, however narrowly or generously "interpretive" is taken, include facts about the author's intentions.

There may still be intentional fallacies; nothing I have said lends support to the view that a literary work really has all and only properties its author intended it to have, nor the view that a literary work is good to the extent that it fulfills its author's intentions, nor the view that what the author says in interpreting his own work must necessarily be taken as authoritative. But to the extent that objections to these excesses, if such they be, have been based on an appeal to the general principle that interpretive statements about a typical literary work are logically independent of statements about the intentions of its author, those objections have not been well taken; *genuinely* fallacious interpretive appeals to the author's intentions remain to be dealt with either one by one or else on the basis of some other principle.

NOTES

Acknowledgment: Earlier versions of this essay were read at Carleton College, Edinburgh University, Manchester University, Wesleyan University, St. Olaf College, Lancaster University, and Skidmore College, and at a meeting of the Pacific Division of the American Society of Aesthetics. I am grateful to the Bush Foundation for a grant under which this version was written.

   1. E. D. Hirsch, Jr., *Validity in Interpretation* (New Haven: Yale University Press, 1967), p. 1. See Chapter 1, p. 11.

   2. Ibid., pp. 46–47. See Chapter 1, p. 16.

   3. John Pick, ed., *A Hopkins Reader* (New York: Oxford University Press, 1953), p. 16. This example, along with many others relevant to the question of the connection between interpretation and intention, is mentioned in Frank Cioffi, "Intention and Interpretation in Criticism," *Proceedings of the Aristotelian Society* 64 (1963–64).

   4. Pick, *Hopkins Reader*, p. 142.

   5. Ibid.

   6. Notice that Hopkins's concern cuts even deeper; he worries that the words not only can express a different wish from the one he intended as well as the one he intended but that they can *only* express the one he did *not* intend as opposed to the one he *did*. That is, he evidently grants that the second conjunct of premise 1 is true, that the line might be read as *not* expressing the wish that Purcell shall have had good fortune but some other wish instead; his fear is that it cannot *also* be read as in fact expressing *that* wish.

   7. Claude Colleer Abbott, ed., *The Letters of Gerard Manley Hopkins to Robert Bridges* (London: Oxford University Press, 1935), p. 173.

   8. Hirsch, *Validity in Interpretation*, p. 8.

   9. Ibid., p. 225. See Chapter 1, p. 17.

   10. Pick, *Hopkins Reader*, p. 304.

   11. Hirsch, *Validity in Interpretation*, p. 46. See Chapter 1, p. 16.

   12. Ibid., p. 47. See Chapter 1, p. 16.

   13. Monroe Beardsley, *The Possibility of Criticism* (Detroit: Wayne State University Press, 1970), p. 26. See Chapter 2, p. 29.

14. Hirsch, *Validity in Interpretation*, pp. 24–25.

15. Jack W. Meiland, "The Meanings of a Text," *British Journal of Aesthetics* 21 (1981).

16. Hirsch, *Validity in Interpretation*, p. 46. See Chapter 1, p. 16.

17. Joseph Margolis has defended in *Art and Philosophy: Conceptual Issues in Aesthetics* (Atlantic Highlands, N.J.: Humanities Press, 1980) a view of works of art as "culturally emergent" entities that suggests that they are not determinate in the present sense. (See Chapter 3, and Michael Krausz's discussion of Margolis's views in Chapter 9.) But Margolis is careful to argue that his view "does not violate any of the usual logical constraints" (*Art and Philosophy*, p. 164; see Chapter 3, p. 48). He does not say exactly which logical constraints he regards as usual.

18. Meiland makes this point in "Meanings of a Text."

19. Beardsley, *Possibility of Criticism*, p. 16. See Chapter 2, p. 24.

20. The bearing of recent (especially Wittgensteinian) discussions of the concept of intention on the Hirschian argument is discussed by Colin Lyas in Chapter 8.

21. Knapp and Michaels's arguments appear in "Against Theory," in *Against Theory: Literary Studies and the New Pragmatism*, ed. W.J.T. Mitchell (Chicago: University of Chicago Press, 1985), pp. 11–30, and in "Against Theory 2: Hermeneutics and Deconstruction," *Critical Inquiry* 14 (1987): 49ff. Selections from these two articles appear in Chapter 4.

22. Knapp and Michaels, "Against Theory," p. 13. See Chapter 4, p. 52.

23. Ibid., p. 14. See Chapter 4, p. 53.

24. Knapp and Michaels, "Against Theory 2," p. 55. See Chapter 4, p. 60. They regard this as the principle that "lies at the heart of [Gadamer's] hermeneutics," but, as they recognize, something like it is equally prominent in the work of speech-act theorists such as Grice and Searle. See "Against Theory," p. 21n.

25. Knapp and Michaels, "Against Theory," p. 16. See Chapter 4, p. 55.

26. Richard Rorty makes essentially this point in "Philosophy without Principles," in Mitchell, *Against Theory*, p. 137n.

27. Knapp and Michaels, "Against Theory 2," pp. 57–58. See Chapter 4, p. 63.

28. Ibid., pp. 54–55. See Chapter 4, pp. 59–61.

29. Ibid., p. 57. See Chapter 4, p. 62.

30. Ibid.

31. Ibid.

32. See, for example, among many others, the discussion of the distinction between "brute" and "institutional" facts, with references to John Searle and Elizabeth Anscombe, by Charles Taylor, in *Philosophy and the Human Sciences* (Cambridge: Cambridge University Press, 1985), p. 19ff.

33. Humpty Dumpty, of course, told Alice that by "glory" he meant "a nice knock-down argument." *Through the Looking Glass*, in *The Complete Works of Lewis Carroll* (New York: Vintage, 1976), pp. 213–14.

34. Beardsley, *Possibility of Criticism*, p. 17. See Chapter 2, p. 25.

35. See Chapter 11.

36. The Revised Identity Thesis also has the advantage of evading the three "conclusive objections" Beardsley has urged against the Identity Thesis in its original form (Beardsley, *Possibility of Criticism*, pp. 18–20; see Chapter 2, pp. 25–28), or so I have argued in "A Revised Identity Thesis," in *Text, Literature, and Aesthetics: In Honour of Monroe C. Beardsley*, ed. Lars Aagaard-Mogensen and Luk De Vos (Amsterdam: Rodopi, 1986).

7

Art, Intention, and Conversation

NOËL CARROLL

I

IN THE NORMAL COURSE OF affairs, when confronted with an utterance, our standard cognitive goal is to figure out what the speaker intends to say. And, on one very plausible theory of language, the meaning of an utterance is explicated in terms of the speaker's intention to reveal to an auditor that the speaker intends the auditor to respond in a certain way.[1] That is, the meaning of a particular language token is explained by means of certain of a speaker's intentions.

Likewise, in interpreting or explaining nonverbal behavior, we typically advert to the agent's intentions. This is not to say that we may not be concerned with the unintended consequences of an action; but even in order to explain unintended consequences, one will need a conception of the agent's intentions. Nor is this reliance on intention something that is relevant only to living people; historians spend a great deal of their professional activity attempting to establish what historical agents intended by their words and their deeds, with the aim of rendering the past intelligible. Furthermore, we generally presume that they can succeed in their attempts even with respect to authors and agents who lived long ago and about whom the documentary record is scant.

Nevertheless, though it seems natural to interpret words and actions in terms of authorial intention, arguments of many sorts have been advanced for nearly fifty years to deny the relevance of authorial intention to the interpretation of works of art in general and to works of literature in particular. Call this anti-intentionalism. Whereas ordinarily we interpret for intentions, anti-intentionalism maintains that art and literature either cannot or should not be treated in this way. Likewise, where characteristically we may use what we know of a person—her biography, if you will—to supply clues to, or, at least, constraints on our hypotheses about her meanings,[2] many theorists of art and literature regard reference to an author's biography as either illegitimate or superfluous.

The realm of art and literature, on the anti-intentionalist view, is or should be sufficiently different from other domains of human intercourse so that the difference mandates a different form of interpretation, one in which authorial intent is irrelevant. In this essay, I scrutinize some of the grounds for drawing distinctions between art and life that advance the thought that authorial intent is irrelevant; and, in contrast, I also try to suggest some hitherto neglected continuities between art and life that might motivate a concern for authorial intention in the interpretation of art and literature.

II

Historically speaking, anti-intentionalism, under the title of "the intentional fallacy,"[3] arose in a context where biographical criticism flourished—that is, the interpretation of such things as novels as allegories of their authors' lives. Authors were geniuses whose remarkable personalities we came to know and appreciate all the more by treating their fictions as oblique biographies.[4] Undoubtedly, this sort of criticism promoted distorted interpretations—as any intentionalist would agree, insofar as it is not likely that Kafka intended to speak of his father in writing The Metamorphosis. But in banishing all reference to authorial intention, to authorial reports of intention, and to the author's biography,[5] anti-intentionalism was an exercise in overkill. That is, in performing the useful service of disposing of what might be better called "the biographer's fallacy," anti-intentionalists embraced a number of philosophical commitments that went far beyond their own purposes, as well as beyond plausibility.

Indeed, anti-intentionalism is often promoted as a means for rejecting critical practices that most of us would agree are misguided. It is generally unclear, however, whether one has to go all the way to anti-intentionalism in order to avoid the errors in question.

For example, anti-intentionalism was advocated as a principle that could dispense with taking outlandish authorial pronouncements seriously. Monroe Beardsley writes "if a sculptor tells us that his statue was intended to be smooth and blue, but our senses tell us it is rough and pink, we go by our senses."[6] This example is meant to serve as an "intuition-pump;"[7] if we agree that a sculptor cannot make a pink statue blue by reporting that it was his intention to make a blue sculpture, then it must be the case that we regard such intentions—and such reports of intention—as irrelevant.

This solution to the case is too hasty, however, and the example need not force the intentionalist into anti-intentionalism. For with cases where the authorial pronouncement is so arbitrary, we may discount it, not because we think that authorial intentions are irrelevant, but because we think that the report is insincere. That is, we do not believe that the sculptor in Beardsley's example really had the intention of making a blue statue by painting it pink.

Intentions are constituted, in part, of beliefs, on Beardsley's own view,[8] and we can resist attributing the belief to an artist that one makes something blue by painting it pink. We need not resort to the hypothesis of anti-intentionalism in such a case, but can instead suspect that the artist was putting us on, perhaps for the purpose of notoriety. That is, competent language users, especially trained artists, are presumed to know the difference between blue and pink. Flouting this distinction leads to the suspicion of irony.

For an actual literary example of the sort of problem that Beardsley has in mind, we could consider Andrew Greeley's sensational novel *Ascent into Hell*. Like many of Greeley's works, this story is a titillating tale of Catholic priests and sex, a kind of soft-core pornography, spiced with religious taboos. Greeley, however, has a note preceding the text of the novel entitled "Passover," in which he offers a symbolic reading of that ceremony, thereby perhaps insinuating that we should take the text of *Ascent into Hell* as an allegory of Passover.

Needless to say, it is difficult to regard the sexual escapades in the book as a serious Passover allegory. But the intentionalist is not forced to accept Greeley's implied intention at face value. One can simply, on the basis of the novel, note that Greeley could not genuinely have the belief that it could be read as that allegory, nor would he have written the text as he did if he had the desire—another component of intentions on Beardsley's view[9]—to render a modern-day Passover theme. In fact, one may hypothesize that Greeley included the red herring about Passover in order to reassure his Catholic readership that his book was not irreligious.

But, in any event, the intentionalist can reject the "Passover" interpretation of *Ascent to Hell* in the face of Greeley's implied intentions by denying that it is plausible to accept the authenticity of Greeley's ostensible intent. Thus the problem of aberrant authorial pronouncements need not drive us toward anti-intentionalism.[10]

Another frequent intuition-pump, employed in early arguments against intentionalism, argues that commending poems insofar as they realize authorial intentions is usually circular. For in many (most?) instances, including those of Shakespeare and Homer, we have no evidence of authorial intention other than their poems. Consequently, if we commend such a poem on the basis of its realization of intentions, and our sole evidence for that intention is the poem itself, then our commendation is tantamount to the assertion that the poem succeeds because it is the way it is because it is the way it is.

We cannot, in these instances, have grounds for discerning failed authorial intentions because the way the artwork is provides our only access to the intention. If it appears muddled, then that is evidence that the artist intended it to be muddled and, therefore, that it succeeded in realizing his intention. That is, commending works of art for realizing authorial intentions when the way work is is our only evidence of intentions threatens to force us to the counterintuitive conclusion that all works of art are commendable.[11]

The unwarranted presupposition here, of course, is that the artwork cannot provide evidence of failed intentions. In the introduction to his *The Structure of Scientific Revolutions*, Thomas Kuhn writes at one point that "having been weaned on these distinctions [the "context of discovery" versus "context of justification"] and others like them, I could scarcely be more aware of their import and force."[12] Clearly, any alert reader will note that Kuhn has said the opposite of what he meant to say. He intended to communicate that he had been *nurtured* on these distinctions, and not that he had been *weaned* on them.[13]

The text itself, in terms of the entire direction of what is being said, makes evident what Kuhn has in mind. Also, we know that the confusion over the dictionary meaning of *weaned*, like the meanings of such words as *fulsome* and *sleek*, are quite common among contemporary English speakers; so it is easy to recognize that Kuhn should not have written what he, in fact, wrote, given his intentions. From the text itself and our knowledge of language usage, we can infer that the sentence failed to realize Kuhn's intentions and that, from his own viewpoint, it is not a great sentence. And, similarly, with artworks—given their genre, their style, their historical context, and their overall aesthetic direction—one can say by looking at a given work that the author's intention has misfired, whether or not we go on to commend or criticize it.

Undoubtedly, as the preceding discussion indicates, one of the deepest commitments of early anti-intentionalism was the notion that authorial intention is somehow *outside* the artwork and that attempts to invoke it on the basis of the artwork itself are epistemologically suspect. Underlying this view is a conception of authorial intentions as private, episodic mental events that are logically independent of the artworks they give rise to in the way that

Humean causes are logically independent of effects. What we have access to, in general, for purposes of evaluation and interpretation is the work itself. The authorial intention is an external cause of the artwork of dubious availability.

However, this view of authorial intention gradually came to be challenged by another view—call it the neo-Wittgensteinian view [14]—according to which an intention is thought to be a purpose, manifest in the artwork, which regulates the way the artwork is. Authorial intention, then, is discoverable by the inspection and contemplation of the work itself.[15] Indeed, the artwork is criterial to attributions of intention.

Searching for authorial intention is, consequently, not a matter of going outside the artwork, looking for some independent, private, mental episode or cause that is logically remote from the meaning or value of the work. The intention is evident in the work itself, and, insofar as the intention is identified as the purposive structure of the work, the intention is the focus of our interest in and attention to the artwork. On the external-episode view, authorial intention is a dispensable, if not distracting, adjunct to the artwork, which adjunct is best ignored. But on the neo-Wittgensteinian approach, tracking the intention—the purposive structure of the work—is the very point of appreciation.

Given the conception of authorial intention as external to and independent of the artwork, the anti-intentionalist claim of its irrelevance to the meaning of the work is eminently comprehensible. But with developments in the philosophies of action, mind, and language, the neo-Wittgensteinian picture of authorial intention seems more attractive. The persuasiveness of anti-intentionalism comes to hinge upon which view of intention in general theorists find more plausible. And to the extent that early anti-intentionalism was based upon a crude view of intention, its conclusions are questionable.[16] Moreover, the more attractive, neo-Wittgensteinian view of intention not only makes authorial intention relevant to the interpretation of artworks but implies that in interpreting an artwork, we are attempting to determine the author's intentions. Thus, at this point in the debate, if anti-intentionalism is to remain persuasive, it must do so not only without presupposing a crude view of intention but also must accommodate the neo-Wittgensteinian picture of intention.

With these dialectical constraints in mind, it seems that two anti-intentionalist strategies have become popular recently. The first relies on adducing ontological reasons based on the nature of artworks to deny the relevance of authorial intention to interpretation. The second argues for the irrelevance of intention by exploring the aesthetic interests that audiences have in art.

That is, the first sort of argument—the ontological argument—advances anti-intentionalism on the grounds of the nature of the artwork, while the second sort of argument—the aesthetic argument—is grounded on what might be thought of as policy considerations about the best way to regard artworks for aesthetic purposes. Both kinds of arguments presuppose that artworks, for one reason or another, are to be or should be interpreted differently from ordinary words and actions.

III

As noted earlier, we ordinarily interpret words and deeds with the cognitive goal of ascertaining the intentions of authors and agents. As the investigations of historians reveals, there seems to be no principled difficulty in such practices even when the agents in question are long dead and the record fragmentary. Thus the question arises, Why should matters stand differently when it comes to art? Should not artworks be interpreted in the way in which we customarily interpret other words and actions? At this point, the anti-intentionalist may attempt to argue that artworks are ontologically different from ordinary words and deeds, and therefore different interpretive practices are appropriate to them; specifically, given the nature of artworks in general and literature in particular, authorial intent is irrelevant to interpretation.

This conviction of ontological difference can be found in different and indeed widely disparate literary theorists. It is, for example, an article of faith of contemporary literary critics who endorse Roland Barthes's notion of "the death of the author."[17] And it is, at the same time, a view that underpins the more traditional approaches of the New Criticism, as that approach was defended by the late Monroe Beardsley.[18] Perhaps this convergence of theorists of different stripes on anti-intentionalism should be less surprising than it seems, for both Barthes and Beardsley arrived at their positions—albeit in different decades and in different countries—while in the process of reacting to what was earlier called biographical criticism.

Though Roland Barthes does not explicitly speak of the issue of intention, he clearly believes that, with a literary text, the reader's activity should not be constrained by the "myth" that the author is confiding in us. One reason advanced in support of this view is that

> writing is the destruction of every voice, of every point of origin. Writing is that neutral, composite, oblique space where our subject slips away, the negative where all identity is lost, starting with the very identity of the body of writing.

No doubt it has always been that way. As soon as a fact is *narrated*
no longer with a view to acting directly on reality but intransitively,
that is to say, finally outside of any function other than that of the
very practice of the symbol itself, this disconnection occurs, the
voice loses its origin, the author enters into his own death, writing
begins.[19]

What Barthes seems to be getting at here is that once writing is divorced
from ordinary usage—that is, when language does not serve the purpose of
acting on reality—the relevance of an author's intention in writing drops out,
and the word sequence is attended to in terms of its play of potential meaning
("the very practice of the symbol itself"). This is a feature of poetry explicitly recognized in modernist writing following Mallarmé, but it implicitly has
been a feature of literature all along ("No doubt it has always been that way.")[20]

Ordinary language is tied to acting on reality, and that is the grounds for
our preoccupation with authorial intent. But when language is detached from
that purpose—when language is aesthetized?—the cognitive goal of fixing
authorial intent becomes feckless. That literary language is not practical sev-
ers its conceptual connection to authorial intention. As soon as language is
employed ("narrated . . .") in what theorists of a more traditional bent than
Barthes would call an *aesthetic* way, the conceptual pressure to make sense of
it in the light of authorial intent dissolves, and the reader can explore it for all
its potential meanings and associations.

In his "Intentions and Interpretations: A Fallacy Revived," Monroe Beardsley, deploying the machinery of speech-act theory, independently evolves an
argument which, though different from Barthes's, also parallels it in pertinent
respects. The argument begins by drawing a distinction between performing an illocutionary action and representing one. When a pickpocket takes
my wallet and I say, "You stole my wallet," I perform the illocutionary act
of accusation. An illocutionary action is generated (according to Beardsley,
following Alvin Goldman) by the production of a text under certain conditions, and according to certain language conventions.[21] In contrast, when a
stage actor, playing a character, says, "You stole my wallet," to another actor,
playing another character, she is not performing an illocutionary action; she
is representing one.

The relation between performing illocutionary actions and representing
them is to be understood on the model of pictorial representation. Just as
Beardsley argues that the relation of a pictorial depiction to its referent is that
of selective similarity, he maintains that the representation of an illocutionary

action resembles the performance of illocutionary action in certain, selected respects (i.e., reproduces certain, but not all, of the conditions requisite for the performance of the illocutionary action). For example, when I accuse a culprit of filching my wallet, I believe that he has taken my wallet; an actor, though repeating much of the formula for accusation, does not believe her fellow actor has stolen anything. Thus, a representation of accusation resembles it in many respects, but not in every respect—for instance, it fails to fulfill the condition of conviction in the culprit's guilt.

Most ordinary discourse is preoccupied with the performance of a multitude of illocutionary actions. Literature, in contrast, specializes in the representation of illocutionary actions. In this respect, once the author's intent to represent illocutionary actions is recognized, thereby acknowledging the neo-Wittgensteinian claim of a conceptual relation between an act and its animating intention, the representation of the illocutionary action is regarded as a selective imitation of the performance of a fictional character—either the literal characters in the text or what has sometimes been called an implied narrator or an implied speaker or dramatis persona.

So when Wordsworth writes about England that "she is a fen," this is not Wordsworth directly performing an illocutionary act of accusation. Wordsworth, in writing poetry, signals his intent to represent the illocutionary act of accusation, which, in this case, is the imitation of an implied speaker's disparaging of England.

The language in the poem is not a performance of an illocutionary act of accusation by Wordsworth. It is a representation of such an action by an implied speaker. Thus the meaning of the language token is not tied to Wordsworth's intention, nor need it be understood in the context of Wordsworth's biography. It is a representation that can be comprehended solely in terms of the conventions of language.

The author of the performance in the text, so to speak, is the implied speaker; since all we know of the implied speaker are the words in the text—since the implied speaker, a fictional entity, has no existence outside the text—there can be no question of his extratextual intentions. There is no extratextual author, so there are no governing, extratextual intentions. Just as the issue of the number of children Lady Macbeth has is underdetermined by the fiction, so there is no access to implied authorial intent beyond the page.

Beardsley agrees that in ordinary language the cognitive goal of interpretation is the discernment of the speaker's intentions. But the language in literature is not a matter of the author's performance of an illocutionary act. It is a representation of the illocutionary acts of characters and implied speakers. And such fictional speakers have no intentions beyond the words on the page, which must, in consequence, be understood solely in terms of the conventions of language (and without recourse to the intentions of actual authors). It is as if in creating fictional characters, through illocutionary-act representation, actual authors' intentions are ontologically detached from the language sequence in favor of the meanings of characters, both literal and implied, which in turn can, for metaphysical reasons,[22] only be a matter of grasping of linguistic conventions (the literal sense of the words, and the conventions or established strategies for comprehending the sense of verbal contexts and metaphors).

The language in a literary text in being represented language—perhaps, this is what Barthes intends by "narrated . . . intransitively"—becomes the linguistic "performance" of the characters—implied and literal—and thereby is disconnected from the intentions of actual authors by means of a fictional frame (Barthes's notion that language is detached from acting on reality). Moreover, the "intentions" of characters have no existence beyond the page and are available solely in terms of linguistic conventions. Stated formally, Beardsley's argument seems to be as follows:

1. If X is a literary work, then X is only a representation of an illocutionary act.
2. Though actual authorial intentions are relevant to whether X is a representation of an illocutionary act, what X is a representation of (its meaning) is solely a matter of the relevant linguistic conventions (the literal sense of words and the conventions or established strategies for grasping the sense of a verbal context and metaphors) *and not* a matter of fixing authorial intent.
3. Therefore, if X is a literary work, then what X is a representation of is solely a matter of the relevant conventions.

Thus, in interpreting the language in a literary text, we will be concerned with the meanings of characters—literal ones, implied authors, or dramatis personae. And since these characters have no existence outside the words in the text, interpreting their meanings is exclusively a matter of convention. The actual author, metaphorically speaking, banishes himself from the text in the process of representing illocutionary actions. This argument grants some role to authorial intention as an ingredient in identifying the author's act as one of representing. But once the representational frame is in place, so to speak, the author's intentions are outside it. And given the ontological status of the representational frame, it is a category mistake to be preoccupied with authorial intent; it is metaphysically irrelevant.

(Moreover, though this argument is stated in terms of literature, one supposes that it can be extended to other art forms, given, for example, Beardsley's analogies between pictorial representation and illocutionary representation—perhaps landscapes are to be understood as vistas seen by implied observers.)

It is absolutely central in this argument that literary language and ordinary language be ontologically distinct. Literary language is a special zone, so, even if in ordinary language authorial intent is a guide to meaning, it is not relevant in literature because literature is not a performance but a representation. In ordinary language, we are prone to say that when a speaker disambiguates her earlier utterance, she has told us the meaning of the utterance. With literature, however, there is no comparable resort to the author's intent, for the relevant speaker is not the living author but various dramatis personae who are ontologically unavailable for comment. If their words are ambiguous, one suspects that Beardsley would be prone to say that the dramatic speaker is being represented as ambiguous.

The crux of Beardsley's argument is, given the distinction between performing and representing, the claim that literature is by definition a matter of representing illocutionary acts.[23] This effectively boils down to the assertion that all literature is essentially fictional. For even if a literary text does not deploy imaginary characters and places, it is involved in presenting its persons, places, and events through the fictional medium of an implied speaker or narrator. Such claims are not unfamiliar.[24] If anti-intentionalism depends on this generalization, however, it is surely in trouble.[25]

Pretheoretically, many works of what we classify as literature fall into the category of nonfiction. Lucretius's Concerning the Nature of Things is one example; The Mahabharata is another. Both appear to be illocutionary acts of assertion, even if what they assert turns out to be false. It does not seem correct to attribute to Lucretius the intention of representing the illocutionary acts of an Epicurean philosopher—he was an Epicurean philosopher philosophizing. Similarly, the authors of The Mahabharata were not imitating the telling of the history of their race; they were telling it. Nor do we need, I think, to travel to the distant past for our counterexamples. When in "Howl," Allen Ginsberg wrote "I saw the best minds of my generation destroyed by madness," there is every indication that, however hyperbolically, he is speaking in his own voice and not representing the illocutionary act of accusation of some "angelheaded hipster." The notion of implied narrators and dramatic speakers, no matter how useful in explicating a great deal of literature, does not afford a necessary condition for being a literary text.[26]

Thus, a literary text is not necessarily a representation of an illocutionary act; it may be a performance of an illocutionary act of assertion, accusation, and so forth. Therefore, the fact that many literary texts involve representations of illocutionary acts does not entail that every literary text must be interpreted without concern for authorial intent in contradistinction to ordinary language.

Of course, it would be a mistake to conflate the representations of illocutionary acts presented through fictional characters with the performance of illocutionary acts by actual authors. It would be an error to identify Emily Brontë with the narrator of *Wuthering Heights*. But that distinction can be readily marked without resorting to the extreme theoretical concession that the literary speaker is always fictional.

Not only are there entire literary works that it seems ill advised to regard as representations of illocutionary acts. There are also many parts of literary works that do not appear to be representations of illocutionary acts: the discourse on whales in Melville's *Moby Dick*, the history of symbols in Hugo's *Hunchback of Notre Dame*, and the philosophy of history in Tolstoy's *War and Peace*. Though housed in fiction, where they undeniably perform a literary function, they are also essays whose authors produced them in order to make assertions. In interpreting these interludes, one needs to approach them as one would any other form of cognitive discourse. Some may be tempted to prefer to read them as representations of illocutionary acts when one finds a particular author's ideas rather harebrained. But such considerations—however cosmetically well intended—are, in fact, irrelevant to the issue of whether the passages in question are performances of illocutionary acts rather than representations thereof. Furthermore, if, as I argue, these are performances of illocutionary acts of assertion, then in such instances, it will be appropriate, as Beardsley would appear compelled to admit, to interpret them with the cognitive goal of discerning what the authors intended.

So far, we have been whittling away at the first premise of Beardsley's arguments by finding poems and passages to which the generalization does not apply and by arguing that in these instances, given Beardsley's own views, interpreting with respect to authorial intention is as appropriate as it is in the case of ordinary illocutionary acts of assertion. But the million-dollar question is, How extensive a problem does this pose for the anti-intentionalist?

My own hunch is that the problem will be very extensive. For once we admit that there can be explicit nonfictional passages (which may range in scale from clauses and sentences to chapters and beyond) housed in fiction— and which are best construed as performances of illocutionary actions—the door is opened to the recognition that there are many implicit or implied propositions in literary works as well, which are also best conceived in terms of performances. *Brave New World* expresses a point of view about what Huxley sees as the prospect of utiliatarian social control. I see no particular advantage in rephrasing this observation in terms of the point of view of a fictional dramatic speaker. And, of course, if it is suggested that we must advert to talk of implied speakers in order to deflect the worries of anti-intentionalism, that begs the question at issue.

Authors, in fact, often make political (Gorky's *Mother*), philosophical (Sartre's *Nausea*), and moral (James's *The Ambassadors*) points through their literary writings. This is a commonly known, openly recognized, and frequently discussed practice in our literary culture. These points are very often secured through oblique techniques—implication, allegory, presupposition, illustration (unaccompanied with explicative commentary), and so on. That is, such points need not be and often are not directly stated. For this very reason, they are one of the most common objects of literary interpretation. And there is no reason to believe that in every case the implicit points found in literary works are merely the notions of a fictional speaker or an implied author rather than the actual author.

This is not to deny that there may be literary works in which the moral, philosophical, religious, political, etc. views are only constituents of dramatic speakers or implied authors. It is only to reject the position that all the implicit points made in literary works are the representations of the implied commitments of fictional speakers.

There may be no general epistemological principle that we can apply to tell whether, in a given instance, the implied point belongs to the actual author or to an implied author. We may have to proceed in this matter on a case-by-case basis, relying on the results of practical criticism (of a sort that at least countenances the applicability of intentionalist hypotheses). But given the practices of our literary culture, that seems a better procedure than negotiating our lack of an epistemological principle by jettisoning the idea that actual authors communicate their commitments to us through literary works[27]—or, to return the issue to Beardsley's idiom, that actual authors do not ever perform illocutionary acts, even in fiction, rather than merely, only, always representing them.

Often it seems that arguments about the relevance of authorial intent to

interpretation become so preoccupied with the issue at the level of word sequences that sight is lost of the fact that much of our interpretive activity is
spent in trying to ascertain the point, often the implicit or implied point, of
large segments of discourse and entire works. For example, we may be concerned with what a whole novel is getting at—its thesis, as Beardsley once
called it.[28] And it seems to me natural, in many instances, to regard the theses
we encounter in literary works as that which the author intends, through the
production of the text, that the reader recognizes as the intended point. If we
can regard implicit thesis projection with nonfictional import as a form of
illocutionary action, there is no reason to think that it cannot be performed
by actual authors. Implicit thesis projection may be a device employed in the
construction of an implied author. But I see no reason to agree that it is always
so employed.

For example, in Donald Barthelme's story "Alice," there is a recurring
strategy of surreal and disorienting lists. In interpreting this strategy, we are
not primarily concerned with elucidating the meaning of words or word sequences, but, and this is more important, in ascertaining Barthelme's point in
employing these lists—that is, we are concerned with why he made the story
this way. A likely hypothesis is that he intended this mode of organization
to suggest the currently fashionable, antihumanist notion that the subject is
decentered.[29] Here the object of interpretation is what Barthelme has *done*, and
even though what he has said in the narrow sense is material to what his has
done, the intentionalist idiom of *action* seems central to the way in which we
characterize thesis projection through artistic strategies.

Not all literature is fictional, and not even all the assertions in fictions
are representations of illocutionary actions. Pretheoretically, literary works,
including parts of some fiction, can involve performances of illocutionary
acts. Thus, if it is an appropriate cognitive goal with respect to performances
of illocutionary acts to read for intentions, then, in certain circumstances,
reading literature for authorial intention is plausible. There indeed may be
times when reading representations of illocutionary acts for authorial intent
is misguided for the reasons Beardsley advances. Nevertheless, those reasons
cannot provide the grounds for a comprehensive anti-intentionalism with
respect to literature (not to mention art in general).

Moreover, if there is implicit thesis projection of nonfictional import—
whereby actual authors express their views about life, society, morality, and
so forth—and a great deal of literary (indeed, artistic) interpretation concerns
the identification of such theses, then intentionalist criticism has a wide arena
of legitimate activity.

So far, I have been concerned to undermine the first premise of my reconstruction of Beardsley's argument. Literary works need not only be representations of illocutionary actions. But Beardsley's second premise also bears scrutiny. Its purpose is to exclude intentionalist interpretive activity on the grounds that its meaning can only be a matter of conventions because its speakers (fictional characters and implied authors) do not exist and therefore have no intentions. And, in any event, even if in some sense "intentions" could be imputed to them, they are not the intentions of the actual author, since he or she is not the speaker.

This premise may have some plausibility if it is narrowly construed to pertain only to the meaning of word sequences. But literary meaning—that is, the object of literary interpretation—need not be concerned solely with the meaning of word sequences even when it comes to the representation of illocutionary acts. Literary interpretation may ask questions about the point of constructing a character in this or that way and thus may investigate the representation of illocutionary acts in a text in terms of the contribution it makes to the point of the character as an element in the overall design of the work.

That is, in representing a character or an implied author and his or her fictional illocutions in a certain way, a theme may be adumbrated. We may ask, why did so-and-so say that in that way at that point in the text—how does it fit into the larger argument of the story or poem? And such questions about the point of character construction and the representation of the illocutionary acts that constitute them seem to me referable to the intentions of the actual author, without risking the kind of ontological gaff Beardsley feels must arise when actual authors are introduced into the interpretation of the meaning of representations of illocutionary acts. Thus, even if it were true that all literary works are only representations of illocutionary acts, that would not preclude intentionalist interpretation of literary meaning in the broad sense.

Of course, we might also wonder whether the actual author is as remote from representations of illocutionary acts as Beardsley supposes. As a historian of philosophy, Beardsley himself, along with an entire profession, appears to find little problem in deriving Plato's doctrine from Socratic dialogues. Surely these are no less representations of illocutionary acts, in Beardsley's terminology, than is the experiential proof of God's existence offered at the end of The Brothers Karamazov. But if we can, at least sometimes, feel justified in treating Plato/Socrates intentionalistically, with respect to illocutionary representations, why should we hesitate treating Dostoyevsky/Alyosha similarly?

Problems arise, then, with both of Beardsley's premises. I have spent more time with Beardsley's formulation than with Barthes's, since I think that it is obviously more developed. Nevertheless, though Barthes does not mobilize speech-act theory, I think that his notion of the death of the author is susceptible to a number of the points made against Beardsley. Barthes apparently maintains that when language is divorced from the goal of acting on reality ("narrated . . . intransitively"), the relevance of the author disappears, and a space is opened for the reader to explore the text in terms of all its intertextual associations. The reader, in a manner of speaking, becomes a writer and the critic, a creator.

I am not sure that once language is used "intransitively," the author becomes irrelevant, since identifying such a use would appear to depend on fixing the author's intention to work in certain genres or forms, namely, those that function intransitively. That is, how will the interpreter know that the writing in question is of the right sort to be read in a writerly fashion without adverting to authorial intentions?

Barthes claims that when writing is divorced from the purpose of acting directly on reality, the author becomes irrelevant. Whether this is persuasive depends on what this divorce from reality amounts to. Does the notion of no longer operating directly on reality reduce to Beardsley-type claims about representations of illocutionary acts or to the notion that literature is essentially fictional? If so, Barthes must deal with the kinds of objections rehearsed already.[30] But if the notion does not dissolve into the view that all writing (literature?) is fiction, then one wonders how often writing is divorced from the purpose of acting on reality. That is, supposing Barthes is correct and once writing is detached from the purpose of acting on reality, the author becomes irrelevant, the crucial question concerns the frequency of this phenomenon.

Barthes clearly thinks it happens a great deal. But, generously construed, the idea of writing acting on reality seems to me to apply quite uncontroversially to much literature that is used to criticize society, to champion moral views, to afford insight into social behavior, to reinforce values, to encourage our sympathies, to elicit our hatred, to give voice to our experience, and so on. If this is said not to be a matter of *directly* acting on reality, we need an account of what Barthes means here. If he has the issue of fiction in mind, we have already provided the counterexamples. Moreover, if narrating intransitively means just any writing where the author is not in the presence of her or his audience—writing detached from the physical context of utterance—that, counterintuitively, implies that such things as book orders do not operate directly on reality.[31]

If Barthes has something else in mind, the burden of proof is on him (or his followers) to produce it. For insofar as it is common practice for authors to strive to affect reality by means of their writing and insofar as they appear in some sense to succeed, then it would seem, given Barthes's own argument, that in certain instances (many?), the author is not dead, and there is no conceptual pressure to treat him or her as such.

Undoubtedly, there may be poems—one thinks of the Exquisite Corpses of the Surrealists—where the writer opens the text to the free play of the reader (though even here the author's intent to enable readers to see the world differently cannot be forgotten). Nevertheless, artistic attempts to secure the death of the author by, so to say, authorial suicide, no matter how interesting and legitimate experimentally, do not force us to concede that, in general, the author is, in every respect, irrelevant to the interpretation of the text—even if we accept Barthes's criterion of acting or not acting on reality as the mark of authorial life and death.

Both Barthes and Beardsley frame their arguments in terms of literature, though I think that it is fair to say that both would advocate anti-intentionalism across the interpretation of the arts.[32] But their anti-intentionalism seems to me to be most persuasive when it is applied to such things as word sequences, whose meanings are extremely conventionalized. In other art forms, where there are not such highly articulated codes of meaning, our interpretations of artistic performances are more akin to discerning the sense of an action than to reading.

If a choreographer mounts a dance in a theater in the round rather than on a proscenium stage, we attempt to figure out the significance of this choice by thinking about what he or she is trying to do with respect to historical and contemporary theatrical practices relative to the work in question. The meaning of "theater in the round" is neither fixed nor semiotically bound to other theatrical "signs" in a way that can be read the way a text may be (either determinately, a la Beardsley, or intertextually, a la Barthes). Instead, its interpretation depends on locating the purpose that the strategy in question serves for what the author is attempting to do.[33] And it is hard to see how such artistic doings—which describe most activity outside literature[34]—can be explicated without reference to the intentional activity of authors.

IV

So far, we have explored anti-intentionalist arguments that preclude reference to authorial intent on the grounds of the putatively special ontological nature of art in general and of literature in particular. Our own position has been that these considerations do not require us in general to treat literature differently from ordinary discourse, except perhaps in certain limited instances—for example, where the meaning of a character's or an implied narrator's literal utterance token, per se, is underdetermined due to the constraints of fiction. But even in the face of these limitations, there are many other cases and aspects of literary and fictional discourse where there is no ontological barrier to the cognitive goal of attempting to discern authorial intention as an object of interpretation. Thus, anti-intentionalism does not, on ontological grounds, afford grounds for believing that authorial intent is irrelevant in every instance of interpretation.

The ontological considerations of the anti-intentionalists, which were canvassed earlier, might be called "reasons of art" in that they declare reference to authorial intent out-of-bounds because of the special nature of art. With respect to discourse, such reasons of art presume that literary discourse is metaphysically different from ordinary discourse in a way that makes reading literature for authorial intent a kind of category error. We have challenged the generality and applicability of this position and concluded that there is no reason why, across the board, reading literary works with the cognitive goal of identifying authorial intentions is inadmissible; indeed, at times—for example with respect to authorial *doings*—it seems the most plausible way to proceed.

There are other "reasons of art" that we have not yet considered. The idea behind the ontological arguments is that it is in some sense impossible to fix authorial intent and that the aim should be abandoned as any other impossible goal should be abandoned. Nevertheless, an anti-intentionalist might admit that the ontological arguments are not generally conclusive, yet adduce reasons of art that show that reading for authorial intent *should not* be pursued, even though it could be pursued. These reasons of art might be called aesthetic. That is, whereas ontological arguments advance reasons of art that maintain that intentionalism is, strictly speaking, impossible; aesthetic arguments admit that intentionalist criticism is possible, but *recommend* that it not be embraced for what might be called aesthetic policy reasons.

Isolating pure aesthetic arguments for anti-intentionalism is a bit difficult, since most anti-intentionalists believe in the ontological distinction between literary language and ordinary language, and as a result they weave their ontological and aesthetic arguments together in ways that are hard to disentangle. The supposed aesthetic advantages of anti-intentionalism are often introduced only to be ultimately backed up by ontological considerations. But it is possible to construct an aesthetic argument without reference to ontological claims about the nature of art in general or of literature in particular.

For example, Monroe Beardsley writes:

> What is the primary purpose of literary interpretation? It is, I would say, to help readers approach literary works from the aesthetic point of view, that is, with an interest in actualizing their (artistic) goodness. The work is an object, capable (presumably) of affording aesthetic satisfaction. The problem is to know what is there to be responded to; and the literary interpreter helps us to discern what is there so that we can enjoy it more fully.[35]

Here, the underlying idea is that an artistic object has a purpose: affording aesthetic satisfaction. This is why we attend to artworks. Our object is to derive as much aesthetic satisfaction as is possible from the object. The role of the interpreter is to show us what there is in the object that promotes aesthetic experience. Nevertheless, one can readily imagine that what an author intended to say by means of an artwork is less aesthetically provocative than alternative "readings" of the work. For Beardsley, these readings, with respect to literature, have to be constrained by what the words of the text mean conventionally. Even with this caveat, it is easy to imagine instances where what the author intended is less aesthetically exciting than an alternate, conventionally admissible reading.

Moreover, since the point of consuming art, and of interpretation as an adjunct to artistic consumption, is to maximize aesthetic satisfaction, we should always favor those interpretations that afford the best aesthetic experience that is compatible with established textual meaning conventions. Furthermore, since aesthetic richness is our overriding concern, we need only interpret with an eye to that which is most aesthetically satisfying and linguistically plausible. Whether or not the meanings we attribute to the text were authorially intended is irrelevant. The proof of the pudding is in the tasting.

Of course, the best reading of the text—the one that is most aesthetically satisfying and also at least linguistically plausible—may coincide with the author's intended meaning, but that is of accidental importance. What is essential for the purposes of aesthetic consumption is that it be the best interpretation—the one that points to the maximum available aesthetic enjoyment—conceivable within the constraints of linguistic plausibility. Thus, for aesthetic purposes, we may always forgo concern for authorial intent in favor of the best aesthetic interpretation.

Where authorial intention and the best interpretation coincide, the reason we accept the interpretation has to do with aesthetic richness rather than authorial intention. Where there may be divergences between authorial intentions and textual meanings (that are richer than the putative authorial ones), we go with the latter because maximizing aesthetic satisfaction is our goal. As a matter of aesthetic policy, the best procedure is always to regard authorial intention as irrelevant because it either adds nothing to our aesthetic satisfaction or it may even stand in the way of arriving at the most enjoyable experience of the work.

On Beardsley's view, there is generally a determinate best interpretation. However, the aesthetic argument can also be mobilized by theorists who eschew determinate meanings, preferring the "play of signification of the text." Here, the argument might begin by recalling that a text can be interpreted either as the utterance of an author or as a word sequence.[36] Read as a word sequence, the text may have multiple meanings compatible with the conventions of language. Given this, the question becomes, What is the best way to read the text—authorially or, so to speak, textually?

In defense of reading the text as a word sequence, one can invoke the Kantian notion that aesthetic experience involves the play of understanding and imagination. That is, taking the text as a word sequence allows us to contemplate it for multiple, diverse meanings and their possible connections. It provides the best way for us to maximize our aesthetic experience of the text, permitting us to track the text for its play of meaning and alternative import. Reading for authorial intent, where the author intends a determinate meaning rather than an "open text,"[37] may obstruct the delectation of the various shifts in meaning that would otherwise be available to the reader who takes the text as a word sequence. Thus, for the purpose of maximizing our aesthetic experience—construed here to be a matter of cognitive play with meanings—the best policy is to attend to the work as a word sequence rather than as an authorial utterance.

The conservative version of this aesthetic argument might hold that texts could be read as word sequences or as authorial utterances and that there is no reason why the intentionalist preference for authorial utterance must be given priority over the possibility of reading the text as a word sequence. Both readings are possible, and neither recommendation is binding.[38] So, if a good reason—like the Kantian aesthetic invoked earlier—can be advanced for anti-intentionalist interpretive practices, then the claims of intentionalism can be suspended. This does not preclude intentionalist interpretation, but only denies that interpretation must always be constrained by intentionalist considerations.

A more radical version of the aesthetic argument would advocate that intentionalist considerations are *always* best bracketed because they stand in the way of, or are irrelevant to, maximizing interpretive play.[39] Concern for authorial intent "closes" down the text; it limits the artwork as a source of interpretive enjoyment; it restrains the imagination (of the audience) unduly. This recommendation may be accompanied by the vague and perhaps confusing cliché that artworks are inexhaustible, insofar as word sequences, ex hypothesi, will tend to have more meanings than authorial utterances. But the argument can proceed without claiming that artworks are literally inexhaustible; only to urge that, for the purpose of making literary experience more exciting, we should treat artworks that way, rather as Morris Zapp in David Lodge's *Changing Places* keeps reinterpreting Jane Austen in the light of every literary theory that comes down the pike. That is, keeping artworks interpretively open—for example, by reading for word sequence meaning rather than authorial meaning—makes for more zestful encounters with art.

The radical version of the aesthetic argument seems to me to underwrite a great deal of contemporary literary criticism. Ironically, where someone like Beardsley supports anti-intentionalism because of his convictions about the autonomy of the artwork and the literary text,[40] contemporary literary critics advocate anti-intentionalism for the sake of the freedom and autonomy of the reader. In Barthes, for example, the "death of the author" corresponds to the birth of the reader.

Admittedly, for Barthes, this is grounded in ontological arguments about the nature of writing. Yet one feels that, with Barthes and his followers, the ontological argument itself is attractive because its conclusion suits their preference for an autonomous reader, one who creatively participates in making the meaning of the text by tracing the multiple and not necessarily converging linguistic trajectories that reading divorced from a concern with authorial utterance allows.[41]

Aesthetic arguments for anti-intentionalism are a subclass of the general view that interpretations are purpose-relative.[42] One could advance anti-intentionalism, then, for purposes other than aesthetic gratification under the banner of purpose-relative interpretation; one could, for example, maintain that anti-intentionalism best realizes some moral or ideological goal, which outweighs whatever aims intentionalism supports.[43] Since I believe that the purpose that critics most often presuppose anti-intentionalism serves best is aesthetic enrichment, however, I focus the discussion on this issue.

With aesthetic arguments, the anti-intentionalist admits, in my reconstruction of the debate, that one could read for authorial intent, but maintains that we have certain aims in pursuing artworks that, so to speak, trump our concerns with authorial meaning. These aims center on the maximization of aesthetic satisfaction. Aesthetic satisfaction is the overriding interest that we have in consuming artworks. So in order to secure said satisfaction, we are best advised to take it that the aesthetically most satisfying interpretation outranks all others, most notably where a competing view is an intentionalist interpretation.

In order to develop this argument fully, the anti-intentionalist needs to say something about aesthetic satisfaction. This may cause difficulties in several registers. The first is the long-standing problem of defining the way in which we are to understand "the aesthetic" in *aesthetic satisfaction*. Moreover, there may be rival views of what constitutes aesthetic satisfaction—Beardsleyan determinate meaning of a certain sort, or the inexhaustible play of meaning in the text. Which of these views must the anti-intentionalist endorse? But even supposing these technical difficulties with characterizing aesthetic satisfaction can be met, I remain unconvinced by aesthetic arguments for anti-intentionalism.

The heart of my disagreement is that it seems unproven that we have overriding interests in maximizing aesthetic satisfaction with respect to artworks. My reason for reservations here have to do with my suspicion that in dealing with artworks we have more interests than aesthetic interests—as "aesthetic interests" are usually construed within the philosophical tradition—and that there is no reason to think that these interests are always trumped by aesthetic ones. Indeed, as I argue, these other-than-aesthetic interests may in fact mandate constraints on the pursuit of aesthetic interest in ways that count against anti-intentionalism and for intentionalism. I would not wish to deny that we have interests in securing aesthetic satisfaction from artworks. But that interest needs to be reconciled with other, potentially conflictive interests that we also bring to artworks.

What are these other interests or purposes? Broadly speaking, I would call them "conversational." When we read a literary text or contemplate a painting, we enter a relationship with its creator that is roughly analogous to a conversation. Obviously, it is not as interactive as an ordinary conversation, for we are not receiving spontaneous feedback concerning our own responses. But just as an ordinary conversation gives us a stake in understanding our interlocutor, so does interaction with an artwork.

We would not think that we had had a genuine conversation with someone whom we were not satisfied we understood. Conversations, rewarding ones at least, involve a sense of community or communion that itself rests on communication. A fulfilling conversation requires that we have the conviction of having grasped what our interlocutor meant or intended to say. This is evinced by the extent to which we struggle to clarify their meanings. A conversation that left us with only our own clever construals or educated guesses, no matter how aesthetically rich, would leave us with the sense that something was missing. That we had neither communed nor communicated.

Not all conversations involve both communion and communication. Probably many firings do not. But what, for want of a better term, we might call serious conversations do have, as a constitutive value, the prospect of community. Likewise, I want to maintain, this prospect of community supplies a major impetus motivating our interest in engaging literary texts and artworks. We may read to be entertained, to learn, and to be moved, but we also seek out artworks in order to converse or commune with their makers. We want to understand the author, even if that will lead to rejecting his or her point of view.

An important part of why we are interested in art is that it affords not only an opportunity to reap aesthetic satisfaction but is an opportunity to exercise our interpretive abilities in the context of a genuine conversation. Clever construals, even if aesthetically dazzling, do not necessarily serve our desire to commune or communicate with another person. Insofar as our pursuit of art is underwritten by, and is an exemplary occasion for, a generic human interest in communicating with others, it is not clear that a concern with aesthetics alone serves our purposes best.

Moreover, in stressing our conversational interest in artworks in terms of understanding the artist, I am not reverting to the notion that we pursue art in order to commune with remarkable personalities. Instead, I am making the more modest claim that art is obviously in part a matter of communication and that we bring to it our ordinary human disposition to understand what another human being is saying to us.

The idea of the maximization of aesthetic satisfaction has a very "consumerist" ring to it. In Buberesque lingo, it reduces our relation to the text to an I/It relationship. What I am trying to defend is the idea that, with artworks, we are also interested in an I/Thou relation to the author of the text. This interest in communicating with others is perhaps so deeply a part of our motive in, for example, reading that we may not have it in the forefront of our attention. But when we pick up Tom Wolfe's *Bonfire of the Vanities*, surely one of our abiding interests is to learn what someone else, namely Tom Wolfe, thinks about contemporary New York. And, the extent to which we have this conversational interest in the text limits the range of aesthetically enhancing interpretations we can countenance. That is, the purpose of aesthetic maximization will have to be brought into line with our conversational interests, which interests are patently concerned with authorial intent.

Furthermore, if I am right about the conversational interests that we have in artworks and literary texts, then our concern with authorial intention will not simply issue from the mutual respect we have for our interlocutor; it will also be based on an interest in protecting our sense of self-respect in the process of conversation. In order to clarify this point, a somewhat extended example may be useful.

In contemporary film criticism, films are often commended because they *transgress* what are called the codes of Hollywood filmmaking, thereby striking this or that blow for emancipation. Within the context of recent film criticism, it is appropriate to regard disturbances of continuity editing, disorienting narrative ellipses, or disruptions of eyeline matches as subversions of a dominant and ideologically suspect form of filmmaking. And given the historical evolution of the language game in which avant-garde filmmaking is practiced, the attribution of such meanings to contemporary films is warranted, especially on intentionalist grounds.

Once interpretations of narrative incoherences in recent films as subversions or transgressions of Hollywood International were in place, however, film critics, such as J. Hoberman of the *Village Voice*, began to attempt to project those readings backward. That is, if a narrative incoherence or an editing discontinuity in a film in 1988 counts as a transgression, why not count a similar disturbance in a film of 1959 as equally transgressive? Thus a hack film by Edward Wood, *Plan 9 from Outer Space*, is celebrated as transgressive as if it were a postmodernist exercise in collage.[44]

Plan 9 from Outer Space is a cheap, slapdash attempt to make a feature film for very little, and in cutting corners to save money it violates—in outlandish ways—many of the decorums of Hollywood filmmaking that later avant-gardists also seek to affront. So insofar as the work of contemporary avant-gardists is aesthetically valued for its transgressiveness, why not appreciate *Plan 9 from Outer Space* under an analogous interpretation? Call it "unintentional modernism," but it is modernism nonetheless and appreciable as such.[45]

One reason to withhold such an interpretation from *Plan 9*, of course, is that transgression *is* an intentional concept, and all the evidence indicates that Edward Wood did not have the same intentions to subvert the Hollywood style of filmmaking that contemporary avant-gardists have. Indeed, given the venue Wood trafficked in, it seems that the best hypothesis about his intentions is that he was attempting to imitate the Hollywood style of filmmaking in the cheapest way possible. Given what we know of Edward Wood and the B-film world in which he practiced his trade, it is implausible to attribute to him the intention of attempting to subvert the Hollywood codes of filmmaking for the kinds of purposes endorsed by contemporary avant-gardists.

An intention is made up of beliefs and desires. It is incredible to attribute to Edward Wood the kinds of beliefs that contemporary avant-garde filmmakers have about the techniques, purposes, and effects of subverting Hollywood cinema. Those beliefs (and avant-garde desires) were not available in the film world Edward Wood inhabited, nor can we surmise that even if Wood could have formulated such beliefs, it would be plausible to attribute to him the intention to implement them. For it is at the least uncharitable to assign to Wood the belief that his audiences could have interpreted his narrative discontinuities and editing howlers as blows struck against a Hollywood aesthetic.[46] That is, it is virtually impossible that Wood could have had the intentions—the beliefs and the desires—that contemporary avant-gardists have about the meanings of disjunctive exposition or the effects of such exposition on audiences.

Historically, it is undoubtedly most accurate to regard Edward Wood's narrative non sequiturs and nonstandard editing as mistakes within the norms of Hollywood filmmaking. One would think that the critic interested in transgression would want to have a way to distinguish between mistakes and transgressions. And the most obvious way to make such a distinction is to require that transgressions be intentional, which requires that the filmmaker in question have the knowledge and the will to violate Hollywood norms of filmmaking as a form of artistic protest. Insofar as it is anachronistic to impute the requisite knowledge (of the discourse of avant-garde theory) or the desire to subvert Hollywood codes to Wood, it is better to regard his violations of certain norms as mistakes. And, in general, it would seem that connoisseurs of artistic transgression would have an interest in being able to distinguish mistakes from subversions—interests that should drive them toward intentionalism.

Nevertheless, it is at this point that an aesthetic argument for anti-intentionalism may be brought to bear. To wit: if a transgression interpretation of Plan 9 from Outer Space yields a more aesthetically satisfying encounter with the film, and our primary purpose in interpretation is in promoting maximum aesthetic satisfaction, why not suspend qualms about intention and take

Plan 9 from Outer Space as a masterpiece of postmodernist disjunction *à la lettre*? Here, the anti-intentionalist might agree that such an interpretation cannot be squared with what it is plausible to say of the film, given the possible intentions of the historical director. But why not sacrifice the distinction between mistakes and transgressions if in the long run it supplies us with more aesthetically satisfying experiences?

That is, the argument against taking *Plan 9* as a transgression rests on the supposition that it is not a reasonable hypothesis of what Wood could have meant in producing the film. But so what? If we drop a commitment to discerning authorial intent, and regard any norm violation as a transgression, would not that make *Plan 9* more aesthetically interesting, and if our premium is on aesthetic interest, would not anti-intentionalist criticism be our best bet?

But I submit that insofar as we have a conversational interest in artworks, we will want to reject this sort of aesthetic argument. For if we take ourselves to be aiming at a genuine conversation, ignoring Wood's palpable intentions, it seems to me, can only undermine our sense of ourselves as authentic participants in the conversation. For, from the point of view of genuine conversation, we are being willfully silly in regarding *Plan 9* as a transgression of Hollywood codes of filmmaking. We are behaving as if we believed that a randomly collected series of phrases, derived from turning the dial of our car radio at one-second intervals, harbored the message of an oracle, and simultaneously we agree that all forms of divination are preposterous.

In his *Concluding Unscientific Postscript*, Kierkegaard notes that a comic moment arises when "a sober man engages in sympathetic and confidential conversation with one whom he does not know is intoxicated, while the observer knows of the condition. The contradiction lies in the mutuality presupposed by the conversation, that it is not there, and that the sober man has not noticed its absence."[47] By analogy, in supposing that Wood is a kind of Godard, we are acting as if a stream of drunken incoherencies constitute an enigmatic code. Indeed, we are placing ourselves in an even more ridiculous position than the butt of Kierkegaard's mishap, for we have voluntarily entered this situation.

In Kosinski's *Being There*, the näif Chance utters all sorts of remarks about his garden, which other characters take to be of great gnomic significance. Since they are unaware that Chance is a simpleton, they are, in effect, applying something like Culler's anti-intentionalist rule of significance[48] to the sayings of a fool. The result, as with Kierkegaard's imagined conversation with the drunk, is comic. Taking something like *Plan 9* to be a radical transgression of Hollywood International seems to me to be a matter of willingly adopting the ludicrous position that those characters suffer inadvertently. It undermines any self-respecting view we could have of ourselves as participants in a conversation. Whatever aesthetic satisfaction we could claim of such an exchange would have to be bought at the conversational cost of making ourselves rather obtuse.

Aesthetic arguments for anti-intentionalism proceed as if aesthetic satisfaction were the only important interest we could have with respect to artworks. Thus, wherever other putative interests impede aesthetic interests, they must give way. But aesthetic satisfaction is not the only major source of value that we have in interacting with artworks; the interaction is also a matter of a conversation between the artist and us—a human encounter—in which we have a desire to know what the artist intends, not only out of respect for the artist, but also because we have a personal interest in being a capable respondent. In endorsing the anti-intentionalist view that aesthetic satisfaction trumps all other interests, we seem to be willing to go for aesthetic pleasure at all costs, including, most notably, any value we might place on having a genuine conversational exchange with another human being. For, as the *Plan 9* example suggests, we are willing to act as if we had encountered a profound, reflexive meditation on the dominant cinema, when, in fact, it is readily apparent that we are dealing with a botched and virtually incoherent atrocity.

Aesthetic arguments in favor of anti-intentionalism presume a species of aesthetic hedonism. They presuppose that aesthetic pleasure or satisfaction is our only legitimate interest with regard to artworks. Here it is useful to recall Robert Nozick's very provocative, antihedonistic thought experiment—the experience machine.

> Suppose there were an experience machine that would give you any experience you desired. Super-duper neuropsychologists could stimulate your brain so that you would think and feel you were writing a great novel, or making a friend, or reading an interesting book. All the time you would be floating in a tank, with electrodes attached to your brain. Should you plug into the machine for life, preprogramming your life's experiences?[49]

Nozick thinks that our answer here will be obviously no, and part of the reason is that we wish to be a certain kind of person and do various things and not just have experiences as if we were such a person and as if we were doing those things. In other words, the pleasure of these simulated experiences is not enough; we have a stake in actually having the experiences in question. Applied to the aesthetic case, what I am trying to defend in the name of conversational interests is the claim that we have an investment in really encountering interesting and brilliant authors, not simply in counterfeiting such encounters. Knowing that *Plan 9* is a schlock quickie, but responding to it as if it were superbly transgressive, is akin to knowingly taking the heroics performed in Nozick's experience machine as if they were actual adventures. It is a matter of sacrificing genuine conversational experiences for aesthetic pleasures. And in doing so, one is willing to lower one's self-esteem for the sake of an aesthetic high.[50]

Of course, the problem I have raised with the use and abuse of the concept of transgression by contemporary film critics brings up general problems with aesthetic arguments in favor of anti-intentionalism. For example, the pervasive problems of allusion and irony are strictly analogous to the problems that we have sketched with respect to transgression. One could render both Richard Bach's *Jonathan Livingston Seagull*[51] and Heinrich Anacker's anti-Semitic, pro-Nazi "Exodus of the Parasites"[52] more aesthetically satisfying by regarding them as ironic. Yet I suspect that we resist this kind of interpretive temptation. And this resistance, I think, can be explained by our conversational interests in artworks. We have every justification for believing that these works are tawdry but sincere, and behaving as though they were ironic—whatever aesthetic satisfaction that might promote—would place us in what we recognize to be an ersatz conversation. We would be, respectively, laughing *with* what we know we should be laughing *at*, and appalled *along with* what we know we should be appalled *at*. Our conversation would not be authentic in either event, and whatever aesthetic satisfaction we secured would be purchased by making ourselves conversationally incompetent. Insofar as one of the abiding values we pursue in encounters with artworks is conversational, we are not willing to turn these particular pig's ears into silver purses.

Stanley Cavell has argued that one of the audience's major preoccupations with modern art is whether it is sincere. Given the dadaist tendencies of contemporary art, the spectator cares whether he or she is being fooled by the artist.[53] The encounter with the artwork is a human situation in which our self-esteem may be felt to be at risk. Likewise, I want to stress that insofar as the artistic context is a kind of conversation, we also may be concerned not only that the artist is given his or her due but that we carry through our end of the conversation. In terms of self-esteem, we have an interest not only in not being gulled by the artist but also in not fooling ourselves. And this interest gives us reason to reject interpretations of artworks that, however aesthetically satisfying they may be, cannot sensibly be connected to the intentions of their authors. The simulacrum of a brilliant conversation cannot be willfully substituted for a brilliant conversation and be a genuinely rewarding experience.

If these thoughts about our conversational interests in works of art are convincing, then they indicate that it is not true that the prospect of aesthetic satisfaction trumps every other desideratum when it comes to interpretation. Aesthetic satisfaction does not obviate our conversational interests in artworks. Moreover, our conversational interest in artworks is best served by intentionalism. Thus, in order to coordinate our aesthetic interests and our conversational interests, the best policy would not appear to be anti-intentionalism but the pursuit of aesthetic satisfaction constrained by our best hypotheses about authorial intent.

These hypotheses, moreover, will often depend on facts available to us about the biography of the artist. That the artist lived in fifteenth-century Italy, for example, will constrain attribution of his supposed intent to explore the themes of Greenbergian modernism in his canvases. Biographical data, in other words, can play a role in hypothesizing the artist's intention, while the recognition of the artist's intention, in turn, constrains the kinds of satisfactions, and, correspondingly, the kinds of interpretations we may advance with respect to artworks.[54] Not only is authorial intention derivable from artworks, *pace* the ontological arguments reviewed in the previous section; authorial intention—and biographical information—are relevant to the realization of the aims, particularly the conversational aims, we bring to artworks. Aesthetic arguments do not show that anti-intentionalism is the best interpretive policy to endorse given our purposes with respect to artworks. For we are interested in art as an occasion for communication with others as well as a source of aesthetic pleasure. And to the extent that communication or communion is among the leading purposes of art, authorial intention must always figure in interpretation, at least as a constraint on whatever other purposes we seek.

NOTES

1. H. P. Grice, "Meaning," *Philosophical Review* 66 (1957). See also Grice's *Studies in the Way of Words* (Cambridge, Mass.: Harvard University Press, 1989).

2. The idea of interpretations as *hypotheses* about authorial intentions is derived from William Tolhurst, "On What a Text Is and How It Means," *British Journal of Aesthetics* 19 (1979).

3. See W. K. Wimsatt, Jr., and Monroe C. Beardsley, "The Intentional Fallacy," *Swanee Review* 54 (1946). This is an expansion of their "Intention," in *Dictionary of World Literature*, ed. J. T. Shipley (New York: Philosophical Library, 1943).

4. See, for example, E.M.W. Tillyard and C. S. Lewis, *The Personal Heresy: A Controversy* (London: Oxford University Press, 1939). Stein Haugom Olsen makes the very interesting claim that the intentional fallacy evolved from the personal heresy but that the shift to intention talk also changed the debate in fateful ways. See Stein Haugom Olsen, *The End of Literary Theory* (Cambridge: Cambridge University Press, 1987), pp. 27–28.

5. Anti-intentionalists have not always been careful to keep the issues of authorial intention, reports of authorial intention, and biography apart. But one should. For example, one may believe that authorial intent is relevant to interpretation and at the same time maintain strong reservations about the authority of authorial pronouncements about the meaning of their artworks. On the distinction between intention and biography, see Colin Lyas, "Personal Qualities and the Intentional Fallacy," *Philosophy and the Arts: Royal Institute of Philosophy Lectures*, vol. 6 (New York: St. Martin's Press, 1973).

6. Monroe C. Beardsley, *Aesthetics* (New York: Harcourt, Brace and World, 1958), p. 20.

7. For a discussion of the notion of "intuition-pumps," see Daniel Dennett, *Elbow Room* (Cambridge, Mass.: MIT Press, 1984).

8. Monroe C. Beardsley, "An Aesthetic Definition of Art" in *What Is Art?* ed. Hugh Curtler (New York: Haven, 1984); and Monroe C. Beardsley, "Intending," in *Values and Morals*, ed. Alvin I. Goldman and Jaegwon Kim (Dordrecht: Reidel, 1978).

9. Beardsley, "Intending."

10. For related arguments dealing with the problem of arbitrary authorial pronouncements, see P. D. Juhl, *Interpretation: An Essay in the Philosophy of Literary Criticism* (Princeton: Princeton University Press, 1980), esp. chap. 7, sec. 4.

11. Beardsley, *Aesthetics*, p. 458.

12. Thomas Kuhn, *The Structure of Scientific Revolutions* (Chicago: University of Chicago Press, 1970), p. 9.

13. If Kuhn had really meant "weaned" here, he should have written "weaned from," not "weaned on."

14. The *locus classicus* of this view of intention is G.E.M. Anscombe's *Intention* (Oxford: Blackwell, 1959). Mary Mothersill provides a brief but useful sketch of the history of these countervailing views of intention in her *Beauty Restored* (Oxford: Oxford University Press, 1984), pp. 15–21.

15. See, for example, Stanley Cavell, "Music Discomposed," in his *Must We Mean What We Say?* (Cambridge: Cambridge University Press, 1976), p. 181. Also see "A

Matter of Meaning It" in the same volume. These originally appeared in *Art, Mind and Religion*, ed. W. H. Capitan and D. D. Merrill (Pittsburgh: University of Pittsburgh Press, 1967). Also relevant is Richard Kuhns, "Criticism and the Problem of Intention," *Journal of Philosophy* 57 (1960). Other arguments in the neo-Wittgensteinian vein include Frank Cioffi "Intention and Interpretation in Criticism," *Proceedings of the Aristotelian Society* 64 (1963–64); and A. J. Close, "Don Quixote and the 'Intentionalist Fallacy,' " in *On Literary Intention: Critical Essays*, ed. David Newton-de Molina (Edinburgh: Edinburgh University Press, 1976).

16. Monroe Beardsley himself seems to have agreed that the earlier view of intention upon which his arguments were based are inadequate—which is one reason why he developed what I call the ontological argument for anti-intentionalism that is examined later in this essay. See Monroe C. Beardsley, "Intentions and Interpretations: A Fallacy Revived," in *The Aesthetic Point of View*, ed. Michael J. Wreen and Donald M. Callen (Ithaca, N.Y.: Cornell University Press, 1982), p. 189.

17. Roland Barthes, "The Death of the Author," in his *Image-Music-Text* (New York: Hill and Wang, 1977). See also Roland Barthes, "From Work to Text," in *Textual Strategies: Perspectives in Post-Structuralist Criticism*, ed. Josue V. Harari (Ithaca, N.Y.: Cornell University Press, 1979).

18. In his *American Formalism and the Problem of Interpretation* (Houston: Rice University Press, 1986), J. Timothy Bagwell argues that the notion of a difference between literary and ordinary language underlies the early anti-intentionalism of Wimsatt and Beardsley. In this essay, I want to extend that insight to Beardsley's later arguments in his "Intentions and Interpretations."

19. Barthes, "Death of the Author," p. 143.

20. There may be an interesting parallel with the New Criticism and even Beardsley's defense of it here. Not only may Barthes's infatuation with polysemy correlate to the New Critical valorization of ambiguity, but also the New Criticism, it can be argued, arose as a critical practice allied with modernism—namely, that of Eliot. Indeed, even Beardsley's treatment of allusion fits nicely with Eliot's willingness to ascribe interpretations retrospectively. Moreover, both the New Criticism and Barthes may be involved in generalizing the critical position appropriate to the works of art they champion to all works of art.

Of course, the analogy I wish to draw is limited. There are also immense differences between Barthes and Beardsley. Barthes moves from the irrelevance of the author to fairly wide-ranging intertextuality, whereas Beardsley, given a commitment to the autonomy of the art work, advances a constrained form of objective interpretation. That is, Barthes's position elicits a great deal of free play on the part of the reader, whereas Beardsley remains committed to the possibility of true interpretations.

On Eliot's retrospective anti-intentionalist interpretations, see T. S. Eliot, "Tradition and the Individual Talent," in *Twentieth-Century Literary Theory*, ed. Vassilis Lambropoulos and David Neal Miller (Albany: State University of New York Press, 1987).

21. Beardsley, "Intentions and Interpretations," p. 190.

22. Characters, implied or otherwise, do not exist *de re*.

23. This view is also advanced by Graham Hough, who traces it to Austin. See Graham Hough, "An Eighth Type of Ambiguity," in Newton-de Molina, *On Literary Intention*.

24. See Richard Ohmann, "Speech Acts and the Definition of Literature," *Philosophy and Rhetoric* 4 (1971); Richard Ohmann, "Speech, Action and Style," in *Literary Style: A Symposium*, ed. Seymour Chatman (London: Oxford University Press, 1971); Barbara Herrnstein Smith, "Poetry as Fiction," in *New Directions in Literary History*, ed. Ralph Cohen (Baltimore: Johns Hopkins University Press, 1974); see also chap. 2 of Barbara Herrnstein Smith, *On the Margins of Discourse: The Relation of Literature to Language* (Chicago: University of Chicago Press, 1978). Indeed, Smith suggests an argument that somewhat parallels Beardsley's in her "The Ethics of Interpretation," in *On the Margins of Discourse*. For Beardsley's defense of the notion that lyric poems are representations, see his "Fiction as Representation," *Synthese* 46 (1981).

25. To be fair to Beardsley, it is important to note that in his "Philosophy of Literature," he appears to admit that there are literary works that are not fictional; this leads him to develop an aesthetic definition of literature—that is, one based on aesthetic intentions rather than on fiction. But it is hard to see that that admission will not undercut the argument in "Intentions and Interpretations." See Monroe C. Beardsley, "The Philosophy of Literature," in *Aesthetics: A Critical Anthology*, ed. George Dickie and Richard J. Sclafani (New York: St. Martin's Press, 1977), p. 325.

26. See John R. Searle, "The Logical Status of Fictional Discourse," *New Literary History* 6 (1974).

27. I suspect that one reason for adopting the notion of an implied author as a general hypothesis applying to all literary works by critical theorists may be an attempt—parallel to phenomenalism—to fend off skeptical, epistemological anxieties. That is, lacking a general principle for telling when one is confronted by the views of an actual author versus an implied author, one opts for a kind of reductionism—there are only, always implied authors. But this sort of reductionism hardly explains the behavior of our literary practices in general—we argue not only about but with Mailer's views on sex, death, and manliness.

In regard to my last point, one might respond in the spirit of Boris Tomasevkij, the Russian Formalist critic. He thinks of the public character of an author as a fictional creation—a fabrication existing in newspapers, published journals, and correspondence. Extrapolating from his position, one might try to say that we are arguing, not really with Mailer, but with the character of Mailer as he exists in our literary culture. But, as intriguing as this idea might be, I think we are often arguing with the real Norman Mailer, not a publicity fabrication or an implied author. See Boris Tomasevskij, "Literature and Biography," in Lambropoulos and Miller, *Twentieth-Century Literary Theory*.

Perhaps another motive for commitment to the generalized application of the notion of the implied author is that it is a means of adjusting to and accepting the intentional fallacy. But in this case, the claim that all literary expression is mediated by implied speakers cannot be used in an argument with intentionalism without begging the question.

28. Beardsley, *Aesthetics*, pp. 409–11.

29. This interpretation is derived from Christopher Butler, "Saving the Reader," in *Future Literary Theory*, ed. Ralph Cohen (New York: Routledge, 1989).

30. Jonathan Culler, a literary theorist in the Barthesian tradition, seems to take it that the literary work is divorced from reality because it is fictional, and therefore not a speech act. It functions differently, as a result, than ordinary language. This view sits strangely with his view that in reading literary texts with their consequent, wide-ranging semiosis we learn about the processes of the production of meaning in general. That is, how can the literary texts be essentially different than ordinary discourse, yet shed light on the processes of ordinary discourse? See Jonathan Culler, *Structuralist Poetics* (Ithaca, N.Y.: Cornell University Press, 1975), pp. 139 and 264–65.

31. Furthermore, if the mark of whether language is acting on reality is the presence of the speaker to the listener, then this would seem to make theatrical utterances a case of acting directly on reality, which is a consequence that I infer Barthes would reject.

32. One wonders, of course, whether Beardsley could extend the distinction between performances of illocutionary acts and representations of illocutionary acts across all the arts, since it is not clear that speech-act theory can be made to fit the cases of pictures, statues, etc.

33. For a more extended account of this, see Noël Carroll, "Trois propositions pour une critique de la danse contemporaine," in *La Danse au défi*, ed. Michele Febvre (Montreal: Editions Parachute, 1987).

34. As well, a great deal of literature will have to be understood in terms of choices and doings rather than solely in terms of manipulations of linguistic conventions. The way in which an author modulates a suspense structure, for example, will have to be explained in terms of what he is trying to do; there are no

fixed conventions to fall back on. Instead, the author will adopt a certain strategy that we will have to interpret intentionalistically. Similarly, the remarks about Barthleme's "Alice" indicate that with what I call strategies, the intentionalistic idiom of action is best suited for much of what we think of as the object of literary interpretation.

35. Monroe C. Beardsley, *The Possibility of Criticism* (Detroit: Wayne State University Press, 1970), p. 34. See Chapter 2, p. 34.

36. For elaborations of this distinction, see Tolhurst, "On What a Text Is," and Jack W. Meiland, "The Meanings of a Text," *British Journal of Aesthetics* 21 (1981).

37. This notion is elaborated on by Umberto Eco in his *The Open Work* (Cambridge, Mass.: Harvard University Press, 1989).

38. I take this to be the point of Jack Meiland's "The Meanings of a Text."

39. It stands in the way of maximizing interpretive play if the authorial intent is determinate; it is irrelevant because if we adopt anti-intentionalist interpretive practices, then whether or not the author intended an "open text," we will read it in that like anyway.

40. For a diagnosis of this, see Mary Sirridge, "Artistic Intention and Critical Prerogative," *British Journal of Aesthetics* 18 (1978).

41. See, for example, the high premium Barthes assigns to "writerly reading" in his *The Pleasure of the Text* (New York: Hill and Wang, 1975).

42. This position has been defended by Laurent Stern in his "On Interpreting," *Journal of Aesthetics and Art Criticism* 39 (1980); and Laurent Stern's "Facts and Interpretations," address to the Pacific Division meetings of the American Philosophical Association, Spring 1988.

43. A moral purpose that anti-intentionalism might be thought to advance is the emancipation of the spectator, a view with respect to interpretation that parallels the aspiration of many modern artists. But one wonders here whether the freedom of the reader here is genuinely moral or whether it is merely a strained moralization of the free play of cognition enjoined by Kantian aestheticism.

Or it might be felt that opening the artwork to interpretative play affords some kind of consciousness-raising heuristic; Jonathan Culler seems to have this view at the end of *Structuralist Poetics* where engaging the nonauthorially constrained play of textual signs teaches the reader something about the process of semiosis in general (p. 264). This claim would depend on a very controversial view of how language, in general, functions.

As well, one could imagine a literary theorist defending anti-intentionalism as securing an institutional purpose. That is, since the literary-critical institution is predicated on the production of interpretations, anti-intentionalism is facilitating because it keeps more interpretive options open. Nevertheless, the job security of literary critics hardly seems like the kind of overriding purpose that would move the rest of us.

Interestingly, intentionalism has also been defended for what might be thought of as institutional purposes. E. D. Hirsch, for example, wants to defend literary criticism as a cognitive discipline, and he believes that this requires determinate meaning, a commitment best served, on his account, by authorial intention. In this respect, Hirsch, unlike P. D. Juhl, is advancing intentionalism as a means to secure an end of the literary institution rather than as a thesis about the nature of meaning. See E. D. Hirsch, Jr., *Validity in Interpretation* (New Haven: Yale University Press, 1967); and E. D. Hirsch, Jr., *The Aims of Interpretation* (Chicago: University of Chicago Press, 1976). See Chapter 1.

44. This is not an invented example. See J. Hoberman, "Bad Movies," *Film Comment*, July–August 1980. Similar arguments appear in Hoberman's "Vulgar Modernism," *Artforum*, February 1982.

Moreover, I should stress that the issue raised by Hoberman's critical practice is not isolated. For it is often the case that the developments of avant-garde art are projected or read backward with respect to earlier works in the tradition. Thus, previously we saw Barthes's tendency to regard Mallarmé's modernist aspiration to efface authorship as a feature of all antecedent writing.

45. Hoberman, "Bad Movies."

46. Intentionalist criticism is guided by what a given text or artwork could have meant to the work's contemporary informed audience. Reference to what the audience could have understood is not to be taken as an alternative to intentionalist criticism, however, but as a means of identifying authorial intent. For, *ex hypothesi*, we begin by attributing to the author the intention of communicating— of getting her audience to recognize her intention. Thus, what we conjecture as the intention of the author, charitably, is something that the author could reasonably believe the audience—that is, the informed audience—could recognize. It should also be noted that included under the rubric of intentionalist criticism is the elucidation of the author's presuppositions, especially the elucidation of the stylistic choice structure through which the author's intentional activity takes place. And again, what an informed audience could perceive as a stylistic option guides our hypotheses about the author's intentions for the reasons already given.

47. Søren Kierkegaard, *Concluding Unscientific Postscript* (Princeton: Princeton University Press, 1941), p. 466.

48. Culler, *Structuralist Poetics*, p. 115.

49. Robert Nozick, *Anarchy, State, and Utopia* (New York: Basic Books, 1974), p. 42.

50. Why, it might be asked, if this analysis is correct, do so many critics seem willing to indulge anti-intentionalist criticism? One hypothesis is that by means of

theoretical devices like unconscious or ideological motivation, they believe that they are getting at the author's actual intentions.

51. This example comes from Denis Dutton, "Why Intentionalism Won't Go Away," in *Literature and the Question of Philosophy*, ed. Anthony Cascardi (Baltimore: Johns Hopkins University Press, 1987).

52. Juhl, *Interpretation*, pp. 121–24.

53. Cavell, "Music Discomposed."

54. Daniel Nathan has argued that intentionalist arguments often depend on having access to contextual information about the text—rather than biographical evidence—and that the anti-intentionalist also may, in principle, have access to contextual information. I think, however, that an example like Edward Wood indicates that biographical information may also be required. For Wood was a contemporary of the Surrealist filmmaker Buñuel, someone who had the intellectual resources and the will to make a transgressive film. Thus, knowing that the filmmaker was Wood, and knowing something about Wood, and that the filmmaker was not Buñuel, is crucial to our dismissal of *Plan 9* as a mistake. See Daniel O. Nathan, "Irony and the Artist's Intentions," *British Journal of Aesthetics* 23 (1982).

Wittgensteinian Intentions

8

COLIN LYAS

I

IT IS OFTEN SUPPOSED that Monroe Beardsley and William Wimsatt argued the total irrelevance to interpretation and evaluation of references to the intentions of artists. Those who object to this usually attempt to demonstrate the relevance of such references to the task of interpretation and, in particular, to the task of determining the meaning of a literary text. But it is unclear whether Beardsley and Wimsatt ever argued the total irrelevance of references by critics and interpreters to the intentions of artists.

They certainly asserted that statements by artists about their intentions have no special authority over the deliberations of critics and interpreters,[1] and this for two different reasons. One is that artists may be in error about their intentions,[2] but this clearly gives no grounds for arguing the total irrelevance of authorial intention to criticism. Another reason is that artists may be in error about whether the works they have produced in fact possess the properties they intended them to have.[3]

Did Beardsley and Wimsatt believe that the fact that artists are not the best judges of whether their intentions are fulfilled is a basis on which to establish the irrelevance to interpretation and evaluation of references to the intentions of artists? Here the evidence is ambiguous. There is an inclination to believe that intention can be dispensed with, and many passages in the Beardsley and Wimsatt canon seem to support this view.[4] At the same time, however, there is evidence that Wimsatt, at least, did not believe that the need to focus on the work, rather than on the prior intentions of the artist, entirely eliminated the possibility of reference to the intentions of the artist. For Wimsatt appeared ready to concede that the work itself might display within it the intention and mind of the artist. For, in what on his own account is a dubiously legitimate external statement about their prior intentions, he tells us that what he and Beardsley *meant* to say in their seminal article "The Intentional Fallacy"[5] was that "the closest one could ever get to the artist's intending or meaning mind, outside his work, would still be short of his *effective* intention or *operative* mind as it appears in the work itself and can be read from the work."[6]

This is a very significant admission, for it undermines what looks to be one of the strongest arguments for the claim that knowledge of and reference to the artist and the artist's intentions can be dispensed with by critics and interpreters. According to that argument, the work is one thing, and the artist, together with his or her mind and intentions, is another and entirely distinct thing. From this it would seem to follow that critics and interpreters, whose task it is to talk about the work of art itself, should entirely ignore the artist and the artist's mind and intentions in order to talk about the intrinsic properties of the work. The passage I have quoted from Wimsatt puts paid to this. For the force of that passage is that work and artist are not always discrete entities. The mind of the artist and the artist's intentions can, so to speak, leak into and be displayed in the work; then, even those critics and interpreters who follow the injunction to talk only of what is in the work may find that this requires them to talk about the intentions and mental qualities the artist displays in that work. This being so, it will no longer be possible to take the work of Beardsley and Wimsatt as designed to prove the total eliminability of references by critics and interpreters to artists and their intentions.

Beardsley writes:

> The first thing required to make criticism possible is an object to be criticised . . . with its own properties against which interpretations and judgments can be checked. The Principle of Independence, as it might be called, is that literary works exist as individuals and can be distinguished from other things. . . . But there is another postulate that is logically complementary to the first: that literary works are self-sufficient entities, whose properties are decisive in checking interpretations and judgments. This is sometimes called the Principle of Autonomy, and it is of course the subject of much dispute.[7]

In the light of Wimsatt's assertions about the aims of his work with Beardsley, it is clear that neither of the principles offered by Beardsley serves to eliminate references to authors and their intentions. One might concede that, by the Principle of Autonomy, works of art are indeed self-sufficient entities against the properties of which interpretations and judgments are to be checked. If Wimsatt is right, however, it may be a property of the work that it display in itself the mind and intentions of the artist; then reference to the work itself may be reference to the mind and intentions of its creator. Beardsley in fact locates the controversy in the wrong place. The dispute is not about the Principle of Autonomy, which seems to say no more than that if a statement is made in which a property is attributed to work, then that statement ought to be verifiable or falsifiable by reference to the actual properties of that work. The argument, if there is to be one, will be an argument about whether displays of mind and intention can be intrinsic properties of works. Wimsatt seems to have conceded that they can be.

I have to say, too, that Wimsatt seems to me to have been right to make this concession. For many of the terms used by critics of works of art seem to refer to qualities of mind displayed in works by their creators. When Wayne Booth, in The Rhetoric of Fiction,[8] speaks of a novel as being undermined by confusion and pretentiousness, he is speaking of a confusion and pretension displayed by the author in the work, and his judgment has to be, and can be, justified, and this is the force of the Principle of Autonomy, by references to what is in the text.

II

Granted that the work of Beardsley and Wimsatt seems not to provide any general argument for the irrelevance of references to artists and their intentions, two strategies seem available to those who are nonetheless suspicious of such references.

One strategy is to argue that Wimsatt was in fact wrong to allow the artist and his intentions to be objectively present in the work. (It is evidence of some confusion of purpose that Beardsley and Wimsatt give some sign of adopting this strategy.) The less radical strategy is to claim that although reference to some intentions is relevant—namely, to those objectively present in the work—nonetheless not every reference to intention is relevant. The quotation I have given from Wimsatt suggests this latter strategy. For while allowing reference to intentions that are operative in the work, he indicates a wish to exclude reference to the intentions that the artist may have had that are not discoverable by reference to the text. If, for example, an author wrote a novel with the intention of making money, and this fact is discoverable only by inquiries into biography that require the critic or interpreter to study something other than the work, then such references are irrelevant to the task of criticism and interpretation. It is at this point that I wish to refer to some of the work of Wittgenstein, for that work bears on the question of the extent to which either of the strategies I have mentioned is likely to succeed. I begin with the more radical strategy.

III

Wimsatt and Beardsley write that "intention is design or plan in the author's mind" (IF, p. 4), a statement echoed in Beardsley's remark that "the artist's intention is a series of psychological states or events in his mind" (*Aesthetics*, p. 17). So far, this is relatively innocuous. It becomes less so when such statements are made in conjunction with assertions like the following: "An art work is something which emerges from the private, individual, dynamic and intentionalistic realm of its maker's mind and personality. . . . But . . . in the moment it emerges, it enters a public, and in a certain clear sense, an objective realm" ("Genesis," p. 116).

Here we find evidence of a philosophical psychology that has two important components. First, there is an element that is most elegantly expressed by one of its leading opponents, Gilbert Ryle. For in Wimsatt's account one has a glimpse of the view that Ryle characterizes thus:

> Every human being has both a body and a mind. . . . Human bodies are in space and are subject to the mechanical laws that govern all other bodies in space. Bodily processes and states can be inspected by external observers. So a man's bodily life is as much a public affair as are the lives of animals and reptiles. . . . But minds are not in space, nor are their operations subject to mechanical laws. The workings of one mind are not witnessable by other observers; its career is private. . . . A person therefore lives through two collateral histories, one consisting of what happens in and to his body, the other consisting of what happens in and to his mind. The first is public and the second is private.[9]

The second element, which is in fact a special case of the first, is the belief that an intention is a discrete event or process or thing that occurs "in" a place called the mind and that is correlated with the physical actions and events and things that happen as the result of someone's possessing an intention as a cause is related to the effect in the physical world. Beardsley, for example writes that two things may be causally connected, "as are presumably the intention and the aesthetic object" (*Aesthetics*, p. 19).

Those who believe the first of these things to be true, namely that there are two worlds, one mental and private, one public and physical, may now, when the theory of interpretation and criticism is under discussion, argue, as indeed Wimsatt seems to do, as follows: The critic and interpreter must be interested in the properties possessed by the public object, the work of art itself. To attend to any other thing is to digress into irrelevance. But now, the mind and the intentions in it are separate things from the public work of art. Consequently, to take any sort of interest in these is to turn aside from the proper task of criticism and interpretation, which is the study of the public work of art itself.

If all this is true, there are two sorts of errors in the work of Beardsley and Wimsatt. First, Wimsatt is wrong to believe that a mind can be publicly discernible, or "operative," in a work. For minds are by definition private. Second, Beardsley and Wimsatt are wrong to suggest, as they sometimes do, that the problem about reference to intention is that knowledge of intention is not available to us. Beardsley, for example, suggests this when he says, "We can seldom know the intention with sufficient exactness. . . . Of the intentions of Shakespeare, Vermeer, the makers of the *Thousand and One Nights*, and the composers of old folk songs we have no evidence at all outside the works they left us" (*Aesthetics*, p. 458). For even if we had the most precise knowledge of intention, it would still be the case, on the view described, that the contents, including the intentions, of private minds were distinguishable from public works of art. Consequently, to take an interest in these mental contents would be to talk about the wrong thing. This, as Beardsley himself says, would be to talk not about the work but "about the worker, which is quite a different thing" (*Aesthetics*, p. 458).

The argument is, then, that minds are one thing, works of art another. From this it follows, first, that minds cannot be displayed in art; and second, that reference to minds is reference to the wrong thing.

This argument constitutes a general argument against reference to the mind of the artist. The argument against reference to intention is a special case of this. An intention is an object located in a mind and not part of the public object which is the work of art. Consequently, those who should be talking about the public object need not pay any attention to the private intention. Beardsley writes, therefore, that

the consequences that follow from making a distinction between aesthetic objects and artist's intentions are very important . . . because they depend on a general principle of philosophy. . . . If two things are distinct . . . then the evidence for the existence and nature of the one cannot be the same as the evidence for the existence and nature of the other. (*Aesthetics*, p. 19)

More simply, we might say, if two things are indeed distinct, then talking about the one is not talking about the other.

I have said that there is evidence of some ambiguity of aim in the work of Wimsatt and Beardsley. On the one hand, we find that they seem committed to the view that a radical separation exists between minds, which are private and hidden, and physical objects, including works of art, which are public and available. This view, if true, would entail that those who talk about works of art are not talking about the minds and the contents of the minds of artists. (Although it would not follow, for reasons we later come to, that we need no knowledge of the minds of artists in order to talk adequately of their works). On the other hand, Wimsatt, at least, appears also to believe that the mind and intention of the artist can be directly observable in the public object that is the work of art.

This leaves us with the question, Which of these views is correct? For if the former is correct, we can conclude with no further ado that to talk about works of art is not to talk about the minds and intentions of their creators; if the latter is true, then reference to publicly displayed features of works of art may involve reference to the minds and intentions of the creators of these works.

The answer to this question is to be found in the philosophy of mind and not in aesthetics. (And one reason why the dispute in aesthetics about the relevance of references to the minds and intentions of artists has been so intractable is that that dispute rests on problems in the philosophy of mind that are equally intractable.)

There are still those who subscribe to the view that mental events occur in one world, physical events in another, and that one can know the contents of a mind only by somewhat shaky inferences (made on the basis of observation of the physical movements of bodies), where the truth of the conclusions of these inferences can never be directly established. Hare, for example, writes:

> More commonly and more basically we represent to ourselves the experiences of others by analogy with our own, judging that situations are similar (someone has just hit his head on a low beam), their physiologies are similar (his skull has about the same dimensions as ours and his nerves are in roughly the same places), and that there-

fore their experience will be similar (he will be liking it just about as much as we did).[10]

Anyone committed to such a view is already committed to the view that to talk of the public work of art is not to talk about the mind and intention of the artist.

Wittgenstein has influenced thinking in aesthetics through the remarks he directly addresses to problems in the arts.[11] A more indirect influence may come from the striking criticism he has offered of any attempt to represent our knowledge of other minds, and hence of knowledge of such things as intentions, as always and in every case a matter of inference (on the basis of the observation of the movements of bodies) about a private world that we can never directly know. With that, there appears to go a belief that minds, and their contents, can show themselves directly in bodies so that, for example, "the human body is the best picture of the human soul."[12]

Whether or not such a view is true is much debated. I am inclined to believe that it is true, and certainly Wimsatt, in referring to the possibility of detecting an operative mind that is displayed in the public lineaments of a work of art, appears to subscribe to it. True or not, to raise, as Wittgenstein did, substantial doubts about the logical privacy of the mental is to raise substantial doubts about any strategy that seeks to eliminate reference to the artist's intentions on the grounds that such intentions exist in a private mental world and can never be directly observed in the work itself.

IV

There is a further contribution that an understanding of some of Wittgenstein's remarks about intention can make to discussions of the relevance of references to the intentions of artists.

I have said that there is evidence, in the work of Beardsley and Wimsatt, of an inclination to think of intention and action as related in the manner in which Hume, for example, believed cause and effect to be related. It is an essential component of this view that cause and effect be independently knowable. This amounts to two claims: first, that which is the cause can be fully known without any reference being made to that which is the effect, and *vice versa*; and second, what we know of the properties of that which is a cause or effect, when such a cause or effect is considered in its own right, gives us no reason to conclude anything about any other object. Hume writes: "It is not the object presented to us, which, considered in itself, afford us any reason to draw a conclusion concerning any other object or event."[13] (This view of objects as logically discrete is echoed in the logical atomism of Wittgenstein, where we read that "from the existence of one state of affairs it is impossible to infer the existence or non-existence of another.")[14] Beardsley speaks of intention and action in ways that suggest an inclination to think of them as discrete objects, related in the manner in which Hume believed objects standing in causal relations are related. "Intention and aesthetic object," he tells us, are "causally related" (*Aesthetics*, p. 19). What we learn about the artist's intention is, at best, "indirect evidence" about the nature of the work. Our ultimate source of knowledge of the work is the evidence gained by "direct inspection of the object" (*Aesthetics*, p. 20).

Here are two beliefs. The first belief is that the artist's intention is some kind of object, or process, or event existing in the internal private realm of the artist's mind. Correlated with this is another discrete object, the work, which exists in the public world. Hence the claim made by Beardsley and Wimsatt that intention is "in the author's mind" (IF, p. 4) and the claim by Wimsatt that, on publication, an artwork "emerged from the private, individual, dynamic and intentionalistic world of its maker's mind" and "enters a public . . . and . . . objective realm" ("Genesis," p. 116). Second, in true Humean style we are told that, given an experience of the ways in which artist's intentions and works of art go together, we may make probablistic inferences from what we know of the one to what is true of the other. If all we want to know is what is true of the work, however, such inferences are unnecessary. For all we need to know in order to know all there is to know about the work can be obtained by a study of it. This is in effect to say that since intention and object are independent objects, a complete knowledge of that object which is the work of art is obtainable without need of reference to that entirely discrete object that is the intention of the artist.

The analysis of intention given by Wittgenstein in the *Investigations* suggests difficulties with both beliefs. First, an object, process, or event seems to be the wrong sort of thing to serve as an intention. For it is in the nature of objects, events, and processes that they have temporal duration and might—indeed, have a momentary existence. A brain process, for example, might occur of a sudden, out of the blue, and be quickly over. We can identify its presence without needing to know the setting in which it occurred. If this is so, then we have a reason for refusing to think of intentions as events, objects, or processes that occur in a shadowy region called the mind, in the way in which physical events, objects, and processes occur in the physical world. For it is essential to an intention, as it is to a hope, that it have a setting. What Wittgenstein says of hope applies equally to intention: "Could someone have a feeling

of ardent love or hope for the space of one second—*no matter what* preceded
or followed this second?—What is happening now has significance—in these
surroundings. The surroundings give it its importance" (*Investigations*, p. 583).

(I do not here wish to deny neurophysiological processes are necessary if
there is to be intending, hoping, or believing. What is to be denied is that to
ascribe an intention to a person just is to refer to a neurophysiological process
that is, in Humean style, merely correlated with an action that follows it. The
error here seems to be equivalent to that of drawing from the true belief that
there can be no value properties in paintings unless some color patches are
physically present the conclusion that talks about the value properties of a
painting can be reduced to physicalist descriptions of the color patches that
constitute it.)

That the ascription of intention makes sense only in a context can be seen
if we think of the absurdity of supposing that an Amazonian Indian could, in
1636, have formed the intention of becoming the first Republican president of
the United States. No evidence of the presence in the brain of such a person,
of neurophysical processes identical with those now present in the brain of
some Republican hopeful, would in the least convince us that the Amazonian
had an identical intention. For, as Wittgenstein writes: "An intention is embedded in its situation, in human customs and institutions. If the technique
of the game of chess did not exist, I would not intend to play a game of chess"
(*Investigations*, p. 337).

Central to our inclination to ascribe an intention to a being is our sense
that that being has the ability to represent to itself that at which the intention is aimed. If we think that cats, albeit in some primitive way, have this
ability, then we can talk of their having intentions. For us, our ability to have
intentions is bound up with our possession of a language in which we can
represent our intentions to ourselves. This is why I can intend (hope) to do
something the week after next in the way in which a cat cannot; and this is
why I can express my intentions, whereas a cat can, in its behavior, give us
evidence only on the basis of which to ascribe intentions to it.[15] We see shortly
that the connection between a setting, and notably a linguistic setting, and the
possibility of intending something creates a difficulty for the kind of analysis
of the role of intention in interpretation favored by Hirsch.

One thing wrong with the claim that intention and action are related as
Humean cause and effect is that that claim seems not to take account of the
fact that it makes sense to ascribe an intention only when an agent is situated
within and aware of a complex social setting. This is related to a difficulty with
a second belief to be found within the overall view of intention and action

as related in the manner of Humean causes and effects. For, according to this belief, intention and action, like any cause and effect, are independently knowable. Thus we have seen Beardsley's inclination to assert that everything that we want to know and say of the work of art, conceived as the effect of a causal intention, can be known and said without any need to know of or refer to that intention.

It is, however, far from obvious that one can complete the description of many actions without knowledge or reference to the intention of the agent. For one thing, the very description of something as an action typically presupposes that it, or some component of it, lay within the control of an agent and to that extent was, in part at least, intentional. For this reason, to be able even to describe something as a work of art, as opposed to a natural object, is to suppose intentional agency.

Since it might be said that to ascribe to a thing the property of being a work of art is not to talk of one of its *important* properties, it is necessary to note that sometimes in order to identify the important properties of an action, or, as we later see, of such results of actions as works of art, it is necessary to know something of the way in which they were intended. We could not call an action a murder if we did not know or assume that a certain intention or state of mind existed in its agent.

In an important respect the proper description of what is done is always related to beliefs about how the agent conceived the action. Thus, to use an example from Winch, behavior counts as voting, not because people put crosses on pieces of paper, for they can be compelled uncomprehendingly to do that, but because they live in a society with certain institutions and comprehend those institutions.[16] It is, therefore, a mistake to believe that the description of an action, or of the result of an intentional action, can be completed without reference to an intention. Some of the things that are true of an action or of the result of an action may be detectable only if we have a knowledge that scrutiny of that action or result alone could not give. Scrutinize the details of a killing as I might, nothing in what is publicly available to inspection in that action need solve the important question whether it is to be called murder.

It is important to realize that what has been said does not commit me to the view that anything agents claim about their intentions has to be admitted. To believe that I can call an action murder only if I have reason to believe that an agent was in a certain frame of mind does not mean that whatever the agent claims about his state of mind has to be accepted. Few murderers would be convicted if this were so. Here we need to distinguish between the claim that we may need knowledge of intention properly to characterize an action and the claim that agents are the most reliable sources of information about their intentions. The latter is dubiously true, and leads, I am sure, to suspicion about references by critics to the intentions of artists. But the dubious nature of this latter claim does nothing whatsoever to establish the falsity of the former. The former commits me only to the claim that I may need to know something about the states of mind of agents if I am properly to characterize their actions. In admitting this, nothing has as yet been said about how I come by that knowledge. In fact I may well believe that the best information about intention comes not from what the agent says but from evidence of an operative mind publicly discernible in the work.

It is equally important to realize that a description of an action in terms of the agent's conception of it, though it tells us something about how the action is properly to be characterized, may not tell us everything about what was done, nor even the most important things about what was done. To adapt an example from Anscombe:[17] I may not realize that in pumping water to a town I am poisoning the inhabitants, but this may be the most important feature of what is going on. Here, indeed, we have another illustration of a point made earlier: an artist, the agent producing the work, may not be the best judge of what is important and interesting about it.

This leads to the following line of thought: We have seen that in the case of killings, an *important* thing about the description of a killing—namely, that it is a murder—might be ascertainable only if we have some knowledge of the state of mind of the agent. Suppose someone now said that the reason for ignoring the intentions of artists is not that the full characterization of actions can be carried out without a knowledge of such intentions, but that no feature of a work that is important in criticism ever requires a knowledge of intention for its recognition. The challenge might then be to find something about works of art that is important to appreciation and that relies for its discovery on a knowledge of intention in the way in which the discovery that an act is a murder depends on a knowledge of intention.

Two examples may suffice to show that the challenge is not impossible to meet. One concerns allusions. In the Gilbert and Sullivan opera The Pirates of Penzance, Major General Stanley, at a loss for a rhyme for the words "din afore" solves his problem by a reference to that "infernal nonsense Pinafore." The audience laughs, not because of the derogatory remark, but because they know that Gilbert and Sullivan are the originators of The Pirates of Penzance and Pinafore and intend that their audience should be aware of this fact and so appreciate the humor of the derogatory reference. Without that knowledge, the point of the joke is lost. Such cases are not uncommon. (A controversial class of them involves self-reference, as when one might think that the poignancy of Milton's "On His Blindness" is heightened by a knowledge that the author was himself blind.)

For a second example, we might consider the way in which, in certain forms of parody and irony, the point of what is happening can only be appreciated if one knows that some kind of imitation is being undertaken. Consider here the way in which the character of Swift's *A Modest Proposal* will be misunderstood unless one assumes a parodic intention on the part of its author. It is not without interest here that Beardsley's discussion of Housman's "1887" appears to connect a decision that the work is ironic with the attribution of an ironic intention, albeit unconscious, to Housman.[18]

V

I have said earlier that a radical effort to clear away references to artists and their intentions might take the form of an effort to demonstrate that the nature of mind and intention made such references otiose. Under the influence of the kind of analysis of mind and intention to be found in the work of Wittgenstein, I have tried to show that there is little to be gained by pursuing this radical approach. We seem, therefore, to have no general argument for the eliminability of references to artists and their intentions.

That said, skepticism about the intentions might take a less radical form. Even granted that there may be critical and interpretive enterprises that are assisted by references to the minds of artists, it is still open to someone to argue that such references are excluded from other areas of criticism and interpretation. Here the strongest argument is to be found in the work of those who have argued that reference to the intention of the artist is not needed by those whose task it is to establish the meaning of a text; and it is this argument that is called into question by Hirsch and Iseminger.[19]

Let us first establish the grounds on which the argument against reference to intentions in determining meaning is founded.

The central consideration is that although words would have no meaning unless there were communities of language users, a word has a meaning independent of the will of any individual language user. We do not give a word a meaning when we speak; we use words as already having a meaning. The question, What meaning does that word have? is no more decided by the will of an individual user than the question, What color is that patch? is decided by the word of the person who painted it. Humpty-Dumpty, indeed, could only give words like "impenetrability" his own special meaning because he had available to him a public language, the words of which have a meaning independent of his will, by which to explain his meaning to others. This being so, it will follow that if an interpreter is puzzled as to the meaning of a word, he does not have to consult the author as to his intentions. All an interpreter needs is the dictionary of the public language.

What is true of individual words, it is claimed, is true also of words in combination. What emerges from a combination of words is decided by reference to the rules governing the meaning and the grammar of the public language. An author may tell us what meaning he or she would like to have seen emerge from a set of words, but this no more determines what *has* emerged than a painter's statement of what he or she would have liked to have seen emerge from a combination of blobs of color determines what has emerged.

This argument is often found in modern discussions of interpretation. It is to be found when Beardsley, for example, tells us that there is a difference between what an utterance means and what a speaker means by it.[20] Equally it is found when he tells us that "texts acquire determinate meaning through the interactions of their words without the intervention of an authorial will" (PC, p. 30; see Chapter 2, pp. 31–32). Hence:

> The goodness in which we take an interest . . . is something that arises out of the ingredients of the poem itself: the ways its verbal parts—its structure and texture—combine and cooperate to make something fresh and novel emerge. The words have to work on us. . . . It is in its language that the poem happens. That is why the language is the object of our attention and of our study when its meaning is difficult to understand. It is not the interpreter's proper task . . . to draw our attention off to the psychological states of the author. . . . His task is to keep our eye on the textual meaning. (PC, p. 34; see Chapter 2, pp. 34–35)

It is found, too, in somewhat different philosophical traditions, as when Sartre writes: "Words . . . finally . . . became things in themselves. . . . And when the poet joins several of these microcosms together the case is like that of painters when they assemble their colours on the canvas."[21]

Resistance to the view that an individual intention can determine the meaning of strings of words is an important part of the project of the *Investigations*. This seems to me to be the point of such remarks as, "Can I say 'bububu' and mean 'if it doesn't rain I shall go for a walk?'—It is only in a language that I can mean something by something." "When I think in language there aren't 'meanings' going through my mind in addition to the verbal expressions." "Suppose I said 'a b c d' and meant: the weather is fine. For as I uttered these signs I had the experience normally had only by someone who had year-in-

year-out used 'a' in the sense of 'the,' 'b' in the sense of 'weather' and so on.—
Does 'a b c d' now mean: the weather is fine?" (*Investigations*, p. 18).

I have indicated some skepticism about efforts entirely to eliminate references to artists and their intentions. That skepticism is, however, compatible
with a belief that there are occasions on which references to intention may
not be necessary or relevant. The current suggestion is that when the problem is one about the meaning of words, then reference to intention is not
necessary. Before I ask whether this is so, it is worth observing that even if it
is so, much that I have said about the possible relevance of reference to artists
and their intentions will survive.

To begin with, let us note that sometimes the term "meaning" is used
when we wish to ask, not what a word means, but what the force of an utterance was. Was it, we ask, a warning, promise, or threat? Usually we ask this
when someone has failed to make the force of an utterance clear. There is one
clear parallel, however, between force and meaning. Whether an utterance
has a meaning is not decided by someone's wish that it have a certain meaning. So too, whether an utterance has a force (successfully conveys a force)
is not just a matter of someone's wanting it to have that force. We decide
whether or not an utterance actually has conveyed its force by criteria that
are independent of the will of the speaker. That speaker, for example, cannot
succeed in promising merely by producing the words "I promise" followed
by a that-phrase. Whether a promise is made will depend on features of the
context of the utterance and the content of the that-phrase. (I cannot, for example, promise you what you and I know you neither want nor need, just by
producing a certain formula with a certain intention.)

All this might suggest that reference to intention is not required when we
are dealing with questions about the force of an utterance. This is not so. What
is true is that whether or not an utterance has a clear force is not decided by
asking a speaker what force he or she wanted it to have. For all that, force
sometimes is made clear by the production of an utterance in a certain context. When it is made clear, then what is made clear is an intention on the part
of the speaker to do something in speaking—for example, to give a warning,
threat or promise. Hence to refer to the force of an utterance is to refer to its
speaker's intention, even though what that force is need not be determined
by asking the speaker what that intention was.

The second thing I wish to point out by way of qualification is that even
if the meaning of the concatenated words of a passage existed independently
of what a speaker or writer might will them to mean, it is nonetheless possible for those words to reveal what Wimsatt calls the "operative" mind of

the author. The words I use may have a meaning independent of my will, but in using them I can display myself. The irrelevance of investigations of intentions when our business is the determination of meaning would not, therefore, entail the irrelevance of references to the authorial mind as displayed in the meaning of the text. Consider, for example, the way in which one might, as indeed Leavis does,[22] criticize the shortcomings of a work in which one detects an unintentional discrepancy between a powerful meaning that an author clearly wants to express and what he or she has actually inadequately managed to articulate.

VI

The essence of the argument offered by Hirsch is that every word sequence, even a long word sequence, is, taken in itself, always indeterminate, since it is always open to more than one assignment of meaning. Clearly we need some determinacy of meaning if language, as a system of communication, is to be possible. Since the word sequence itself does not supply us with a determinate meaning, something else must make that sequence mean *this* rather than *that*. That discriminating force is the act by which an utterer wills *this* rather than *that* meaning.

There is a possible interpretation of this claim that renders it liable to objection in the light of remarks that I have earlier made about intention and meaning. Suppose that a form of words, for example, "I like my secretary better than my wife," could be used to say either that one likes one's secretary better than one's wife does or that one prefers one's secretary to one's wife. It would be a mistake to believe in such cases that one might by an act of intention make such a set of words mean one of these things rather than the other. For it is a condition of having an intention that some set of words should bear a certain meaning and that one be able to represent that intended meaning to oneself. How is that to be done in the present case? Presumably one brings before the mind a form of words that has the meaning one wishes to express. This cannot be the phrase "I like my secretary better than my wife," for that is the very phrase the meaning of which is indeterminate. So one has to bring before the mind another, elucidatory phrase, such as "I like my secretary better than my wife does," and intend that as the meaning of the indeterminate phrase. Then, however, a dilemma appears. For either the elucidatory phrase is indeterminate in meaning, or it is not. If it is indeterminate, as every word string must be on Hirsch's account, then a further act of intention will be required in order to give it the determinate meaning that is to be wished onto the original phrase. That act of intention will consist in the representation to oneself of a further phrase, the meaning of which will again be indeterminate. If it is supposed that all word sequences are indeterminate, it is difficult to see how this regress can be ended. Suppose, in contrast, that the elucidatory phrase brought before the mind has a determinate meaning, as seems to be true with the phrase "I like my secretary better than my wife does." This immediately casts doubt on the belief that word sequences are all indeterminate unless preceded by an act of willing a particular meaning for them. Moreover, if one brings before the mind a phrase with a determinate meaning, one must immediately realize the impossibility of willing this as the meaning of the indeterminate phrase with which one began. For the original phrase genuinely was indeterminate in meaning, whereas the new phrase is not. How, then, can the latter be wished on the former as its meaning?

What the argument here shows is that if an utterance is indeterminate in its meaning (ambiguous perhaps), this indeterminacy is a real property of that utterance. A statement by its utterer about what he or she would have liked to have meant by an utterance merely uses a further determinate statement to tell us which of the various meanings of an indeterminate statement the utterer had hoped, unsuccessfully, to make clear.

By exactly this argument, Beardsley and Wimsatt seek to demonstrate the irrelevance of reference to intention when the question is, What meaning does that utterance have? The argument appears in the earlier "The Intentional Fallacy." It reappears later when Beardsley writes that "an ambiguous text does not become any less ambiguous because its author wills one of the possible meanings. Will as he will, he cannot will away ambiguity (PC, p. 29; see Chapter 2, p. 31). The same argument seems to me to establish that when a work does have a determinate meaning, it does not get that meaning as the result of some *prior act* of willing or intending that meaning. For, as we have seen, this leads to a regress of acts of willing the meaning.

If the meaning of a work or utterance is indeterminate, no act of will can make it determinate. It does not follow from this, however, that when an utterance or work *does* have a determinate meaning, we can distinguish between that meaning and what the utterer wished to say. Indeed it looks more plausible to say that where the meaning of a set of words is unambiguous, this will be because those words articulate the intention of the speaker. Given a knowledge of the context in which they are spoken, our words can display our intentions as much as our actions can. Unless words could thus display our intentions, they could never have a determinate meaning. We could talk only of what they *might* have been used to say. The point is related to a point about action. There is a sense in which the answer to the question "What was he doing?" specifies the answer the agent would give; and in the same sense the question what was he saying may have to make reference to what the agent would acknowledge.

If Hirsch wishes to say that when I speak I bring before my mind an indeterminate string of words and then intend a determinate meaning for them, then I can make no sense of this. But if the claim is that when we say that a string of words has a determinate meaning, we do so because we recognize in those words an intention to say a certain thing, this looks more plausible.[23] If there is an inclination to deny it, that will probably be because of an inclination to think of an intention as a private act of will that precedes and is logically separable from some publicly available set of words; then the question will arise why, if the words are publicly available, we need to bother with the private intention. But here, as Wittgenstein remarks in paragraph 337 of the *Investigations*, "we are constructing a misleading picture of 'intending.'" This picture leads us to forget the way in which an intention may manifest itself in actions and words, and the way in which, when it does, it can determine at least part of the proper description of those actions and words.

So it may seem that there is some truth in the claim that to refer to the determinate meaning of a set of words is just to refer to an intention embodied and made manifest in them. Even if this is true, however, the relevance of reference to intention in criticism and interpretation has not yet been shown. For it is possible to argue that although there are situations in which we are interested in determinate meaning, and hence in intentions, the situation in which we take an interest in a literary text might not be one of them.

It seems to me that one of the rules of procedure that govern the conversational interchanges in which we give information is the rule that enjoins us always to look for the most relevant determinate meaning of an utterance. The heroine of the Alice books, for example, is continually frustrated by the refusal of those she meets to abide by this rule:

> Here the Red Queen began again. "Can you answer useful questions?" she said. "How is bread made?"
>
> "I know *that!*" Alice cried eagerly, "You take some flour—"
>
> "Where do you pick the flower?" the White Queen asked. "In a garden or in the hedges?"[24]

If, however, we wanted to find one mark whereby to indicate the difference between the informative interchanges and literary art, we might say that a literary text allows us to treat it in the way in which the White Queen inappropriately responds to Alice's utterances. That is why we are invited to look for more meaning than the artist may have intended. The text becomes all the things it could have meant and is not confined to any determinate thing that actually was meant. Hirsch may be right to this extent; in our dealings with informative discourse we are interested in determinate meaning, and the determinate meaning is the meaning the speaker successfully intended. Nevertheless, for literary discourse it may be inappropriate even to try to distinguish between, to use Hirsch's own words, "what an author does mean by a word sequence and what he could mean by it."[25] In this way, even if there is truth in Hirsch's account, the link between intention and meaning can be loosened.

There are, however, constraints on the loosenings that are possible here. One is that in our interpretations we are always confined to what could have been meant by the words we are dealing with. Whatever Housman's poem could have meant, it could not be read as, to borrow the title of a poem by Cowper, a hymn of praise to the merits of the halibut. Again, the intention of an author may come through so clearly and unambiguously as to discourage us from looking for more complex overall interpretations. Keats's "Ode to Autumn" seems to me to be in this category, although even here minor investigations into the possible alternative meanings of the constituent parts of that poem are not excluded. Yet again, a poem may exhibit the kind of ambiguity that arises from imprecision of meaning, or there may be sheer unclarity, as there is when we try to work out what Milton meant by "that two handed engine at the door" in the poem "Lycidas." For here the problem is not one of deciding which of a variety of clearly statable possible meanings we might assign to the words but one of not being able even to determine what the candidates might be. Loosening the tie between the author's intention and meaning does not rescue such cases from obscurity. Nor are these words rescued from obscurity merely by evidence that Milton wanted them to mean something or other. What would rescue the phrase would be evidence that there was at the time of publication some intention to say something that could have been made clear by these words, rather than by some other words of a different meaning that the author, subsequent to the publication of his poem, uses to make clear what he would like to have said. If this is so, then Beardsley and Wimsatt are right: if the words do not have a certain meaning, then the authorial will cannot give them one. But this is compatible with the claim that to say that the words of a text have a determinate meaning is to say that a speaker makes his intentions clear in them.

NOTES

1. See, for example, Monroe C. Beardsley, *Aesthetics* (New York: Harcourt, Brace and World, 1958), p. 26. Quotations from this work hereinafter cited as *Aesthetics* in the text.

2. Ibid.

3. Ibid., p. 20.

4. Ibid., p. 29.

5. W. K. Wimsatt, Jr., and Monroe C. Beardsley, "The Intentional Fallacy," in Wimsatt, *The Verbal Icon* (New York, 1954). Quotations from this work hereinafter cited as IF in the text.

6. W. K. Wimsatt, Jr., "Genesis: A Fallacy Revisited," in *On Literary Intention*, ed. D. Newton-de Molina (Edinburgh: University of Edinburgh Press, 1976), p. 136. Quotations from this work hereinafter cited as "Genesis" in the text.

7. Monroe C. Beardsley, *The Possibility of Criticism* (Detroit: Wayne State University Press, 1970), p. 16. Quotations from this work hereinafter cited as PC in the text. See also Chapter 2, p. 24.

8. Wayne C. Booth, *The Rhetoric of Fiction* (Chicago: University of Chicago Press, 1961), p. 81.

9. Gilbert Ryle, *The Concept of Mind* (New York: Barnes and Noble, 1949), p. 11.

10. R. M. Hare, *Moral Thinking* (Oxford: Clarendon Press, 1981), p. 127.

11. Ludwig Wittgenstein, *Lectures and Conversations on Aesthetics, Psychology, and Religious Belief*, ed. Cyril Barrett (Oxford: Blackwell, 1966).

12. Ludwig Wittgenstein, *Philosophical Investigations* (New York: Macmillan, 1953). Quotations from this work hereinafter cited as *Investigations* in the text.

13. David Hume, *A Treatise of Human Nature* (London: Dent, 1911), 1:139.

14. Ludwig Wittgenstein, *Tractatus Logico-Philosophicus* (London: Routledge and Kegan Paul, 1966), proposition 2.062.

15. G.E.M. Anscombe, *Intention* (Ithaca, N.Y.: Cornell University Press, 1963), p. 37.

16. Peter Winch, *The Idea of a Social Science* (London: Routledge and Kegan Paul, 1958), p. 50.

17. Anscombe, *Intention*, p. 37.

18. Beardsley, *Aesthetics*, p. 26.

19. See Chapters 1 and 6.

20. Beardsley, *Aesthetics*, p. 25.

21. Jean-Paul Sartre, *What Is Literature?* (London: Methuen, 1950), p. 8.

22. F. R. Leavis, *The Common Pursuit* (Harmondsworth: Penguin Books, 1962), p. 26.

23. To do justice to Iseminger's more careful statement of an intentionalist position (see Chapter 6) one has to distinguish two claims about the connection between intention and determinate meaning. One is the claim that a determinate meaning is willed onto an utterance token by a prior, and separately identifiable, act of willing or intending that that token have meaning. The other is the claim that we can assign a determinate meaning to an utterance token because we recognize in the act of uttering that token, in the particular circumstances of its utterance (and not all the relevant circumstances need be such that we can read them off from the text alone), an intention to say a particular determinate thing. The former claim seems to me to fall afoul of the Humpty-Dumpty objection. The latter need not do so. It is unclear to me which claim Hirsch wishes to make. It is equally clear to me that Iseminger's more careful statement of an intentionalist thesis is not committed to the first, and more suspect, of the claims I have described.

24. Lewis Carroll, *The Annotated Alice,* ed. Martin Gardner (Cleveland and New York: The World Publishing Company, 1963), p. 322.

25. E. D. Hirsch, Jr., *Validity in Interpretation* (New Haven: Yale University Press, 1967), p. 46. See Chapter 1, p. 16.

9

Intention and Interpretation: Hirsch and Margolis

MICHAEL KRAUSZ

I

IN THE PREFACE, Gary Iseminger asks us, "What is the connection, if any, between the author's intentions in (while) writing a work of literature and the truth (acceptability, validity) of interpretive statements about it?"[1] Before discussing E. D. Hirsch's and Joseph Margolis's treatment of some aspects of this question, I first raise some questions about the question itself.

The Author.   To which author shall we address ourselves? The historical author? The reconstituted author? A postulated author? The work may have been produced over an extended period of time, perhaps in interrupted stages. Are we to assume that the author is one and the same person? While that person may bear the same spatiotemporal identity, need he or she embody the same persona over time? No one person or persona might be identified as the author of the pertinent work. Indeed, the author might *assume* various and perhaps competing personae. She or he may be literal at one sitting, ironic at another, and of yet further stances at succeeding sittings. Such considerations make problematic whether the author speaks with a single voice. The very idea of an author seems to suggest a kind of fixity or stability of voice from which the work is supposed to have been issued. But we cannot presume such fixity, stability, or singularity of voice—this even though the authorial voice may or may not have been emitted from a self-identical human person.

Intentions.   The overriding question seems to presume that intentional states of an author cannot be equivocal and that they should be determinate. But intentions may be ambiguous or indeterminate, reflecting essentially mixed intentions of a particular person at a particular time. Further, the question seems not to recognize intentionality in its social sense, as opposed to intentionality in its individual sense. Social intentionality is embodied in the institutions of a given tradition and thereby in its cultural artifacts. It is not reducible to individual intentionality. Indeed, we cannot make sense of individual intentionality independent of social intentionality. Now, when we consider that individual intentions are in this way parasitic on social contexts or traditions, and if social intentionality may be essentially indeterminate, then that indeterminacy will be reflected in the individual intentionality of a particular person at a particular time. So, if a particular person wishes to transmit the feel of "the Baroque" or "the American" in a poem or musical performance, say, and if the feel of "the Baroque" or "the American" is indeterminate, then the content of the individual intentions will reflect the indeterminacy of the socially intentional. Such indeterminacy makes delineating determinate individual intentions problematic. Further, we must consider the possibility that what comes to be produced can embody genuinely emergent properties, ones not or not fully intended in the individual sense at all.

Writing.   Is the act of writing to be distinguished from the fact of authorship? Do intentions precede the act of writing? Are the author's intentions to be located in the act of writing itself? Where do we locate the beginning of the writing? The author's intentions might be understood as *prior* to the act of writing, *in* the act of writing, or indeed, *following* the act of writing. This suggests the possibility that a work might not have come to be written at a particular time at all. It may have been written over a long period of time, in many discrete and separable periods. And the kinds of intentions that may have preceded (or been simultaneous with or followed) those particular acts of writing may have been different. And the periods between acts of writing might be important in speaking of intentions behind a work of art or literature.

Work of Literature.   How are we to construe a work of literature? I resist any foundational, timeless, ahistorical account of what constitutes a work of literature or art (or a culturally embodied entity generally), one that resists the vagaries of historical transformation or interpretive transfiguration. Also, questions arise concerning value assumptions about the very idea of literature. For example, insofar as we should not count trash as literature, what sorts of value judgments are in play when deploying the concept of literature, and what are their grounds? Finally we come to the thrust of the overriding question.

The Truth. Here the definite article prompts the question whether there is one truth. Even if we were to substitute "acceptability" or "validity" as the salient valuative notion, the general question is concerned with the singularity of that valuative notion. This is counterposed with the possibility of a multiplicity of acceptable interpretations.

Consider the possible substitutability of "acceptability" or "validity" for "truth." While acceptability emphasizes the consensual nature of what is taken to be an ideal condition for interpretation, truth, as classically construed, suggests that there might be a fact of the matter independent of the consensus of a pertinent community. So there appears to be an important difference between the acceptability of an interpretation and the truth of an interpretation. Correspondingly, validity, like truth, smacks of an objectivist ideal condition of singularity. So understood, we should separate truth and validity (where construed objectively) from acceptability. Now, let us round out the overriding question.

Interpretive Statements. The question asks us to reflect on the truth of interpretive statements about works of literature. Here we find an implied distinction between interpretive statements, on the one hand (perhaps themselves counted as something of a natural kind), and that about which those statements are made. But is there a sharp distinction between a work of literature (or a work of art) and interpretive statements made? According to an imputational or constructionist view, the work of art turns out to be a construct of interpretation. So whether there is a sharp distinction to be drawn between interpretive statements and what they interpret is itself contentious.

So much for some general (and here unexplored) issues prompted by the overriding question. Now let us reconsider some of them as they arise in discussions of E. D. Hirsch and Joseph Margolis.

II

In a characteristic passage, Hirsch says:

> Meaning is an affair of consciousness not of words. Almost any word sequence can, under the conventions of language, legitimately represent more than one complex of meaning. A word sequence means nothing in particular until somebody either means something by it or understands something from it. There is no magic land of meanings outside human consciousness. Whenever meaning is connected to words, a person is making the connection, and the particular

meanings he lends to them are never the only legitimate ones under the norms and conventions of his language.

One proof that the conventions of language can sponsor different meanings from the same sequence of words resides in the fact that interpreters can and do disagree. When these disagreements occur, how are they to be resolved? Under the theory of semantic autonomy they cannot be resolved, since the meaning is not what the author meant, but "what the poem means to different sensitive readers." One interpretation is as valid as another, so long as it is "sensitive" or "plausible."[2]

Hirsch's logical moves are reconstructable in the following way. (1) Conventions of language can sponsor different meanings; (2) such multiplicity is to be eliminated by the willful fixing of particular meanings by particular persons; (3) meaning is an affair of consciousness of words; (4) and without so fixing meanings, we face a "chaotic democracy of readings."

Number 1 is correct. (2) is misguided because of Hirsch's unargued presupposition that all interpretive discussion should end with full convergence. Further, (2) falsely presumes that particular persons are required to fix meanings—whether they be singular or multiple; and (2) falsely presumes that when they do, particular persons may not simultaneously fix different meanings allowable by the conventions of language. Thus the equation of consciousness with individual consciousness is mistaken. Finally, multiplicity of meaning need not be seen in terms of chaos. On the contrary, such multiplicity may be seen better in terms of fidelity to practice and critical discourse between ideally contending interpretations. (Some of these points are developed in our discussion of Margolis.)

Let us consider the question of the determinacy of meaning. The Oxford English Dictionary (1961) defines "indeterminate" as "2. not fixed in extent, number, character or nature." This definition, which I embrace, does not arise from an epistemic lack. It is at odds with others that do. Correspondingly, I understand indeterminacy as a feature of the object of interpretation, not of epistemic uncertainties about an interpreter's knowledge of its would-be determinate character.

E. D. Hirsch favors a different view. He says:

> Reproducibility is a quality of verbal meaning that makes interpretation possible: if meaning were not reproducible, it could not be actualized by someone else and therefore could not be understood

or interpreted. Determinacy, on the other hand, is a quality of meaning required in order that there be something to reproduce. Determinacy is a necessary attribute of any sharable meaning, since an
indeterminacy cannot be shared: if a meaning were indeterminate,
it would have no boundaries, no self-identity, and therefore could
have no identity with a meaning entertained by someone else.[3]

Hirsch is right to require reproducibility and shareability for interpretation. But he is mistaken when saying that indeterminate meaning cannot fulfill
these conditions. And this mistake deflects him from examining an interesting avenue of inquiry that ultimately leads to his embracing the false doctrine that indeterminate meaning could have no boundaries, no self-identity,
no identity shareable by different people. Surely, the distinction between determinate and indeterminate is a matter of degree on a continuum rather than
one of two binary terms. It would be best to speak of one meaning being
more or less determinate rather than determinate or not. These terms should be
understood as comparative, not absolute.

This mistake, then, leads to a tangled confusion in the passage immediately
following that just quoted. Hirsch goes on to say:

But determinacy does not mean definiteness or precision. Undoubtedly, most verbal meanings are imprecise and ambiguous, and to call
them such is to acknowledge their determinacy: they are what they
are—namely, ambiguous and imprecise—and they are not univocal
and precise. [I would have called this "indeterminate"—MK.] This is
another way of saying that an ambiguous meaning has a boundary
like any other verbal meaning, and that one of the frontiers of this
boundary is that between ambiguity and univocality. [But surely the
point is that the boundary is indeterminate—MK.] Some parts of the
boundary might, of course, be thick; that is, there might at some
points be a good many submeanings that belonged equally to the
meaning and not to it—borderline meanings. However, such ambiguities would, on another level, simply serve to define the character
of the meaning so that any overly precise construing of it would
constitute a misunderstanding.[4]

In this case, quite a lot rides on terms. If it is more plausible to read equivocation, ambiguity, and the like as indeterminacy, and if—as Hirsch concedes—
the meanings involved in such instances are self-identical or sufficiently so
for critical discourse, then, contra Hirsch, it would seem that at least certain

sorts of indeterminacies could fulfill his general requirement for self-identity of a soft kind, or "unicity" as Margolis puts it.[5] So conceived, Hirsch's sentences following his most recently quoted passage turn out to be wrong. He says: "Determinacy, then, first of all means self-identity. This is the minimum requirement for sharability. Without it neither communication nor validity in interpretation would be possible."[6]

I have suggested, contrariwise, that certain kinds of indeterminacies or, if you like, indeterminacies-of-sufficient-determinacy may satisfy the requisite requirements of self-identity or unicity. Clearly, Hirsch's distinction is based on a rather wooden understanding of self-identity, one that does not concede the sufficient determinacy of such indeterminacies as examples provided by Margolis. Margolis says that

> nothing could be referentially fixed that did not exhibit a certain stability of nature; but how alterable (or by what means altered) the life of a person or the restored *Last Supper* or the oft-interpreted *Hamlet* or the theoretically intriguing *Fountain* or the marvelously elastic *Sarrasine* may be is not a matter that can be decided or that is actually determined, merely by fixing such texts or artworks as the reidentifiable referents they are.[7]

To reiterate my qualms about Hirsch's account of determinacy, indeterminate meanings of sufficient determinacy may indeed be sufficiently self-identical (exhibiting unicity) for requisite interpretive purposes. It is therefore not required, as Hirsch proposes, that they be "changeless" and determinate in his sense.

From here, Hirsch goes on to affirm that a will is required to fix meaning for it to be determinate in his sense, leading up to his defense of authorial meaning as capturing the meaning of a work. Again, his presupposition that there should be a single ideally admissible interpretation of a work is objectionable, as is his further presumption that meanings in general are to be fixed only by single persons, *rather than* communities, institutions, traditions or, generally, essentially social agencies.

Hirsch urges us to fix singular meanings of texts in order to avoid an "anarchy" of multiplism. To do so, he urged us to retrieve the intentions of the creator of the text. Besides the epistemological difficulties of access to those intentions (pointed out by the New Critics and others not in other ways sympathetic to their views) the meaning(s) of texts just are not stable in the way Hirsch presumes—stable, that is, over the contexts of interpretation in which the original creator(s) or receiver(s) may have operated or do operate. That is, with the recontextualization of the text, the object of interpretation is differently imputed in different context. This sort of shifting accounts for an instability of the object of interpretation, and it makes the Hirschian program of fixing the meanings of a text—meanings invariant with respect to interpretive contexts—quite impossible. This brings us to an issue central to the views of Joseph Margolis.

III

Margolis does not require closure between competing interpretations such as to eliminate all logical tension between them. In contrast, Beardsley and Hirsch, however interesting and important the differences between them, agree that ideally there ought to be full convergence.

Of them, Margolis says that they have favored "exclusively correct and comprehensive interpretations; but no one has shown why nonconverging interpretations cannot be legitimately defended."[8]

This, in a nutshell, is Margolis's challenge. Margolis wants to capitalize on the possibility that nonconverging interpretations can be legitimately defended, not as an interim or tolerable condition approaching an ideal condition of full convergence, but as a condition that is *ideally* admissible. Margolis holds that this condition reflects the nature of cultural entities and their interpretations.

Margolis's view about the possibility that nonconvergence may be ideally admissible is tied to his view that one cannot clearly individuate a given work of art or cultural entity; one cannot clearly say what is in a given work and what is not. He holds that cultural entities are "ontically" indeterminate.

Margolis criticizes Beardsley's idea that interpretations must be true or false and says that Beardsley has not shown why this should be so. On the contrary, Margolis demonstrates the possibility that two incongruent interpretations might both be plausible, though not both true. The question of truth (in its bipolar sense) characteristically does not arise in such discussions. So while the search for the true interpretation is formally available, characteristically it is not pertinent. Instead, as regards the imputation of cultural entities, such other values as plausibility, aptness, and the like are the terms in which such discussions are characteristically pursued. Margolis holds that we may hold to incongruent interpretations as being simultaneously plausible. Yet they may not both be true. Following Aristotle, then, Margolis holds that we cannot ask for more precision than the subject will allow, and allowance for nonconvergent interpretations, as an ideal condition, accords with this observation.

About imputational interpretation, Margolis says:

> There is no reason why, granting that criticism proceeds in an orderly way, practices cannot be sustained in which aesthetic designs are rigorously *imputed* to particular works when they cannot be determinately *found* in them. Also, if they may be imputed rather than found, there is no reason why incompatible designs cannot be jointly defended.[9]

Since interpretations may impute and not just find aspects of artworks, there is no reason to think that incompatible works cannot be defended; a given work may be imputed (i.e., constituted) in different ways. Here arises the question of the identity of imputed works. Insofar as works may be imputed in different ways in different circumstances, one wonders whether or not the results of such imputation are sufficiently divergent that one no longer has a basis for talking about different interpretations of *one* work as opposed to different interpretations of *different* works. In the latter case, the condition of competition between the two interpretations would not obtain. This latter condition would amount to an innocuous pluralism. Margolis wishes to capture the idea that under different imputations of works of art we may still talk of one work of art.[10] This is possible on the condition that there is in place a soft notion of identity, "unicity," much as there is for a "self" undergoing "self-development." For example, while the self changes and transforms, the notion of self-development is not an oxymoron. Between stages of self-development, the self could not be self-identical in a strict Leibnitzian sense, otherwise many selves would be generated. Self-development requires a softer view of self-identity. As well, such unicity obtains for the identity of a work of art; the "same" work is imputed and interpreted differently in different circumstances. At least such a condition of unicity is required for competition between two interpretations of the "given" work.

The question of unicity is closely tied to Margolis's view of admissible incongruent interpretations, as evidenced in the parenthetical remarks in the following:

> Thus, musical interpretations A and B of Brahms's *Fourth Symphony* or literary interpretations A and B of *Hamlet* are incompatible in the straightforward sense that there is no interpretation C in which A and B can be combined. But *that* is not to say that A and B cannot both be plausible. (The equivocation on "A" and "B" is benign enough.) When, therefore, I say that "we allow seemingly incompat-

ible accounts of a given work . . . to stand as confirmed," I mean to draw attention to the fact that the accounts in question would be incompatible construed in terms of a model of truth and falsity, but are not incompatible construed in terms of plausibility.[11]

Now, let us call the view I have sketched so far Margolis's "substantive view." He characterizes it as relativist. And he defines "relativism" as the view that rejects bipolarity. Correspondingly, when reclaiming the Protagorean motto "man is the measure," Margolis understands it, not (as has been customary) as implying that truth is relative, but that through his interventions with the world man determines conditions answering to his interpretations. I comment on this later.

As I have indicated, Margolis groups appropriateness and aptness along with other such values as plausibility and probability. This, I believe, is unfortunate, since the latter notions are elliptical for "plausible, with respect to truth," or "probable, with respect for truth." Yet aptness and appropriateness need not suggest such a reading (and these notions do seem especially pertinent when discussing properties to be imputed to the object of interpretation.) To say that such-and-such an interpretation is appropriate or apt need not invite saying that it is true. Now, having distinguished values that are elliptical for some cognate of truth and those that are not, concentrating on aptness and appropriateness, we may ask whether the claim that A was more apt than B entails that B was not more apt than A. It would seem that one could not hold both that A was more apt than B and that B was more apt than A on a given measure of aptness. And on different (perhaps incommensurable) measures of aptness, the matter might better be seen in terms of equivocation. Indeed, as Margolis holds, the bipolar model of truth is not sufficient to capture his aim of admitting incongruous interpretations that may be entertained simultaneously. But even aptness and appropriateness may exhibit the exclusivity or bipolarity just considered. It is one thing to concede the possibility of incommensurable measures. It is another thing to say that, with respect to given measures, judgments of A over B or B over A are nonexclusive. I agree with the first concession. Margolis urges the stronger second option. To this, Margolis might say that the first concession amounts to the stronger second option. But then it would be unclear what kind of overarching measure it would be that would at once be nonexclusive (bipolar) and also could perform the discriminatory task of assigning A over B or B over A.

Alternatively, we may offer an account consistent with Margolis's motivation to preserve both claims (that A is better than B and that B is better than A) simultaneously entertained. To do this, I suggest, might involve an overdetermination of measures that are not themselves subsumable under a univocal overarching measure. Here it would be the measures that would be incongruent. That is, drawing on familiar features of incommensurability, one might construe incongruence as a case in which, for a given object of interpretation in an informed discussion of contending interpretations, there may be in play a number of measures that themselves—for reasons peculiar to their own nature—resist being subsumed under an overarching measure. They, in turn, would not be rankable according to a univocal metameasure. Here it would be the measures (aptness, etc.) that would be incongruent, thereby rendering the pertinent interpretations incongruent.

Take the case of the upbeat to the Allegro Con Brio section of the first movement of Beethoven's Symphony No. 1. According to the measure of faithfulness to the score, the upbeat should be played in the Adagio tempo still literally governing it. Yet, according to the measure of aesthetic consistency (the figure is repeated often within the Allegro at the Allegro tempo), it should be played according to the Allegro tempo, despite its appearance still literally in the Adagio section. Here, the measures of "faithfulness to the score" and "aesthetic consistency" are incongruent with respect to each other, and there is no available overarching measure at hand that could conclusively rank their measures in turn. Yet, a proponent of each interpretation may argue for the plausibility, reasonableness, aptness, appropriateness, etc., of his interpretation. Each may provide good (though inconclusive) reasons for his interpretation. But with respect to each measure, interpretation A is better than B, or B is better than A.

The point can be exemplified in another case, E. D. Hirsch's example of Wordsworth's Lucy poem, "A Slumber Did My Spirit Seal," as interpreted by Cleanth Brooks and alternatively by F. W. Bateson.[12]

> A slumber did my spirit seal;
>   I had no human fears:
> She seemed a thing that could not feel
>   The touch of earthly years.
>
> No motion has she now, no force;
>   She neither hears nor sees,
> Rolled round in earth's diurnal course
>   With rocks, and stones, and trees.

From Hirsch's discussion, here are excerpts from two commentaries on the final lines of the poem; the first is by Cleanth Brooks, the second by F. W. Bateson:

> [The poet] attempts to suggest something of the lover's agonized shock at the loved one's present lack of motion—of his response to her utter and horrible inertness. . . . Part of the effect, of course, resides in the fact that a dead lifelessness is suggested more sharply by an object's being whirled about by something else than by an image of the object in repose. But there are other matters which are at work here: the sense of the girl's falling back into the clutter of things, companioned by things chained like a tree to one particular spot, or by things completely inanimate like rocks and stones. . . . [She] is caught up helplessly into the empty whirl of the earth which measures and makes time. She is touched by and held by earthly time in its most powerful and horrible image.

And Bateson says,

> The final impression the poem leaves is not of two contrasting moods, but of a single mood mounting to a climax in the pantheistic magnificence of the last two lines. . . . The vague living-Lucy of this poem is opposed to the grander dead-Lucy who has become involved in the sublime processes of nature. We put the poem down satisfied, because its last two lines succeed in effecting a reconciliation between the two philosophies or social attitudes. Lucy is actually more alive now that she is dead, because she is now a part of the life of Nature, and not just a human "thing."

In this case what is the object of interpretation is unstable. In a strict Leibnitzian construal of identity, they are not talking about the same thing. In a "unicity" sense, they are. The issue turns on Bateson's affirmation of a "pantheistic magnificence of the last two lines" or (even conceding its presence) its salience. The fact is that the last two lines could be read in Bateson's way, but they need not. Yet Bateson seeks to make intelligible the whole of the poem. The reading of the whole is underdetermined by the text, and the text is consistent with the reading. In so interpreting the poem, though, Bateson is imputing or constituting an object of interpretation (the "pantheistic" object of interpretation), and it is that about which Bateson might speak when placing the Lucy poem in the larger context of Wordsworth's corpus. The point is that, these same formal remarks are true of Brooks's interpretation. The issue turns, finally, on the commonality of the object of interpretation. That is, is the poem-as-pantheistic the same as the poem-as-dead-lifelessness? If not, then the object of interpretation would have been bifurcated, and no claim of competition between the interpretations could be sustained. An innocuous pluralism would obtain. But this seems most implausible. Alternatively, one needs to concede that the objects of interpretation are self-identical in a non-Leibnitzian sense of unicity. The objects of interpretation are sufficiently common for interpretive purposes. But the poem answers to each of the incongruent interpretations.

The readings are incongruent because measures presumed by each interpreter are themselves incongruent. For Bateson, the text reads one way. For Brooks, it reads another. It reads differently for each because of the differences in the measures embodied in the critics' general disposition to Wordsworth's work, their conception of this poem in relation to the rest of Wordsworth's corpus, and, inevitably (among other things) their own attitude and dispositions to such things as the sealing of spirits, having human fears, having feelings at all, the processes of earthly years, the absence of motion and force, silence and darkness, the earth's astronomical regularities, and the evocations of its natural objects.

The general point as regards incongruence, then, is that without bifurcating the object of interpretation, one must allow self-identity of the object of interpretation understood in nonstrict (unicity) terms, as Margolis says. But in allowing the admissibility of incongruent interpretations, one should unpack the notion of incongruity along the lines of the incongruity of the measures. This strategy, I suggest, sidesteps the "reductive" issue mentioned at the outset of this discussion.

Now, putting aside the adequacy of this account of incongruence, I am also concerned about Margolis's characterization of his "substantive" view that, ideally, incongruous interpretations are admissible. He calls it relativist. Surely, that should be a separate item on his philosophical agenda, for the substantive point could remain even if one characterized it as nonrelativist.

Margolis says: "It takes little imagination to see that admitting that judgments which are incompatible on the model of assigning truth-values (true and false) may be jointly defended in terms of the assignment of other values is tantamount to the adoption of a form of relativism."[13]

In holding that his construal captures the spirit behind Protagoras's much misinterpreted view (the greatest misinterpreter being Plato), Margolis seeks to undo the bad press that relativism has gotten throughout its history.[14] This in itself may be an important suggestion, and it raises interesting questions about why and how it is that historians of ideas might have gotten it so wrong for so long. But one wonders why Margolis ties this rhetorical–historical question so closely to what I have called his substantive point. Two forthcoming books of Margolis may well address themselves to this question. One, on metaphysics, is yet untitled. The second is entitled *The Truth About Relativism*. But we should elaborate our misgivings about Margolis's construal, one on which he insists.

Margolis's argumentative strategy goes along the following lines: He argues for the substantive thesis of incongruent or incompatible interpretations, providing reasons directly pertinent to it. Then, to lend further "credence" to that position, he associates it with the doctrine of relativism. The traditional criticism of that doctrine has been that it is either incoherent or false. So Margolis then sets out to correct the traditional view by indicating that the doctrine, appropriately adjusted *and* faithful to its original spirit, is neither incoherent nor false. But why not just leave the adjustment as is, without invoking any putative historical connection to classical relativism? Why cloud the case for incongruent interpretations with the difficulties associated with the history of relativism? As interesting as Margolis's suggestion is about relativism's original spirit, it remains historically contentious, still to be taken up as a separate research project in its own right. There seems to be no philosophical payoff in Margolis's arguing for the characterization of his substantive point as relativist *while* articulating the substantive view. The substantive point could be conceded without its characterization as relativist.

Relativism is characteristically associated with the view that one may assign *contradictory* truth values to interpretations of a given object of interpretation. It is a rhetorical matter whether one wishes to stipulate that incongruence or incompatibility rather than contradiction should be characteristic of relativism. But why need Margolis have taken on the rhetorical job of arguing for the propriety of construing relativism in this way? What difference would it make to his substantive view were one to say, "Well, if *that's* what relativism is, then, all right, have your relativism"? Alternatively, if one were to insist that relativism should be understood as the thesis that allows for the possibility of assigning contradictory truth values to competing interpretations, then Margolis's view would not be relativistic. Why not leave this question of construal as a distinct matter, and affirm that what is important in Margolis's view is his allowance that there may be incongruent or incompatible though not logically contradictory interpretations of a cultural object of interpretation? In this respect, it seems that Margolis's argumentative strategy is needlessly overburdened.

These concerns aside, though, I am in substantial agreement with Margolis's view concerning constitutive or imputational interpretation, and the ideal admissibility of incongruent interpretations, given the qualifications already indicated. Now we can see how Margolis's views bear on those of Beardsley and Hirsch.

Both Hirsch and Beardsley assume that the intentional is only individual, as opposed to social. As singularists, they both agree that the ideal interpretation involves the full convergence of initially competing interpretations toward the elimination of all but one. Their difference concerns the procedures in that singularist program.

From Margolis's point of view, such a difference is intramural. Margolis does not require the ideal of full convergence to begin with. He disassociates himself from the Hirschian view that it is the individual author's intentions that should be the criterion for the singularly right interpretation. As well, Margolis dissociates himself from the Beardsleyan account of the internal autonomy of the work and its examination to find singular meaning. Instead, in representative cases, what is internal or external to a work of art is systematically elusive. This is not due to some sort of epistemic lack. What is internal or external is essentially indeterminate. The meaning of a work of art is imputed, but constrained by the culturally intentional contexts in which it appears. For that reason, no artwork can be fully understood independently of a theory of culture.

IV

In this essay I have claimed:

1. Hirsch's and Beardsley's differences are motivated by a shared assumption that the range of ideally admissible interpretations needs to be singular. This assumption is mistaken, owing partly to their view that intentionality can be understood only in individualist and singularist terms.
2. Concession to multiplism does not necessitate Hirsch's dreaded "anarchism."
3. Margolis is right to embrace multiplism.
4. Margolis is right to embrace an imputational function of interpretation.

5. Margolis is right to observe that objects of interpretation may be indeterminate but self-identical and reidentifiable.
6. Margolis is right to allow that incongruous or incompatible interpretations may be ideally admissible.
7. But, contrary to Margolis's treatment, incongruity may be better understood in terms of multiplicities of measures.
8. Finally, support for Margolis's correct thesis of the ideal admissibility of incongruent or incompatible (as opposed to contradictory) interpretations seems not to be gained by attaching it to and simultaneously defending a relativist construal of it.

NOTES

Acknowledgment: I gratefully acknowledge suggestions of Gary Iseminger, Joseph Margolis, and Richard Shusterman.

1. See Preface, p. ix.
2. E. D. Hirsch, Jr., *Validity in Interpretation* (New Haven: Yale University Press, 1967), pp. 3–5. See Chapter 1, p. 13.
3. Ibid., pp. 44–45. See Chapter 1, p. 14.
4. Ibid. See Chapter 1, pp. 14–15.
5. Joseph Margolis, "Reinterpreting Interpretation," *Journal of Aesthetics and Art Criticism* 47 (1989): 237–51.
6. Hirsch, *Validity in Interpretation*, p. 45. See Chapter 1, p. 15.
7. Margolis, "Reinterpreting Interpretation," pp. 241–42.
8. Joseph Margolis, *Art and Philosophy: Conceptual Issues in Aesthetics* (Atlantic Highlands, N.J.: Humanities Press, 1980), p. 157. See Chapter 3, p. 41.
9. Ibid., p. 160. See Chapter 3, p. 45.
10. See Margolis, "Reinterpreting Interpretation," for example.
11. Margolis, *Art and Philosophy*, p. 164. See Chapter 3, pp. 48–49.
12. Hirsch, *Validity in Interpretation*, pp. 227–28. See Chapter 1, pp. 19–20.
13. Margolis, *Art and Philosophy*, p. 160. See Chapter 3, p. 45.
14. See Joseph Margolis, "The Truth about Relativism," in *Relativism: Interpretation and Confrontation*, ed. Michael Krausz (Notre Dame: University of Notre Dame Press, 1989).

10

Interpreting with Pragmatist Intentions

RICHARD SHUSTERMAN

I

AT LEAST THREE DIFFERENT and influential theories of interpretation claim to be pragmatist. Knapp and Michaels's theory is rigidly intentionalistic and author bound, while Richard Rorty's contrastingly emphasizes the production of nonauthorial readings. The third, advanced by Stanley Fish, submits (and dissolves) both author and reader to the notion of the interpretive community as the authority determining the proper meaning of a text. In this essay I investigate two of these rival theories, examining them in the light of more general pragmatist principles. The purpose of this exercise is not to award a prize for the most authentically pragmatist theory but to reach a better understanding of interpretation and its variety.[1]

II

Knapp and Michaels's theory of interpretation is paradoxically advanced in a polemic "Against Theory," where "theory" is narrowly defined as "the attempt to govern interpretations of particular texts by appealing to an account of interpretation in general."[2] The gist of Knapp and Michaels's strategy is to argue that the whole project of theorizing about interpretation rest on the mistake that there is something to theorize about, a question of what in general a text means and how it should be interpreted. Only on the assumption that there exist alternative possibilities of what textual meaning and interpretation could be, "the illusion of a choice between alternative methods of interpreting," could theory situate itself in the space of this question and take for itself the function of assessing and deciding between these possibilities (AT, p. 18).

Since most interpretive theorizing has centered on the question of whether a text's meaning should be identified with the intention of its author, Knapp and Michaels challenge the very validity of this question by insisting that it is logically impossible for textual meaning to be anything but authorial intention. And if there is no possible alternative or choice, there is simply no place for theory to try to argue that literary interpretation should or must be intentionalist. In this way they distinguish their position from more traditional intentionalist theories (e.g., Hirsch's) and claim not to be theorizing at all but simply reporting on a conceptual necessity about textual meaning and interpretation, namely, that "what a text means and what its author means are identical" and hence that interpretation must necessarily be "faithful to the historical author's intention" (AT, pp. 19, 103).[3]

But in both ordinary and critical discourse "meaning" and "authorial intention" are not conceptually identical. We know this not only because the issue of intentionalism is hotly debated, but by the mere fact that we can meaningfully ask whether a given text really conveys the author's intention. Yet Knapp and Michaels eschew such homespun empirical facts and argue transcendentally that the conceptual identity of textual meaning and authorial intention follows logically and necessarily from the very nature of language.

They ground their argument on a now widely held view (developed from Austin by Grice and Searle) which insists that linguistic meaning must be understood in terms of intentions and the speech-acts that embody them. Though analytic philosophy often eschewed intentionalism for relying on entities that seem too spectrally private and because intentional contexts resist standard truth-functional accounts of meaning, it shows growing recognition that sentence and utterance meaning cannot be fully explained in purely extensional, referential terms and thus that language must be in some sense intentional (even if our intentions are in turn viewed as essentially dependent on language). We need not resolve this general issue here. For even if we agree with Knapp and Michaels that "meanings are always intentional," this still does not entail their conclusion that "what a text means and what its author intends it to mean are identical" and that "the necessary object of interpretation," indeed "of all reading," "is always the historical author's intention" (AT, pp. 101, 103). We must be careful not to confuse the view that all textual meaning is in some sense intentional with the very challengeable assertion that the meaning of a text is identical with the historical author's intention or intended meaning.

But this is precisely Knapp and Michaels's mistake. By conflating "meaning" with "authorially intended meaning," they thereby preclude the possibility of someone's speech or writing failing to mean what it was intended to mean, a possibility that is indeed a very frequent actuality. Rejecting this conflation, one could still grant the basic intentionality of language, which Knapp and Michaels seem right to emphasize. One could grant this first in the holistic sense that there could be no linguistic meaning without a background of human intentionality, no "possibility of language prior to and independent of intention" (*AT*, p. 19). But one might plausibly hold further that every individual linguistic text requires some particular intention for its meaning. A string of letters accidentally produced by a computer or by waves on the sand (as in Knapp and Michaels's example) would still depend for its meaning on an intentional act, here the intention of the reader to see and use the marks as a meaningful text, as language rather than mere marks.

Nevertheless, even if we follow Knapp and Michaels in denying that "there can be . . . intentionless meanings" and in asserting that (in some sense) "what is intended and what is meant is identical," this still does not entail that "the meaning of a text is simply identical to the author's intended meaning" (*AT*, pp. 15, 17, 12). All that follows is that the meaning of the text is inseparable from some intention (or group of intentions) or another. But the necessary meaning-securing intentions could belong to readers of the text (or collectively to an interpretive community) rather than to its original "historical author" with whose intention Knapp and Michaels identify the text's meaning.[4]

The only way for them to secure this identification would be to count any of a text's (sense-making) readers as its (meaning-giving) author. But such a drastic remedy undermines the whole idea of intentionalist, author-oriented interpretation by dismantling the very notion of author. Knapp and Michaels understandably reject this move, confining "the author" to "the historical author" and confining his or her meaning-giving intention still more narrowly to that of the "particular occasion" when he or she produced the text (*AT*, pp. 103, 141). For them there can be no issue of choosing whose meaning-given intention is more fruitful for our purposes or which intentional context is more useful to employ in dealing with the work (though these are pragmatist considerations par excellence). There is only "the empirical difficulty of deciding what its [historical] author intended" (*AT*, p. 142).

Knapp and Michaels are, of course, aware that the literary interpreter often claims and seems to be concerned with meanings other than the historical author's. To counter this recalcitrant empirical evidence, they do not argue that such nonauthorial interpretation is ultimately counterproductive for criticism—a legitimate and characteristically pragmatist argument of cost accounting. Instead, they take the road of high theory and transcendental argument that they pretend to eschew. They simply relegate the finding or making of other meanings to a realm altogether outside the activities of reading and interpretation by treating this as the writing of another work: "*replacing the authorial intention with some other intention . . .* [is] rewriting and is no longer interpretation at all" (*AT*, p. 103).

To justify this relegation, Knapp and Michaels claim that the same text cannot logically bear two different intentions or interpretations. To interpret an intention other than the defining one of its author is thus to interpret or write a different text. What we ordinarily take as a text's different possible meanings or expressed intentions should be construed as the meanings of different texts. A text simply cannot have different meanings, they argue, because sameness of text requires sameness of meaning, which itself is defined as sameness of intention. Thus, their case for outlawing all plurality of interpretation and identifying textual with authorial meaning ultimately rests on a theoretical argument concerning the issue of textual identity. Only by strictly identifying its meaning with its historical author's particular intention can the text be adequately individuated, only the intention of "a particular author on a particular occasion . . . [can be] what gives a text its identity as a text" (*AT*, p. 141). But, conflating referential and substantive identity, they offer no real argument for this being the only workable criterion of individuation; and, once again, in stark opposition to their theory, the plain fact is that texts are not so individuated as to preclude divergent intentions or interpretations.[5]

Finally, even if we agree to individuate the text in terms of a particular authorial intention, this still will not exclude a plurality of interpretations or possible meanings. For, first, intentions themselves share much of the indeterminacy of the language in which they are typically formulated, and thus they themselves can be differently interpreted. Knapp and Michaels simply assume that intention will ground the meaning and the identity of a text in something fixed and transparent that itself neither needs interpretation nor allows divergent ones. But we have no reason to believe that such a transparent, language-neutral, self-interpreting, and unambiguous idiolect of intentionality does or even could exist. And since intention itself is indeterminate and variously interpretable, it cannot guarantee the disambiguation and univocal interpretation of a text. Second, the individuating intention might in fact be the generation of textual polysemy and multiple interpretation whose specific varieties are not already foreseen and foredetermined. Certainly the intentional production of an ambiguous open text is characteristic of contemporary art and aesthetic interpretation and partly distinguishes them from more practical discourse where univocity of intention and interpretation is more important. It is therefore not surprising that Knapp and Michaels un-questioningly assimilate literary texts into more ordinary speech-act situa-tions, just as they take issue with the practice of interpretive theory that helps nourish the notion of the open, polysemic text.

Though problematic and unconvincing, Knapp and Michaels's intention-alist theory is nonetheless instructive for pragmatist hermeneutics, for it seems to go most wrong where it goes against the spirit of pragmatism it pur-ports to represent. First, their position denies the possibility of any choice of what interpretation could be, allegedly "describ[ing] the way interpretation *always* works," and must necessarily work, irrespective of the intentions and activities of literary critics and institutions (*AT*, p. 105). And in denying any choice of the ways we can interpret, Knapp and Michaels similarly disallow any change or development of what interpretation could be so as render it more serviceable and satisfying of our (changing) needs. This rigid interpre-tive monism runs counter to the pragmatist tradition, which challenges the putative necessities of thought and the fixities of a static universe and instead aims to emphasize and enlarge the realm of choice in cognition and action.

The pragmatist attitude, says James, is pluralistic and open, "looking away from . . . *supposed necessities*" and instead recognizing and furthering the role of choice and the range of possibilities in carving out the objects of our world "to suit our human purposes."[6] Pragmatism is also a forward-looking philosophy, which emphasizes future consequences and the importance of change.[7] Its insistence "not upon antecedent phenomena but upon conse-quent phenomena, not upon the precedents but upon the possibilities of action" is what (in Dewey's words) distinguishes pragmatism from "historical empiricism."[8] Knapp and Michaels reveal themselves more as old-fashioned empiricists not only in their backward-looking and static account of meaning but in their attempt to prove its necessity by appeal to the alleged conceptual truth that textual meaning necessarily means authorial intention, an appeal that involves Quine's first dogma of empiricism, the belief in unchallengeable analytic truths of meaning.

In sharp contrast to pragmatism's meliorism, Knapp and Michaels's ne-cessitarianism proudly eschews any aim of improving interpretive practice. For, like the project of theory it opposes, their "anti-theory" can have "no consequences for the practice of literary criticism" except for the practice of theory itself which it seeks to arrest (*AT*, p. 99). But if interpretation is always necessarily the same enterprise of discovering authorial intention, and inter-pretive theory can therefore have "no practical consequences" (*AT*, p. 25), why all the fuss? The mere fact that theory sometimes distracts us from practice simply cannot justify the vehemence of Knapp and Michaels's will to extirpate theory and to establish the conceptual identity of textual meaning and authorial intention. Instead, their impassioned urgency in claiming theory's futility and the necessity of intentionalism betrays the fearful recognition of both theory's power to transform interpretive practices and its past success in generating different interpretive modes free from authorial intention. The anxiety is that such interpretive pluralism and instability of meaning will undermine the convergence necessary for conceiving literary criticism as a cognitively respectable discipline. To shore up such interpretive convergence, Knapp and Michaels seek at once to homogenize and outlaw interpretive difference by maintaining that such difference is only apparent and yet prohibiting it as logically illegitimate. By relegating nonauthorial interpretation to the category of writing and by denying the very possibility of interpretive change, they seek to fix and limit the scope of interpretation and thus constrain what a text can mean or be. That "the object of all reading is always the historical author's intention" assures in principle a fixed and common interpretive aim and object (*AT*, p. 103).[9]

III

Recognizing that critical discourse would be incoherent without the possibility of individuating and reidentifying texts, theorists typically assume that such identity can be understood and sustained only by fixing it in some permanent substantive stratum, some unchanging essence of the text that lies outside social practices, which are flexible and open to change. Knapp and Michaels, like the more traditional intentionalists, anchor it in the author's intention, while textualists like Beardsley and Goodman locate it in the text itself.[10] Both parties are guilty of confusing the need for individuation and referential continuity with the demand of fixed substantive identity. Certainly, however much we allow our interpretation of a text to differ, we must allow for the reidentification of the same text among this difference in order to talk about "the" text (and indeed "its" different reception) at all. The ordinary referential and predicative functions of discourse simply require this bare logicogrammatical identity of individuation. But such identity does not entail that what is identified on different occasions is completely or even substantially the same.[11] For practical purposes of discourse, we can agree that we are talking about the same thing while differing radically as to what the substantive nature of that thing is, whether it is a bird, a plane, or indeed Superman. Agreement about referential identity can be secured by agreeing on a certain minimum number of identifying descriptions, or it can be (and most often is) simply assumed by our deeply entrenched cultural habits of individuation. In distinguishing between referential and substantive identity, we can similarly distinguish between change in the object interpreted and change of the object interpreted, where the former need not (but can, if sufficiently extreme) involve the latter. A novel interpretation or authorial revision can make a poem new without making it an altogether different poem in the referential sense of individuation.

For Dewey, interpretation and knowledge are always rendering changes in the objects they appropriate. But if there are sufficient background continuities through these changes, we continue to identify and refer to them as the same object. Such objects are not fixed but are "relatively constant" or stable; and the degree and nature of the desired stabilities depend on our (changing) purposes of individuation.[12] Textual objects are cultural entities that are constituted and reconstituted as individual objects by the social and linguistic practices and traditions of the culture that they serve. Their individuation and identity (referential and substantive) rest on nothing beyond such practices and are thus as open to change as these practices are. Recognizing this, we can easily explain how the work's substantive identity of properties and meaning can change significantly over time, although the work has already been written or "completed" by its author and although we continue to identify it as the same work. Nor would we need to continue agonizing over the question whether, given such change, it really is the same work, assuming the question must have a definite answer, as indeed it should if we assume the work exists as an antecedently determinate and independent object of reified meaning.

Instead, on the pragmatist account I have been sketching, the literary work turns out to be a continuous and contested construction of the efforts to determine its understanding and interpretation; that is, of efforts to determine how and what the work will be taken to be, which amounts, pragmatically speaking, to how and what it actually is. Though such efforts to determine understanding can perhaps be said to begin with the author (if we forget the memorable fact that literary and linguistic traditions are already determining his determining efforts), the intentions that continue to guide and shape understanding extend far beyond his authorial control.

In challenging the assumption that we need some substantive fixity beyond discursive practice to allow coherent individuation and fruitful inquiry, Deweyan pragmatism opens the literary work to change, entrusting its identity and meaning to the changing practices and purposes of its community of interpreters. Rorty and Fish follow this flexible, future-looking, and practice-dependent direction. Contemporary pragmatism should therefore welcome their recognition of interpretive change and difference; but it also must carefully consider the limits and price of their endorsement of variety and change.

IV

In many ways, Richard Rorty[13] presents the most striking contrast to Knapp and Michaels' necessitarian and authorially backward-looking theory. While they regard textual meaning as something permanently defined by the past intention of its historical author, Rorty regards it as something to be continually redefined by the future, by the intentions and practice of future readers. While Knapp and Michaels think interpretation has one necessary object and purpose, Rorty insists that the objects and ends of interpretation are always "a matter of choice" (PP, p. 134), always the product of a recontextualizing redescription aimed to "get us what we want" by reweaving our web of beliefs and desires (CP, p. 150). For Rorty, what we want from literature and its criticism is variety and novelty: new meanings, new vocabularies, "new ways of speaking" (CP, p. 150), while Knapp and Michaels seek conformity and fixity to past meaning in the name of critical truth. Though they require a fixed substantive identity without which talk about the text would make no sense, Rorty rejects this need to "postulate an object," "an enduring substrate of changing descriptions," as the only and necessary base for critical communication. Instead, he dissolves the objecthood of texts into "nodes within transitory webs of relationships," foci of "possibilities for use" (TL, p. 12; CP, p. 153).

But if not as an enduring substantive object, how is the text identified for purposes of critical discourse? Employing the pragmatist strategy sketched above, Rorty argues that discursive practice itself provides sufficient individuation for critical communication to be fruitful. To establish identity of reference so that our different interpretations and changing descriptions can be directed at and illuminate the same text, we need not assume some substantive and permanent identity or essence of the text—"the very text itself, or the true meaning of the text"—which provides the permanent reference for predication and the permanent criterion of interpretive adequacy. "All that is required is that agreement be obtainable about what we are talking about—and this just means agreement on a reasonable number of propositions using the relevant term" (TL, p. 12). This agreement between interpreters, an agreement (not necessarily explicit) on a requisite number of discursive applications of the text's name (or pronominal substitutions thereof) can provide us with the required individuating focus or logical referent on which to structure our further discussion and debate about what we have thus identified. Instead of a static substantive identity, the work becomes an organizing focus and field for the production of discourse. Yet it is only constituted as a focus by agreement in ways of talking or reacting that pragmatically identify it as the same work while allowing its descriptions and interpretations (but never simultaneously all of them) to change without necessarily implying that we have changed the object of discourse.

This pragmatist dereification of the objects of interpretation may initially seem strange and perhaps even viciously circular. Yet there is nothing here but the familiar linguistic turn, namely, that individuation of linguistic items like texts depends on further linguistic practices and that there is simply no way outside of language to talk about any individuals at all, a view that does not necessarily entail reducing all the world and its experience to language. But though the strategy of common individuation through discursive agreement seems perfectly acceptable in itself, it is arguably incoherent when combined with Rorty's one-sided emphasis on discursive "diversification and novelty" and his radical privileging of the autonomously private over the shared (CIS, pp. xiv, 77).

Rorty repeatedly insists that what should be paramount in our use of language is neither the realist goal of discovering the truth nor even the Habermasian goal of cooperative problem solving to promote consensus of belief, but instead the goal of private perfection through individual original creation. The primary aim is "to make things new," "to make something that never had been dreamt of before," to achieve autonomy over oneself and one's world "by inventing a new language" which redescribes these things in one's "own terms," so as to escape the oppression of shared "inherited descriptions" that involve a Bloomian anxiety of inflence, "the horror of finding oneself to be only a copy or replica" (CIS, pp. 13, 27–29).

This linguistic strategy, Rorty believes, is particularly right for literary works and criticism, since what we "want [of] both these works and the criticism of them [are] new terminologies" (CP, p. 142). And to ensure that there are no constraints on proliferating new vocabularies to stimulate "the intellectual's private imagination," Rorty maintains that we need "no common language in which critics can argue" (CP, p. 158). But in denying such common language, Rorty seems to deny the very conditions of propositional agreement that, by his own account, allow him to talk about texts at all or indeed any reidentifiable object. For us to have objects of interpretation that we can talk about, no matter how transient they are and no matter how differently they are interpreted, there must be some agreement on propositions and thus some common language or discursive practice to provide it. To deny any common language is to deny any effective referential individuation, hence any effective discourse. This is just an aspect of the Wittgensteinian case against private language, which Rorty in fact endorses.

There are two ways for Rorty to meet this objection. One is by adapting Davidson's account of metaphoric meaning and his "passing theory of language" [14] to argue that we need no common set of linguistic norms to reach provisional agreement on propositions and hence on object individuation, since we can do this through intuitive predictions of meaning based on context and on our previous habits of linguistic understanding, which are essentially stable and conservative. But the rejoinder is that those habits would be undermined and unprojectible if language were as radically innovative, protean, and privatized as Rorty urges it to be.

Another way for Rorty to outflank this inflection of the private-language argument is to separate a public use and a private use of language. The former is shared and serves the basic needs of linguistic community (including individuation of objects). The latter need not and should not be shared if we aim to maximize diversity, novelty, and autonomy, but it can be sufficiently anchored or related to shared public language so as to escape the force of the private-language argument. Rorty's recent advocacy of an ethics of individualist self-creation and self-perfection within a liberal polis rests on such a distinction between public and private language, one that privileges the private use or personal dialect as more valuable and significant to our lives but nonetheless recognizes its dependence on public language to keep the whole linguistic and societal project afloat. [15] In the same way, with respect to our question of textual identity, Rorty could hold that the shared public language provides sufficient agreement for identification of the text, while leaving critics completely free to spin their own private vocabularies and webs of significance in filling out the meaning or content of what has been publicly identified, without fear of dissolving this identified focus. This strategy would reflect the actual practice of criticism, where we typically have no problem in agreeing which text we are discussing, though every problem in agreeing what it precisely means.

But any strategy that so heavily relies on "a firm distinction between the private and the public" (CIS, p. 83) cannot help but be as problematic as the firmness of that shifty distinction. What Rorty calls the critics' private vocabularies and ways of readings are always more than private, and not merely because they are always somewhat prestructured by the public language and interpretations they inherit. They are also public in the important sense that they are typically published and essentially designed for publication. The new vocabularies and readings Rorty valorizes are from the outset thoroughly motivated by the aim of making themselves not only public but publicly accepted and influential. The autonomous private reader or "strong textualist" Rorty praises is explicitly identified with Harold Bloom's "strong misreader" whose novel transformative interpretations aim to escape the domination of already influential readings by becoming influential themselves. The strong misreader, we recall, is one "whose readings will matter to others as well as to himself."

Hence, for all their initial divergence from the public's shared interpretations (which allows Rorty to distinguish them as "private"), these readings and the vocabularies in which they are formulated cannot be regarded as merely private. Rorty cannot therefore argue that their private status renders them logically incapable of disrupting "public" ways of reading or threatening the shared public discourse used for the very individuation of texts to be read. The undeniable fact is that such innovative "private readings" (whose intrinsic public status is standardly highlighted by their authors' publishing and institutional affiliation) do impose themselves on the reading public, and they challenge (for better and for worse) its familiar, shared, and perhaps cherished understandings of literature. Since our individuation of textual objects depends on our literary interests and values, radically changing our understanding and experience of texts can result in changing their individuation. We may no longer find them worth individuating in the same way, no longer care about distinguishing their authentic copies from drastically abridged or bowdlerized versions. In other words, though we can and must distinguish individuation of the work from the particular meanings and content interpretively ascribed to it, the latter can sometimes reciprocally modify our determining the former. Applying this lesson to Rorty's strategy, we realize that although widely variant private readings can swing free of each other and remain focused on a shared "publicly" individuated text, if such interpretive swinging is long and violent enough, the initial organizing focus can be unhinged.

Rorty's so-called private readings exceed and violate the private in a more general way. Collectively, they create a field that structures and constrains the range of acceptable public response to texts, valorizing some as currently informed and up-to-date, while deprecating others as naive and old-fashioned. This structuring works not only within the critical profession but in fact marks off (so as to dismiss) the large and valuable range of more truly "private" reader response that lies outside its regulated borders, at once classifying and declassing such response as "unprofessional." What facilitates this dismissive exclusion of unprofessional reading and interpretation is a twofold confusion common to contemporary theory. The conflation of reading with interpretation is coupled with an implicit identification of all legitimate forms of literary interpretation with the interpretive forms legitimated by the literary critical profession. The upshot is that all reading worthy of the name must conform to the conventions and aims of professionalized interpretation. Since such interpretation is supposed to make a novel contribution to our understanding of the text, and since it is always explicitly articulated (hence is as much a matter of writing as of reading), any interpretive effort that fails to issue in an innovative interpreting text should not qualify as interpretation.

The deplorable drift of such totalizing professionalism and preoccupation with novelty is that all legitimate reading must also be writing and that interpretation must be professionally original to have any value. This attitude brutally constrains the possibilities of value in reading and interpretation. First, it suggests that these activities can be properly practiced only by a professionalized elite. Second, it denies crucial values even to the members of that elite. For these professionals are always both more and less than professionals. As concrete individuals, they are always more; and since they can hardly be specialists with respect to all literatures and authors, they are inevitably also mere lay readers as well. Surely, outside their specific area of scholarship (but I suspect also in it), professional critics can find value in familiar shared readings, and indeed in the very fact that they are so shared. Community of response is one of the irreducibly social goods that art can foster, though art can also generate divisiveness when its appreciation becomes too far removed from the common sphere of experience and instead posited in the hands of an institutionalized priestly class of professional appreciators.

By Rorty's own pragmatist standards, the case for interpretive innovation must be made in terms of evaluative cost accounting rather than by appeal to transcendental conceptual necessity. His argument for hermeneutic novelty seems to be that it provides greater pleasure and autonomy. Both points can be challenged. Though I am not clear how reading pleasure should be measured, my (professional and nonprofessional) experience suggests that trying to crank out academic papers with novel interpretations is not always more satisfying than simply reading a literary work as an amateur focused on its more common understanding. Certainly this should be the case for nonprofessional readers, whose claims, if not existence, seem neglected here. More important, even if the pleasures of "strong misreading-writing" are indeed superior, we must not let the best become the enemy of the good by rejecting the value of ordinary readings because of the greater thrill of extraordinary ones. Here, as elsewhere, what mars Rorty's interpretive theory is not the advocacy of innovative individualist reading, but its one-sided, virtually exclusive valorization, which neglects and demeans the common. Pragmatists should be pluralists.

The argument that novelty is the best or only expression of autonomy seems similarly suspect. True autonomy, one would think, should allow us the choice of whether we wish to seek novel interpretations or whether we prefer just to have a good read, experiencing the work without producing a significantly innovative interpretation or even a formulated one at all. Though Rorty equates it with autonomy, the demand for novelty of interpretation betrays an obvious obeisance to the pressures of academic publication and professional advancement, compounded by an abiding and unquestioning bondage to the late romantic and modernist aesthetic that only has eyes and praise for the radically new.[16] Moreover, both the professional and the aesthetic demand for rapid and relentless innovation can themselves be seen as obeying a greater master, as dependent cultural reflections of capitalism's increasing demand for new commodities to produce continued profits.[17]

NOTES

1. I do not have space here to consider Fish's theory, which shares some problems with Knapp and Michaels's and others with Rorty's. I critically examine his theory and compare it with these others while formulating my own interpretive theory in *Pragmatist Aesthetics: Living Beauty, Rethinking Art* (Oxford: Blackwell, 1992). Joseph Margolis develops a new pragmatist theory of interpretation in his book *The New Puzzle of Interpretation* (Chicago: University of Chicago Press, 1992), so the failure of Rorty's, Fish's, and Knapp and Michaels's theories does not entail the failure of pragmatist interpretive theory as a whole.

2. See Steven Knapp and Walter Benn Michaels, "Against Theory," in *Against Theory*, ed. W.J.T. Mitchell (Chicago: University of Chicago Press, 1985), p. 11. Parts of this work are reprinted in Chapter 4. (Future page references are to the original and are cited as *AT*.) There are good reasons to deny this narrow construal of theory and their related presumption that theory cannot include any "essentially empirical" account, no matter how general. For this view sharply departs from ordinary usage in a way that begs the question against theory by making theory seem much more narrow, rigid, and objectionable than it has to be. Moreover, Knapp and Michaels seem caught in a reflexive contradiction, since their own

allegedly antitheoretical position on interpretation—that "the meaning of a text is simply identical to the author's intended meaning"—is itself nonempirical and theoretical, despite their protestations to the contrary (AT, pp. 12, 98–100).

3. There is another and somewhat different way to argue against the possibility of theory by denying the validity of its question of how in general we should interpret a work. Rather than assert (as Knapp and Michaels) that there can be no alternatives to make the question meaningful, one could maintain that there are too many interpretive alternatives to make it answerable. One might assert that because interpretive strategies will and should always depend on the particular changing situations, contexts and purposes of interpretation, the question of a general strategy is an illegitimate one, and so therefore is the whole idea of theory that seeks to answer it. But the theorist could rightly counter that to say interpretation should always be contextual is itself a general answer of sorts, and moreover the fact that a question can be given no one definite answer does not mean that it cannot be profitably addressed in theoretical discourse and that such theoretical discussion cannot have positive results for practice.

4. The question of whose intentions will determine meaning suggests that meaning and interpretation are also deeply issues of power. One underlying theme of my subsequent critique of Rorty and of Knapp and Michaels is the undemocratic character of their interpretive theories.

5. In a sequel entitled "Against Theory 2: Hermeneutics and Deconstruction" (Critical Inquiry 14 [1987]: 49–69), Knapp and Michaels extend their intentionalist critique to the hermeneutic theories of Gadamer and Ricoeur, the semiotic conventionalism of Goodman and Elgin, and the deconstructionist contextualism of Derrida. (Further references to this essay, part of which is also reprinted in Chapter 4, are cited as AT 2.) Their basic line of argument does not change, however; there is just no way "that a text can mean something other than what its author intended," nor can there be "any plausible criteria of textual identity (e.g., in terms of syntax, linguistic conventions, or traditions of identification) that can function independent of authorial intention" (AT 2, p. 50), simply because without some determining intention, texts could neither mean nor be identified as such.

I should also note that Knapp and Michaels misrepresent Beardsley's anti-intentionalism as holding the view that textual meaning is "permanent and unchanging" (AT 2, pp. 51, 68). On the contrary, the 'fact' that a text's meaning can change (through changes in its words' meanings) long after its author is dead is one of Beardsley's central arguments to prove that textual meaning is not logically identical to authorial meaning. See Monroe C. Beardsley, The Possibility of Criticism (Detroit: Wayne State University Press, 1970), 19, reprinted in Chapter 2.

6. William James, Pragmatism and Other Essays (New York: Simon and Schuster,

1963), pp. 27, 28, 11, 118. James thinks those objects and facts we accept as given regardless of our choice and against our will are really the product of the past choices
and interpretations of our ancestors that we are drilled to accept: "the world *we*
feel and live in will be that which our ancestors and we, by cumulative strokes of
choice, have extricated from" raw experience. See William James, *The Principles of
Psychology* (New York: Dover, 1950), pp. 288–89. Peirce and Dewey similarly affirm
possibility and pluralistic choice against the necessities of a static universe and
fixed concepts to deal with it. The essentially pluralist spirit of pragmatism has
been recently emphasized by Richard Bernstein, "Pragmatism, Pluralism, and the
Healing of Wounds," *Proceedings and Addresses of the American Philosophical Association* 63
(1989): 5–18.

7. James describes pragmatism as essentially facing "forward towards the future" and defines the "pragmatic method" as "*the attitude of looking away from first
things, principles, categories, supposed necessities; and of looking towards last things, fruits, consequences, and facts.*" His pragmatism similarly insists that the goal of knowledge is not
to copy existing reality but "that existing realities may be changed" to provide us
more satisfactory experience. James, *Pragmatism and Other Essays*, pp. 100, 27, 99, 26.

8. John Dewey, "The Development of American Pragmatism," in *Philosophy and
Civilization* (New York: Capricorn, 1963), p. 24.

9. Yet within this frame of fixity in principle, Knapp and Michaels can still
allow for the existence of interpretive variety in practice by leaving completely
open the so-called empirical question not only of what the historical author intended but who the historical author actually is. It could even be, they say, "the
universal muse" (*AT*, p. 103). They thus, like Hirsch, allow for the professional pressures of interpretive productivity while assuring us that ultimately interpretation
converges on a fixed and common object of truth, which preserves the pretense
of criticism as a collaborative enterprise aimed at cumulative knowledge.

10. I provide a detailed critique of Goodman's textualism in *The Object of Literary
Criticism* (Atlantic Highlands, N.J.: Humanities Press, 1984), pp. 130–45, where I treat
the concept of work-identity as a "range concept" that is open and pragmatically
contextual.

11. Joseph Margolis makes essentially the same point in "Reinterpreting Interpretation," *Journal of Aesthetics and Art Criticism* 47 (1989).

12. John Dewey, *Art as Experience* (Carbondale, Ill.: Southern Illinois University
Press, 1987), 327; and Dewey "The Practical Character of Reality," where Dewey argues that since "all existences are in transition," the function of knowledge is not
"impossible copying" but "to make a *certain* difference in reality" (pp. 40, 46–47).

13. I shall be referring to Richard Rorty's works parenthetically, using the following abbreviations: *Consequences of Pragmatism* (Minneapolis: University of Min-

nesota Press, 1982), CP; "Texts and Lumps," *New Literary History* 17 (1985): 1–16, TL; "Philosophy without Principles," in Mitchell, *Against Theory*, PP; and *Contingency, Irony, and Solidarity* (Cambridge: Cambridge University Press, 1989), CIS.

14. See Donald Davidson, "What Metaphors Mean," in *Inquiries into Truth and Interpretation* (Oxford: Blackwell, 1984), and Donald Davidson "A Nice Derangement of Epitaphs," in *Truth and Interpretation*, ed. E. Lepore (Oxford: Blackwell, 1986), pp. 433–36.

15. Rorty declares in no uncertain terms: "The language of self-creation is necessarily private, unshared, unsuited to argument" (CIS, p. xiv). I examine his individualistic ethic of self-creation at length in *Pragmatist Aesthetics*.

16. Rorty in fact sees pragmatism as "the philosophical counterpart to literary modernism, the kind of literature which prides itself on its autonomy and novelty rather than its truthfulness to experience" (CP, p. 153).

17. The connection between the demand for interpretive novelty and the pressures of professionalism is even clearer in Fish's interpretive theory, which I discuss in *Pragmatist Aesthetics*. In that book I offer my own pragmatist account of interpretation, which does justice to nonprofessional modes of literary understandings and challenges the hermeneutic dogma that all understanding is interpretation.

11

Irony, Metaphor, and the Problem of Intention

DANIEL O. NATHAN

> As emotions were the first motives which
> induced man to speak, his first utterances were
> tropes. Figurative language was the first to be
> born, proper meaning discovered last.
>
> —Rousseau,
> *Essay on the Origins of Languages*

I

WHATEVER ONE MAKES OF Rousseau's view of
the motivation and speech of early humans, the relationship between the
literal and the figurative remains controversial. If one makes the plausible
assumption that with metaphor and irony the direct, literal, or "ordinary"
meanings do not by themselves make sense of the tropes, it is no surprise to
feel set adrift in search of a way to meaning. And, in part, it is just such wan-
derings that have led many to set their compasses mistakenly on the author's
intention. This essay considers the reliability and proper role of intention
in the interpretation of figurative language and finally lands on familiar anti-
intentionalist territory, claiming that even in cases of metaphor and irony, the
meaning of a text must remain logically independent of the intent of its historical author. The focus here is on irony and metaphor because they are likely
the most difficult cases for the anti-intentionalist, but also because they stand
as the marks of the literary. Consequently, the weakening of the intentionalist position here would have broad implications for literary interpretation in
general.

II

Metaphor and irony can seem especially problematic for anti-intentionalism, the view that the actual intention (attitudes, beliefs, etc.) of the author can play no logical role in determining meaning. Classic statements of anti-intentionalism, like that of Wimsatt and Beardsley, reject such "external" elements as those of the text's genesis and instead emphasize the "internal" properties of the text, its words and literary structure, and the sufficiency of public conventions of usage to resolve questions of meaning. But problems are hinted at in a typical characterization of what is required to understand instances of metaphor or irony. One might say, in the simplest possible terms, that the meaning of a figurative expression cannot just be "read off" the meanings of the words that make it up. Instead, some "extra" interpretive move appears necessary to capture the special twist of language at work. In metaphor, speakers manage to communicate to their hearers despite the fact that, as Searle paradoxically puts it, "they do not say what they mean." "Strictly speaking, whenever we talk about the metaphorical meaning of a word, expression, or sentence, we are talking about what a speaker might utter it to mean, in a way that departs from what the word, expression, or sentence actually means."[1]

So, with metaphor, the meaning is said not to be exhausted by the mere juxtaposition of the literal meanings of the vehicle and tenor, a juxtaposition that may only produce something false, trivially true, or apparently meaningless. In irony, the twist is a full 180 degrees: the straightforward literal meaning is precisely the opposite of the appropriate, so-called intended, meaning. It can then be argued that without appeal to something external to the text, namely, the specific intent of the author, one is threatened with having not merely an impoverished or incomplete interpretation but one that is either directly contrary to the real meaning or else falsely entails that the expression lacks any meaning whatsoever.

This suggestion that figurative language poses a special problem for the anti-intentionalist requires closer examination. How might the argument actually proceed? First, it is assumed that anti-intentionalism requires that the meaning of a text is to be identified with the meaning of the word sequence that constitutes it, and that this word-sequence meaning is fully analyzable in terms of linguistic combination rules plus the lexical definitions of the individual words, and of course in any event without necessary recourse to the author's intent. But, the argument continues, such an approach strips many, perhaps most, literary uses of language of any possibility of correct understanding. Consider one of Hirsch's examples of irony: "Now there's a bright idea!" (uttered presumably with a sneer, perhaps in response to a stupid suggestion). The meanings of the words alone provide absolutely no clue to the ironic character of this minitext, since the very same English words, in the same order, by the same system of linguistic rules (modern English) are straightforwardly used to compliment, not to sneer. Thus, basing an analysis of the meaning solely upon the word-sequence meaning fails to account for the actual ironic meaning of the utterance. Instead, it produces an interpretation diametrically opposed to the correct one. Only an analysis that considers such extratextual information as the larger extralinguistic and situational context, a context that includes the author's background and intention, can issue the proper interpretation. The twist on the straightforward word-sequence meaning that we find in cases of irony necessitates an appeal to authorial intent. The text, it is claimed, is ironic only and essentially because the author *meant* it ironically.

The parallel argument regarding metaphor might run as follows: As Max Black said, the meaning of any metaphor that is not dead is not "part of its standard meaning, and is therefore to be found neither in dictionaries or encyclopedias."[2] Interesting metaphors have meanings that are "typically new or 'creative,' not inferrible from the standard lexicon."[3] So it has seemed natural to some to claim that only by virtue of the fact that the author *means* the new figurative sense can it be derived. Perhaps this is what led Black to say that there can be "no objection in principle" to invoking what the author means.[4]

At least, an intentionalist might so argue. As mentioned in the opening, it is apparent in both metaphor and irony that, in Wayne Booth's words, "literal, discrete, or 'ordinary' meanings alone will not make sense of the passage."[5] Perhaps one should qualify this a bit by saying that when literal meanings do make sense of the passage, they make the wrong sense. There is a "straight" reading of an ironic text and a literal reading of certain metaphors that coincidentally happen to be literally true, such as "Gorbachev is no teddy bear." Of course, in neither case is the reading appropriate.

But to infer from this that one must appeal to author's intention is clearly to leap across the horns of a false dilemma. Certainly, establishing meaning often requires more than what the metaphorical or ironic phrase or sentence provides when taken in isolation. With metaphor and irony, as in most linguistic expression, meanings are context dependent, and the question becomes whether or not the larger context need include the author's intention. Anti-intentionalism does not entail a literalist position on metaphor; it does not lead to an a-contextual, literal interpretation of figurative language. Who would have thought otherwise? So it is not obvious that interpretation must appeal to the author's intention to turn the corner of a new figure. At least, not as long as the context is understood to include a properly wide range of linguistic clues, clues ranging from the complete text in which the phrase or sentence occurs to the connotative richness of the words at the time of expression and even to such elements as vocal intonation when dealing with oral utterances. Even these considerations reflect only part of the relevant context once that is properly worked out, a point I return to later. All these contextual clues are publicly accessible; arguably, none are logically tied in any obvious way to the historical intention of a particular author. (Though, of course, there are causal connections.) If, based only on consideration of those limited and public contextual factors, one cannot justify the ironic construal of a statement, then the propriety of so construing it is properly open to question, perhaps indeed no matter what the author's intention is taken to be.

This anti-intentionalist response, whatever its ultimate merit, clearly raises a number of questions. There needs to be further clarification of what is to count as the relevant, larger, public linguistic context, and whether that context can be understandable given the exclusion of authorial intention. Some elucidation of the notion of intention itself is surely required. There are theorists who claim that the reference to context suggested earlier can be correctly understood only as an appeal to the actual intentions of the author, either because what is to count as the relevant context is ultimately determined by the historical author's intention or because the only reason context is important at all is as an indication of what the author intended by the words he used. Though there is not adequate space in the present essay to do so, each of these issues and claims must finally be examined in depth. Here we do little more than hint at their complexities. Before doing even that, however, we must look more closely at Hirsch and the intentionalist analysis.

III

Explaining the workings of irony and metaphor can turn out to be problematic for intentionalist positions as well. To see this, suppose we take the intentionalist view to assert that an expression means what its author meant by it. Of course, few intentionalists would leave that to mean that the author's intent is both a necessary and sufficient condition for meaning;[6] otherwise, "Eileen loves all animals" could, just by authorial fiat, mean that the average maximum temperature in Auckland is 63 degrees Fahrenheit. Additionally, on such a view, it would be impossible for the author to misspeak, to intend one thing and say another. Typically, then, to avoid such apparent absurdities, the intentionalist will try to work the position out so that the author's meaning is somehow limited by the range of conventional, literal meanings of the words that constitute the expression. This is played out differently by different intentionalists.

Hirsch thus refers to the "codetermining influence" exerted by linguistic norms. The author "cannot successfully make words mean just anything he wants them to."[7] Hirsch asserts that when there is an inconsistency between word meaning and author intention, the expression does *not* mean what the author intended, nor what the words mean, nor is it ambiguous between those two possible candidates for meaning. Instead, such an expression, on Hirsch's view, is simply meaningless. He is forced into such a claim because on the first option intent effectively trumps and is not limited by linguistic rules at all—thus it would set us back to naive intentionalism and its flaws. If he were to take the second option, then word meaning would trump, and his position would collapse into anti-intentionalism. The third choice (ambiguity), like the first, would entail a version of naive intentionalism, for an expression would have one of its multiple meanings established by authorial fiat alone, with no connection to any linguistic norms for that portion of its meaning. Beyond this, Hirsch would likely see such an alternative as not really solving the problem of determining meaning. So a fourth option seems needed, and thus such problem cases are purged from the ranks of meaningful expressions.

Besides the potential unsatisfactoriness of Hirsch's move here, there is some difficulty making sense out of his use of the idea of a "codetermining influence." With it, I take Hirsch to assert that the meaning of an expression is constrained by the rules of language or by Hirsch's possibly weaker "principle of sharability"; which is to say that "the willed type has to fall within known conventions."[8] Thus the norms of language, while on Hirsch's view never adequate to determine meaning by themselves, do serve to narrow the range of meanings available to the author.

But even this seemingly sensible idea appears to cause problems for Hirsch when it comes to figurative language and ironic expressions in particular. Consider what he has to say about ironic expressions, given his overly narrow construal of linguistic conventions with respect to their role as a codetermining influence: In one of his examples he suggests that the two statements "That's a bright idea?" and "That's a bright idea!" while differing in ironic content, cannot be distinguished based on linguistic conventions alone (they are the "very same text").[9] But such an extraordinarily limited construal of linguistic norms, besides making anti-intentionalism into a straw man, sets up an unpleasant dilemma for Hirsch, of which he appears unaware: on one reading of this limited conception of linguistic norms, as a codetermining influence they can narrow down the range of possible meanings of expressions to their several conventional (presumably literal—more about that later) meanings plus the negations of these meanings. Hence, to allow the author to be ironic in his use of the bright-idea text, we must be able to construe "bright" to mean stupid. But the problem for Hirsch is now obvious: linguistic norms can hardly serve as a limiting factor at all, for every expression is now left to mean either what the text says or the negation of what the text says. Because the only remaining determining influence is authorial intent, *any* expression would become ironic just by virtue of the author *meaning* it to be; that is, all is once again left to authorial fiat. This of course has the implication that interpreters can never know (or even have a well-founded belief) that a work is, for example, not ironic. Even the immediate presence of the author can be of no help here, since author testimony, however closely it follows our conventions of sincerity, might itself always still be ironic.

A second, and even less promising, reading of linguistic norms as a codetermining influence would take them to narrow the range of possible word meanings to their literal, a-contextual senses. (No inclusion here of the negations of those meanings.) If we now take seriously that the author is limited by linguistic norms of this sort, then no expressions can ever be ironic. Should the author mean for the text (*any* text) to be ironic, the conflict between author intent and the constraints of Hirsch's narrow reading of conventional linguistic norms makes the author's expression meaningless, not ironic. I think the proper conclusion to draw from all this is that unless linguistic conventions are construed broadly enough to produce the ironic (or metaphorical) meanings independently—that is, to do the twisting themselves—then they cannot effectively function as a codetermining influence for Hirsch, and he can make no sense of figurative expression. If, however, they *can* do the work independently, then that undermines Hirsch's broader position by obviating any talk of author's intent.

IV

There are times when Hirsch seems to realize there is a problem with the role of intention on his analysis. As a consequence, he attempts a shift to a different sense of "intention" and, at certain points, even appears to endorse what amounts to an anti-intentionalist position.[10] But he waffles on this shift and often slides confusingly between the two different senses of the term.

Thus, sometimes "intention" is understood in a way that makes it simply a public matter—what was previously referred to by "sharable meaning"—and sometimes he appears to take it in the old style as some complex of conscious and unconscious states of the author's mind during the creative process. It is of course the latter interpretation that troubles the anti-intentionalists; the author's conscious or unconscious state of mind is what they deny to be relevant to the proper understanding of a text, and so that is how I shall read the Hirschean notion.

One way of approaching this Hirschean shift is to see it as another interesting effort on his part to limit the role of authorial intention (that is, to deny its sufficiency for meaning), in order to avoid the absurdities that naive intentionalism seems to entail. Thus, after raising some standard objections to naive intentionalism,[11] Hirsch argues that the interpretation cannot rest on whether the author had that meaning in mind, for "if that is the principle, all hope for objective interpretation must be abandoned." Why? Because "in most cases it is impossible (even for the author himself) to determine precisely what he was thinking of at the time or times he composed his text."[12] It is therefore worth examining whether this new effort has greater success in dealing with problems of figurative language.

Hirsch adapts as his central notion the Husserlian one of a "horizon," using it to explain what he calls the "supra-personal" (or "impersonal") character of verbal meaning. Verbal meaning is then defined as "that aspect of a speaker's 'intention' [sic] which, under linguistic conventions, may be shared by others."[13] And, once again, "the meaning is determined once and for all by the character of the speaker's intention."[14] Here it must be kept in mind (though it is not clear that Hirsch himself consistently does so) that the object before the historical author's mind (his thoughts, his intention in the more standard sense) is a distinct things from the intentional object in Husserl's sense, for those actual historical thoughts surely cannot be confined by the linguistic conventions that determine the sharable meaning of the intentional object that is the text. That is, after all, the substance of Husserl's rejection of what might be called "psychologism," the need to know the contents of the author's mind at the time of composition. Since Hirsch emphasizes that the actual mental state of the author is inaccessible and, in any event, will not tell us the implicit meaning of his work, he appeals to the new principle ("horizon") to take us beyond the most superficial level of meaning.

If we now infer that Hirsch's distinction between implicit and explicit meaning corresponds to, or even parallels, that of the metaphorical versus the literal or the ironical versus the straightforward, then the relevance to our immediate subject is obvious. But even if there were no direct parallel, the principle, in its role as a constraint on possible meanings, bears crucially on the project of generating a version of intentionalism adequate to handle figurative language.

It is, on Hirsch's view, the "horizon" that *"defines* the author's intention as a whole"[15] and thus defines the implicit meanings of the text, as well as its explicit ones. The author cannot be presumed to be consciously aware of all of the implications of his expression, and the so-called horizon, what Husserl took to be a system of typical expectations and probabilities, permits the interpreter to begin to unpack certain of the deeper meanings of the text. In the case of a single word, Hirsch says the boundaries of possible authorial meaning (the "author's horizon") are established by consulting the "linguistic horizon," the possible meanings of the word according to the conventions of the language at the time of composition. The linguistic horizon "strictly bounds" the possible implications of the word within the text. This linguistic horizon is nothing new (and would raise the very problems already mentioned), but there are broader horizons within Hirsch's field of view, ones that determine the genre of the work and that, as mentioned, reflect the author's meaning as a whole. Hirsch next permits the reader to determine the literary genre in which to locate the text, and one of these now more global horizons of textual meaning will be the basis for various interpretive moves to follow. And to achieve this determination, Hirsch says in somewhat circular fashion that interpreters must ask, "What are the implications of the typical components of the whole meaning under consideration?"

Here, then, is how the interpretive process works so as to avoid the need to delve into the psychology of the author. The interpreter begins by positing a genre: "casual conversation, command, scientific prose, lyric poem, novel, epic, etc."[16] The genre posited establishes a "general horizon" given the "typical meaning components" that characterize it. This horizon is then narrowed somewhat (though, according to Hirsch, not enough to specify the meaning uniquely or to disambiguate the expression satisfactorily) by means of what Hirsch calls the "typical meanings of the author's mental and experiential world." Note that "typical" is the operative term here—in both cases. It is the notion that essentially purports to free interpreters from the task of psychological inquiry into the actual and explicit thoughts of the author.

But the problems are rife. In the first place, it is not apparent that the interpreters are freed from detailed and specific psychological inquiry. How, after all, could one otherwise determine what was typical within the *author's* "mental and experiential world?" Presumably, one is not seeking the typical mental world of just *any* unspecified author or even that of an average author of the time, but of the exact author of the exact document in question. What counts as typical for that historical person is straightforwardly a function of his or her actual and explicit thoughts. The psychological inquiry is thus unavoidable.

A second difficulty lies in the identification of the genre. How is this to be accomplished? If, as we are told, the reader simply *posits* it, then we are left with a number of questions. If "positing" is adequate at this level, then in what sense is the reader taking seriously the idea that the author's subjective act (intention) is the specifier of meaning—that without it there is no meaning?[17] For it is certainly within the realm of possibility that the reader may posit a genre that had never been intended by the author. Letters to student newspapers are frequently interpreted by competent readers as serious comments despite what we later discover to be the ironic intentions of the author. Would Hirsch take that "positing" to be appropriate? Is it an option for the reader to posit as lyric poetry some casual conversation that she or he encounters? Or are we to understand that there are *grounds* for genre classification? If we were to take the view, consistent with other aspects of Hirsch's general position, that the genre depends on the author's classification (that being on his view the only secure grounds), then the damning psychologism returns anew. If, alternatively, we depend on "typical" genre classifications (whatever that means), then there can be no guarantee that the result will in any way correspond with the author's chosen genre, and hence once more no guarantee of the meaningfulness of the text on Hirsch's account of meaningfulness.

In any event, "typical" will not bear the burden Hirsch places on it. Effectively, depending on how it is explicated, its use either contradicts the most basic tenets of his position or takes one no closer to the analysis of meaning, due to its inability to handle maverick interpretations. Since the author may intend a new or atypical genre or, within a genre, have in mind an unusual meaning component, there are not adequate grounds for inferring that typical genre or typical meaning components will not actually exclude the author's meaning. Unless, that is, one substitutes typical meaning for authorial meaning entirely as formally sufficient to establish verbal meaning. But to do that cannot satisfy Hirsch, since it undercuts the entire intentionalist project.

There is one other possible retort available to Hirsch. He could claim that reliance on typical genre and typical meaning components still takes seriously the general necessity of the author's subjective state without becoming embroiled in psychologism as long as we take the text to be an infallible guide to the unconscious thoughts of the author. But, surely, the reasons for being reluctant to move to such a position are manifold. Most important, the suggestion that anything is an infallible guide to the unconscious mind of the author is implausible. That a single text (or even a corpus of texts) constitutes such a guide is yet more implausible. Further, if one understands the textual horizon as a guide to the implications of the text, implications that stretch beyond (as Hirsch realizes) what was consciously meant by the author, one must assume at least a compatibility or consistency between the conscious meanings and the implied meanings for Hirsch's intentionalism to have any bite. But there is no particular reason to make such an assumption. In the oft-cited example of A. E. Housman's poem "1887," there was no apparent compatibility between Housman's conscious meaning (as he expressed it in the controversy that followed) and the standard critical assessment that the poem is an ironical statement about the loss of English lives in careless wars. Even if the critics' judgment is mistaken, the potential of incompatibility clearly remains.

In the final analysis, the concept of horizon on which Hirsch relies to justify his suggestion that "author's meaning does not impoverish meaning, [it] simply exludes what does not belong to it" can do no real work for Hirsch. Its use depends on an equivocation over two different senses of "intention" and on logical maneuvers that are not consistent with Hirsch's essential notion of author's meaning or with the metaphysical tasks it is designed to perform. To achieve the exclusions he seeks while stopping short of psychoanalysis of the author, Hirsch must replace author's meaning with "typical meaning." But "typical meaning" is a notion that can be only contingently related to the intention of the historical author and one that ultimately amounts to a conceptual surrender to anti-intentionalism. In contrast, the notion of authorial intention required by Hirsch's intentionalist program still faces the problems of psychologism and arbitrariness in establishing meaning, given its lack of any clear and necessary connection to public linguistic convention.

V

If one supposes that all or some of the meaning of figurative language comes by way of implication, rather than directly, then there are other interesting intentionalistic accounts to consider. One argument, first presented by Paul Ziff, and recently revived by P. D. Juhl, concludes that "to understand what is said by implication it is not enough to understand what is said in the statement sense. One may have to have some knowledge of the speaker's beliefs, attitudes, convictions, opinions and so forth."[18] The conclusion rests essentially on the following rather powerful case: "If on being asked to play tennis a person replies, 'I have work to do,' what has he said by implication?

That depends on him: no general answer is possible here. If the speaker is an ordinary sort then perhaps he was saying by implication that he couldn't play. But he needn't be an ordinary sort. Perhaps he's a queer sort who plays and is delighted to play only when he has work to do."[19] Thus we are led to infer that a single semantic string, "I have work to do," can be either an expression of desire to play or one of refusal to play, and which one it is can be determined only by the attitude of the speaker.

My general response is that this case turns out to be less special than it appears, for, much as with simpler cases discussed in earlier parts of this essay, an enriched conception of context can provide all necessary tools for understanding what is said by implication. So this example only serves to remind us of the breadth of the relevant context required for proper interpretation to occur at all. The relevant context must be understood to include a variety of background assumptions, as it does in all linguistic interpretation. I argue that, contrary to Ziff and just as in other linguistic interpretation, general answers can be given, and those answers need not depend in any way on the particular attitudes at the time of the actual speaker. Essential to my claim is that while certain background assumptions surely must be made for interpretation of implication to proceed, these background assumptions are logically of no different order from those at work in understanding ordinary statements.

Consider the ordinary statement "We sell alligator shoes."[20] Seeing the correct interpretation of this statement to be "we sell shoes made from the skins of alligators" and not "we sell shoes to be worn by alligators," requires certain normal background assumptions, namely, that alligators do not typically wear shoes. That kind of background assumption is not a linguistic one, nor really akin to any of the variety of contextual elements mentioned in the early sections of this essay. But it must be considered part of the general context within which this ordinary statement needs to be understood. Furthermore, while it is not linguistic, it is public and not fundamentally a function of the idiosyncracies of the actual speaker. Assumptions such as these are part, a necessary part, of the repertoire of any normal speaker of the English language.

In a similar fashion, the tennis case raised by Ziff calls forth certain background assumptions about the world, one of them being that people who report that they have work to do are not typically encouraging a game of tennis. So, against this background, a general statement can be made about the implication of the reply "I have work to do." Absent any explicit cancellation of the background assumption, one can justifiably infer that the reply amounts to a refusal to play, just as in the absence of defeating our assumptions about footwear for alligators, we can justifiably look for shoes made of alligator skins beneath the "We sell alligator shoes" sign. The meaning in the latter case and implication in the former are in similar ways, and for similar reasons, determinate. Ordinary sort or not, the speaker is saying by implication that he could not play.

One must *do* something, not just intend something or have an unconventional attitude, in order to defeat the ordinary background assumptions at work in the linguistic setting. Both speaker and hearer must in fact rely on the existence and bearing of what amount to default background assumptions.[21] We clearly do not consider "We sell alligator shoes" to be ambiguous between the two meanings cited precisely because the ordinary (or default) meaning suffices unless explicitly defeated by the speaker or in some other fashion contextually undermined. Without some contextual grounds for questioning the ordinary meaning, without some evidence canceling or altering the default assumptions, those assumptions will play their role in determining meaning. That is not to say that in all instances the resultant meaning will be as unambiguous as in the alligator example, only that these additional background factors can similarly take us a good distance toward the understanding of implicative meaning. And, in particular, in the tennis example there is no reason to suggest it is ambiguous in any way.

The presence and relevance of these default assumptions cast doubt on Juhl's claim that one needs "to recognize the speaker's intention in order to understand what is said." Juhl says that in the case of the fellow who plays only when he has work to do, the reply "I have work to do" actually *means* that he would be delighted to play tennis. While we can mutually agree that it plainly has that meaning when the speaker adds an explanation that he especially likes to play when he has work to do, Juhl makes the far stronger claim that if the reply meant that after the explanation, then it meant that before it as well, "its meaning does not change." But Juhl's assertion of sameness of meaning is highly questionable given that the context is changed with the addition of the explanation and that the particular aim of the explanation is precisely to defeat the normal background assumptions. It is reasonable to see the defeat of those background assumptions as bringing about that very change in the meaning of the reply. Without the added text, then, the meaning is different. (To one unwilling to grant that much, the argument at least provides an alternative explanation of how a change in meaning can be plausibly maintained.) And if one does not acknowledge the necessity of explicitly defeating normal background assumptions in order to effect a change in meaning, then ordinary discourse would seem impossible inasmuch as speakers may in every case intend to ignore an infinite variety of background assumptions.

Finally, there is still another category of background assumption, quite distinct from the sort of factual assumptions about the world mentioned to this point, that I would argue must come into play in any linguistic setting. It is that of speaker competency; not that of any particular individual, but more hypothetically. The notion of a hypothetical speaker is needed for the project of interpretation even to get under way. The competency at issue is hypothetical in the sense that it cannot be defeated by any facts about the actual historical author. That the background assumption is best understood as involving only a hypothetical speaker is most obvious in the speech of fictional characters, but it is also reflected in the fact that it is correct to describe actually incompetent speakers as having said things that they do not mean. Were this presumption taken to be about the competency of the actual speaker, then in the latter case we would have to say of the speaker, not that he said something he did not mean, but that he said nothing at all (a position discussed earlier as one taken by Hirsch). A competent speaker, it should be noted, knows that his utterances cannot be assumed to take on meaning by virtue of some private mental act, but must bear meaning by virtue of the conventions of usage of the system that he shares with his hearers and within which he speaks. Hence, despite sounding like the sort of background assumption that would give succor to intentionalists, the presumption of speaker competency appears to cancel out the credibility of intentionalism at the outset.

Where, then, have we arrived? Juhl has used Ziff's example to argue that the context "will be able to disambiguate an utterance if and only if it constitutes evidence of speaker's intention." [22] But much of the earlier discussion is aimed at showing that it is at best only an abstracted intention of a hypothetical, competent speaker and not the actual intention of a particular speaker that belongs in the second half of this biconditional. [23] Better put, given a context that includes standard background assumptions, the implications of the reply in the tennis example are never really ambiguous to begin with. And, further, when the background is understood to play a disambiguating role, the abstract intention involved will simply be that of a competent speaker and not necessarily that of the *actual* speaker.

Thus, Juhl errs when he concludes that "to know the context of an utterance is . . . a matter of understanding how *the speaker views* the situation in which his utterance occurs." [24] If the actual speaker views the situation abnormally, that is, believes the context to be other than the way it is viewed by default, and takes no measures to defeat those standard conditions (or, alternatively, in fact defeats those conditions without appropriately accounting for that change), then those *actual* views can carry no weight in establishing the relevant context. That is why it remains possible for students (and others) to inadvertently write ironic letters to the editor, and (in a more familiar case mentioned by Knapp and Michaels) for a passenger to say "go"—and have it *mean* "go"—despite intending all along for it to mean "stop."

Each of these arguments against Juhl's intentionalism requires that we take for granted the now vastly broadened conception of relevant context—a context that includes not only lexical meanings, grammatical and textual settings of words, verbal intonations and emphases, systems of associations and connotations, but also the kinds of innumerable background assumptions suggested in the preceding discussion. The fundamental question with which we began could then perhaps be reframed to that of whether this broad context must also include the author's intent. What I hope the argument thus far has shown, however, is that such inclusion is no more necessary for grasping implicated meaning or the richness of meaning in metaphorical and ironical expressions than it is for ordinary meaning; and the case remains to be made for ordinary meaning.

VI

Interpretation is in general and essentially a matter of asking "why," of seeking an explanation of whatever it is we have before us. That applies to the interpretation of metaphors as it does to the interpretation of any literary or artistic work. The discovery of the intention of the actual author makes up part of one important sort of explanation, namely, causal explanation. As such, it is attractive within literary interpretation in a number of ways: Causal explanation is a reasonably familiar type of explanation—we are accustomed to it from daily life as well as from the social and natural sciences. And it has a comforting sense of concreteness about it, probably just because it is a common species of scientific explanation. But beyond these facts about causal explanation, intentionalism attracts because works of art are inherently intentional objects, being the products of human beings. And Hirsch finds intentionalistic interpretation especially appealing because, in his view, the principal alternative to intentionalism would lead to a sort of interpretive anarchy.

Nonetheless, even when it comes to intentional objects, the "why" question can be answered in a number of ways, not all of them as threatening as Hirsch and others might imagine. Most important, instead of asking "why did this particular author . . . ?" we might ask, "Why would anyone . . . ?" One might think of the move to this new question as a shift from asking for the efficient cause of what we have before us to asking for its final cause.[25] If we did this, we would be seeking not the most probable reading (as Hirsch would have it) but the maximally explanatory one—the one that explains all that we have here, or at least does so to the extent possible. It is this interpretive approach that I would urge. It is the single approach that is compatible with our talk in the previous section of a hypothetically competent speaker. And that hypothetical conception is a richer one than that of the actual speaker, for reasons that I hope become further apparent in this final section.

Richard Wollheim insists, in one of his defenses of intentionalism, that "criticism is concerned to find out not just what the work of art is like but what it is like by design."[26] There are sound instincts here. But, what those instincts ought to call forth are not facts about the life of the author but certain institutional conventions, certain demands of the concept of art itself, specifically ones that require us to see everything in the text before us as if it were purposeful. Not to discover what design or purpose was at work in the actual creation of the object, but instead to explain what seems purposeful about the object, what can be explained as though it had been done on purpose, whether it actually was so or not. In seeing this point, it is crucial to understand that no discoveries about the mental life of the actual author would seem to override the judgment or the requirement that lies behind it. Even aside from the depth of these conventional demands, however, there are other reasons for the approach that I am suggesting.

On Hirsch's view, the literary work is in a sense limited, and not just in a way that resists interpretive anarchy. For his intentionalism entails that the work can mean only what the author intended it to mean. If author's intent is not compatible with the meaning it would have as established by public conventions of usage, then the work simply has no meaning. But why should we limit literature in this way? Should not literature be allowed to transcend, exceed authorial intent, to be "extravagant and subversive" or "uncanny and exorbitant" (to use Jonathan Culler's descriptors), stretching beyond literary traditions and the capacity of any single will or intellect?[27] Hirsch allows that the work may be more than the author consciously envisioned, but why not also more than the depths of his particular unconscious mind might intend? And why, after all, should literary theory require (as Hirsch's seems to) an a priori commitment to a notion of unconscious intent at all?

The art world has always had room for marvelous accidents as well as (though not so often clearly distinguished from) works of genius. Those who engage in the public enterprise of art accept the existence of the accidental, both when it takes the form of failure, as in the expression of an inferior thought, and when it is fortuitous, generating some positive result that the artist did not or could not have foreseen. But, for Hirsch and others, the category of accidents would disappear because, on his view, they would have to be either subsumed mysteriously within genius or dismissed as meaningless.

Here, interestingly because of the nature of the practice of art itself, acceptance of the notion of a hypothetical or ideal author necessarily shows respect for the actual author's intent, or at least one essential aspect of that intent. The actual author must always intend, while not necessarily that his work transcend his specific "meaning," at least that its meaning be borne in a sufficiently public fashion that he need not personally accompany it to explain the meaning he placed there. Actual authors intend to create a work that can stand on its own, to send their work off complete, capable of being understood by its audience. This is not merely an accidental desire of some artists, but plausibly one of the most fundamental of any artist's actual states of mind and part of what it means to engage in the human and public enterprise of art. Paradoxically, this actual and apparently essential intention is one part of the mental state of the artist that intentionalism seems to disregard entirely.

Hirsch worries throughout his work about the absence of adequate alternatives to his author-centered theory of meaning. In fact, the argument he gives rests crucially on the assumption that there are only two choices: his intentionalistic view or the end to "validity" in interpretation, that is, the interpretive anarchy he perceives in any other critical approach. He concludes that if we relinquish the actual author's meaning as the standard, then we are left with reader's idiosyncratic, "solipsistic" meaning.[28] While there is a dilemma here, it turns out not to be exactly the one he constructs.

In fact, there is an important similarity in both Hirsch's author-centered approach and the reader-centered one he fears. What the two views share is that they are both fundamentally subjectivist approaches to meaning. They are subjectivist in the sense that each defines the correct interpretation in terms of the mental state or the mind of some actual and particular individual. The most basic problem, as I see it, lies in the element of subjective incorrigibility that must arise in any such account. Just as one can recognize in the reader-centered view the threat of anarchy that so alarms Hirsch, we can also see that the source of the threat rests in the fact that, on the subjectivist analysis, the reader cannot be mistaken, cannot misinterpret. To most, I suspect, this incorrigibility seems even more implausible than the anarchy seems obnoxious. But the incorrigibility is precisely what is shared by Hirsch's author-centered theory, a subjectivist cousin of the reader-centered one. As I tried to demonstrate in previous sections, Hirsch's theory entails that the author at some level cannot be mistaken, cannot misspeak. Hirsch's view allows that the author can sometimes utter things that are meaningless, but he can never mistakenly say anything that he did not mean to say. That should strike people as equally absurd.

The most obvious and natural alternative to these subjectivist standards would be some sort of intersubjectively based theory. One such intersubjective standard makes the correct interpretation turn on a social practice or convention, including linguistic convention, either alone or in combination with a real or hypothetical agreement between persons. The kind of hypothetical notion at work in various parts of this essay aims to draw on just such an intersubjective standard.[29] Throughout, I have been suggesting that we seek (we necessarily presuppose) a concept of an idealized, hypothetical author, an author who can be held responsible for everything in the text, being aware of all the relevant context, conventions, and background assumptions, an author for whom we may imagine everything is there by design, on purpose. For when we approach a work of literature, like any work of art, we approach it as if it were made to be entirely understood. To the extent that we can do so, we are obligated to see all of it as purposeful, whether in fact it was or not.

While the notion of an ideal author is more than merely consistent with the kinds of principles defended in previous sections, it is certainly not the only nonsubjectivist approach available. So questions still must arise about making such a choice. Why not talk instead of a hypothetical agreement of ideal readers? Why, that is, bother with talk about an author at all? Why need we encourage talk about "abstract intentions" once free of the need to talk of actual intentions?

Basically, I think there are at least two kinds of reasons why it remains essential to maintain some notion of an author within any interpretive analysis. First, there are reasons having to do with the very concept of art because of the connection suggested earlier to that concept. The nature of the enterprise dictates such an interpretive approach, for the notion of intentionality is imbedded in art's character as a normatively driven human activity. If we focus only on the response of readers, even "ideal" readers, works of literature are not differentiated from natural objects, and thus they need not be seen to be what they are, namely, the productions of human beings as part of an ongoing human enterprise. And second, the "why" question demands talk of an author. The mere agreement among readers ignores the assertion (assuming it was correct) that what we seek is the maximally explanatory reading. If we are asking, "Why would anyone have done this?" the question demands an answer in terms of human purposes. Given the weaknesses of ordinary intentionalism, appeal to a hypothetical author is the only adequate response to these aspects of literary interpretation.

NOTES

1. John R. Searle, "Metaphor," in *Metaphor and Thought*, ed. Andrew Ortony (Cambridge: Cambridge University Press, 1979), p. 93.

2. Max Black, "How Metaphors Work: A Reply to Donald Davidson," in *On Metaphor*, ed. Sheldon Sacks (Chicago: University of Chicago Press, 1979), p. 190.

3. Ibid. Some of Black's concerns about the way metaphors are capable of creating new meaning are answered afresh in an important recent work on the topic by Eva Feder Kittay. In her book *Metaphor* (Oxford: Oxford University Press, 1987), Kittay introduces the notion of "semantic fields" and explains how both the vehicle and topic in metaphor must be understood to belong to entire systems of relationships, the complex transfer of which begins to explain both the difficulty and reward of interpreting metaphor. The attempt, then, to see some property as standing within some other wholly alien system of relationships, like trying a found key in a system of locks, could indeed produce something new, perhaps the discovery of some completely unanticipated relationship.

4. Black, "How Metaphors Work," p. 191.

5. Wayne Booth, "Metaphor as Rhetoric: The Problem of Evaluation," in Sacks, *On Metaphor*, p. 52.

6. Iseminger interprets Knapp and Michaels as doing just this, however. See Chapter 6.

7. E. D. Hirsch, *Validity in Interpretation* (New Haven: Yale University Press, 1967), p. 27.

8. Ibid., p. 66.

9. Ibid., p. 235. He goes on to say that "it is both incorrect and futile to inquire, 'What does the language of the text say?' " Only an inquiry into what the author probably *meant* makes sense here, Hirsch says.

10. "Textual meaning itself must not be identified with the author's or reader's psychic acts as such." Ibid., p. 217. While in isolation this quotation could be interpreted to be compatible with a moderate intentionalist position, the material that follows it shows its separation of meaning from psychological states of the historical author to be much more closely in line with anti-intentionalism.

11. Ibid., p. 216.

12. Ibid., p. 220. Hirsch overstates the problem here. Surely authors of simple texts, which encompass most of the texts people write, have a pretty good idea about what they were thinking. So do the readers of those texts. The surfaces of the texts themselves likely provide adequate clues as long as we limit ourselves to the conscious thoughts of the authors.

13. Ibid., p. 218.

14. Ibid., p. 219. No scare quotes appear around "intention" here, but there is also no clue given why they appeared earlier.

15. Ibid., p. 221; emphasis mine.

16. Ibid., p. 222. This is Hirsch's only list of examples, and the reader is left to wonder whether metaphor or satirical essay or ironic treatise would be encompassed within the "etc."

17. Ibid., p. 225. See Chapter 1, p. 18.

18. Paul Ziff, "What Is Said," in *Semantics of Natural Language*, ed. Donald Davidson and Gilbert Harman (Dordrecht: Reidel, 1972), pp. 712–13, and quoted in P. D. Juhl, *Interpretation: An Essay in the Philosophy of Literary Criticism* (Princeton: Princeton University Press, 1980), p. 97.

19. Ibid., p. 713 and p. 96, respectively.

20. This example comes from J. A. Fodor and J. J. Katz, "The Structure of a Semantic Theory," in their book *The Structure of Language* (Englewood Cliffs, N.J.: Prentice Hall, 1964), p. 489.

21. The phrase "default assumptions" comes from Kittay, *Metaphor*, p. 55 and passim. I am indebted to this book for the more sophisticated conception of context and of how metaphor works that I hope is reflected in this section of my essay.

22. Juhl, *Interpretation*, p. 97.

23. Of course, I am not denying here that contextual meaning provides evidence of actual intent. I claim only that the potential of context to disambiguate does not *entail* actual intent to do so (thus intent is not necessary for contextual meaning) nor does the actual intent to do so entail meaning (thus intent is not sufficient either) even in cases of apparently ambiguous expressions. There is no inconsistency here. On the contrary, the evidentiary principle I do accept (and that seems so generally unexceptionable) seems to militate against the entailment claim: should not a contextually ambiguous meaning serve as evidence of the intention to be ambiguous? It seems that one might have to relinquish the evidentiary principle in cases of apparent ambiguity. For if actual intent is both necessary and sufficient to ground any disambiguation, then the role of this sort of public evidence becomes obscure at the least.

24. Ibid., p. 99; emphasis mine.

25. Nehamas, among others, brings up this contrast. See Alexander Nehamas, "The Postulated Author: Critical Monism as a Regulative Ideal," *Critical Inquiry* 8 (1981).

26. Richard Wollheim, "Criticism as Retrieval," in Richard Wollheim, *Art and Its Objects*, 2nd ed. (Cambridge: Cambridge University Press, 1980), pp. 190–91.

27. Jonathan Culler, "Issues in Contemporary American Critical Debate," in *American Criticism in the Post-Structuralist Age*, ed. Ira Konigsberg (Ann Arbor: University of Michigan Press, 1981).

28. Hirsch, *Validity in Interpretation*, p. 236.

29. This talk of a hypothetical author, distinct from the actual author, with hypothetical intentions is certainly not new. It has appeared previously in one guise or another in my own work as well as the writings of Kendall Walton, Alexander Nehamas, and Wayne Booth, variously labeled "ideal author," "apparent artist," "postulated author," and "implied author." See Kendall Walton, "Style and the Products and Processes of Art," in *The Concept of Style*, ed. Berel Lang (Philadelphia: University of Pennsylvania Press, 1979); Nehamas, "The Postulated Author"; Booth, *The Rhetoric of Fiction* (Chicago: University of Chicago Press, 1961); and Daniel O. Nathan, "Irony and the Artist's Intention," *British Journal of Aesthetics* (1982).

12

Allusions and Intentions

GÖRAN HERMERÉN

I

UNDER WHAT CONDITIONS SHALL we say that a literary text or a work of art contains an allusion to another text or artwork or that a particular allusion succeeds or is understood? These are the main questions I discuss in this essay. Before proposing an analysis of allusions, however, in a more informal and intuitive way I discuss allusions and some related notions and call attention to some demarcation problems, which I hope pave the way for the subsequent discussions.

II

Erwin Panofsky, in his book on Dürer, writes as follows about the horse in Dürer's famous engraving *Knight, Death and Devil*:

> The horse, on the other hand, is patterned after one (or more) of Leonardo's studies for the monument of Francesco Sforza. Its proportions are remodeled according to a canon of Dürer's own invention . . . , but its gait retains more of the Italian rhythm than is the case in the *Small Horse* of 1505 or the drawing *Death on Horseback* of the same year.[1]

Thus we can say that Dürer *adapted* Leonardo's studies for his own purposes or that he used these studies as his model. But does it follow that he also alluded to these studies? If not, why not?

First, we have to take into account the possibility that there are unclear borderline cases between allusions and adaptations. Besides, the evidence required to settle the issue whether a particular motif is an allusion or an adaptation may not always be available. Usage may also vary between art historians belonging to different theoretical camps and traditions. But let us concentrate on the typical cases and on the center of these concepts rather than on their periphery.

For simplicity, let us compare "X is an allusion to Y" to "X is an adaptation of Y." In both cases there is a certain minimal resemblance—or systematic difference—between X and Y, which is impossible to specify a priori in general terms but which I return to later. Moreover, in both cases the person who created X must have been familiar with Y before he created X. The difference seems to be that allusions are always intentional, whereas adaptations do not have to be intended in the same sense: the artist who created X may not be aware of the fact that he used Y as a model or a starting point.

Moreover, and perhaps more important, as far as adaptations are concerned, it is not necessary to be aware of the fact that the artist has adapted Y, or some part of it, to be able to understand his work richly and fully. But this is essential at least as far as successful allusions are concerned. Those who miss the allusion miss an important aspect of the meaning or point of the work in question.

Why "successful"? The meaning-expanding function of allusions noted earlier characterizes successful allusions, and it may be (although this is an empirical hypothesis) that most allusions *are* successful and thus help to enrich the meaning of the work. But I would hesitate to build this clause into the definition of the concept of allusion for the simple reason that I do not want by definitional fiat to legislate that all allusions are good ones.

To put it differently, though the observations made earlier are relevant in this context, we must leave the possibility open that there are works of art that are overdone or oversaturated with allusions. A work can be spoiled if the author tries to squeeze too many allusions into it. (And literary critics can spend too much time hunting allusions!) Thus it is important to distinguish between a discussion of the definition of the concept and an analysis of how typical or successful allusions function.

III

The notion of allusion is sometimes defined in terms of the notion of reference. For example, in the *Oxford English Dictionary* allusion is defined as "implied, implicit, indirect, or hidden reference." A similar definition has also fairly recently been endorsed by Harold Bloom.[2] Since definitions of this kind have lexicographical support and have been suggested by distinguished critics and scholars, they deserve to be discussed in this context.

The key problem here is the notion of reference. It is defined as follows by Michael Wheeler: "A *reference* is a word, phrase or passage which directs the attention to an adopted text but which does not share stylistic similarities with it."[3] In discussions of references it is helpful to distinguish between (1) the referring expression, (2) what it refers to, and (3) the relations between the expression and whatever it refers to. Wheeler's definition concentrates on (1) and (3), but his definition raises some important problems.

First, it may be argued that this definition is too unprecise in one important respect. Wheeler does not in his definition specify whose attention is directed toward the adopted text. Surely it cannot be enough—for X to refer to Y—that there is one person whose attention is directed to Y when he reads X. Besides, the reactions of all readers are not, as it were, equally relevant; they may be more or less idiosyncratic. Additional restrictions are required to rule out irrelevant reactions.

Second, this definition leads to curious results if it is combined with Wheeler's idea that there are two kinds of allusions: quotations and references. The expression "the author of Waverly" refers to Sir Walter Scott; it does not allude to Scott. Analogously, the words: "So we beat on, boats against the current, borne back ceaselessly into the past" are a quotation of the last sentence of Scott Fitzgerald's *The Great Gatsby*, not an allusion to that sentence.

It would help, of course, to distinguish between "marked" and "unmarked" quotations in the way Wheeler does, and between more or less complete quotations. Nevertheless, it is too strong to say, as Wheeler does, that allusion "is the generic term for quotations and references and for the act of quoting or referring."[4] But if "quotation" and "quoting" are replaced by "unmarked and more or less complete quotations" (and "unmarked and more or less complete quoting," respectively), his thesis becomes less open to criticism.

Third, it is easy to trade in a misleading way on more well-established and well-defined senses of "reference" that are of little relevance here, such as, "an expression refers to something if and only if there is a code or convention according to which the expression stands for that thing." Combined with the quotations above ("is the generic term"), this definition seems to be both too wide and too narrow in this context. It *includes* examples of symbolism, which ought to be excluded; and it *excludes* cases that ought to be included, where an author alludes to, for example, Greek ideals by alleged Greek quotations that he has made up himself.

In the latter case there cannot be a convention of the requisite sort, since the expression is presented for the first time in the work in question, and in the former case the distinction between allusion and symbolism is blurred.

IV

The Swedish literary historian Gunnar Tidestrom has argued that Milton was one of several important points of departure for the Nobel Prize winner Harry Martinsson's remarkable poem *Aniara*.[5] In particular, Tidestrom suggests that there is an echo in this poem of such lines in *Paradise Lost* as "the . . . Chrystall wall of Heav'n" (6. 860) and "Heav'n opn'd wide / Her ever during Gates . . . / On golden Hinges moving" (7. 205). Did Martinsson intend to make us think of these lines when he wrote (freely translated), "The solar system closed its gates of the purest crystal"? How do we know? Is this an example of a parallel, of an adaptation, or of an allusion? How does it differ from an allusion in a scientific context?

Such concepts as allusion, parody, travesty, adaptation, quotation, reminiscence, echo, and plagiarism (1) are all vague and (2) are used in different ways by different writers. But (3) only a rough outline is necessary for my limited purpose. I want to stress that (4) no claim is made to describe the usage of any particular writer or group of artists with precision, and (5) what I intend to do is only to make explicit how I am going to use some of these terms. Further (6) I claim that my proposal represents a fruitful way of defining the concept and (7) that this proposed definition accords fairly well with what is at least one standard usage of a considerable number of critics and writers.

In view of this, it becomes important to make clear the nature of the problems we are discussing and to distinguish between questions such as these:

1. How is the term "allusion," as a matter of fact, used by certain critics?
2. What is the best or most fruitful definition of that concept, given the interests and problems of scholars?
3. What is worth inquiring about? Is the author more interesting than the text or the reader?
4. What can be proved? Can we find out what the artist intended?

Here I concentrate on the second question, but I occasionally, though briefly, touch on all these issues.

The way the concept is defined is bound to have important consequences for what are counted as examples of allusions, for what arguments are relevant to support or to counter hypotheses about allusions, for what methods should be used in studies of allusions, and so forth.

For example, if the notion of allusion is defined in terms of the author's intentions, historical and biographical methods will be relevant. If, however, the notion of allusion is defined in terms of the associations readers make when they study the text in question, different methods will have to be used. If, finally, the notion of allusion is defined in terms of the reaction of "ideal" readers, a normative element is inevitably introduced, since these readers will define the "proper" way of understanding the text in question.

Moreover, the definition chosen will also have important consequences for what are to be regarded as failures. Under what conditions shall we say that an author tried but failed to allude to something in a literary text?

V

It would be desirable to have a clear idea of the difference between allusions in artistic contexts (e.g., poems, paintings) and allusions in ordinary life and in scientific reports, where one author may allude to a discovery made by another, use a title to allude to the title of another work,[6] and so on. But this distinction turns out to be elusive and difficult to pin down.

For instance, is a particular aesthetic intention of the author required in artistic contexts? Or a particular aesthetic response by the reader? Or something else? This is not easy to say, and it raises a number of more general questions about the distinctions between art and nonart, between the aesthetic and the nonaesthetic. In this context it suffices to say that the universe of discourse is confined to works of art in various art forms and genres as well as to artists, poets, playwrights, and so on, and that normal input and output conditions in the contemporary art world obtain.

These conditions may be specified by describing the standard conditions under which works of art are created, studied, and appreciated in our culture, in addition to such obvious requirements as that both artist and beholder, and both author and reader, have no physical impediments that make painting, writing, reading, and viewing works of art or literature impossible.[7]

These requirements can be supplemented in various ways. For example, for literature, Nicholas Wolterstorff has suggested the following illuminating and concise description:

> The fictive stance consists of presenting, or offering for consideration, certain states of affairs—for us to reflect on, to ponder over, to explore the implications of, to conduct strandwise extrapolation on. And he does this for our edification, for our delight, for our illumination, for our cathartic cleansing, and more besides.[8]

Similar can be said, *mutatis mutandis*, for the visual arts. A more detailed description of these input and output conditions would no doubt provide us with an opportunity to distinguish more precisely between literary allusions and allusions in ordinary language or scientific contexts. But to pursue this topic further would carry us too far afield. What is needed is neither more nor less than a full-fledged theory of literature and literary discourse, and similarly for the visual arts.

Thus the complications are many and obvious. They include that input and output conditions may vary from culture to culture and from time to time. It is possible that the analysis to be suggested here will hold also for allusions in works created in other cultures than our own, but I think it best to leave this open. It is an empirical question whether allusions in the sense outlined here occur only in (or also outside of) our contemporary Western art world.

VI

What are the formal features of the concept of allusion? It is clearly asymmetric—if X alludes to Y, Y does not allude to X. Transitivity is more difficult, however. If X alludes to Y, and Y alludes to Z, does X allude to Z? It may, but it does not have to. The author's depth of intention may vary from case to case. My intuitive guess, however, would be that such transitive allusions are rare.

Moreover, can an author or an artist allude to his own earlier works? The answer seems clearly to be yes. This kind of allusion may also be rare, but there is no reason to legislate against it on conceptual grounds. If a painter like Picasso can make variations and paraphrases of his own earlier works, it is difficult to see why it should be logically impossible for someone to allude to his or her own works.

Finally, "allude" is a one–many relation in the sense that one motif or string of words may allude to several things; and it is a many–one relation in the sense that one and the same thing can be alluded to in several different ways.

Within these formal constraints, however, a number of definitions can be worked out, as we see shortly. These definitions should, it appears, be compatible with the following statements:

1. It is possible that an author intended to allude to something but failed.
2. It is possible that a work can contain an allusion even if nobody discovered the allusion.
3. It is possible that a work can contain an allusion even if nobody read that text.

Finally, it will be desirable to keep the clauses in the definitions to be proposed as descriptive as possible so that the question whether they are satisfied in a particular case can be settled by people with different literary tastes and conflicting political opinions. Thus, I do not take for granted that allusions by definition are always a good thing.

There may be particular problems with music when it comes to allusions. The kind of intentionalistic and causal concept that I propose may appear to be more fruitful in interpretations and explanations of literature and the visual arts than in music. For the time being, therefore, I leave open the question whether this kind of analysis can also be applied to music.

VII

Before I go into further details, I would like to outline four different approaches or analyses. Each of them may contain some grain of truth, but each of them also has its own peculiar weakness. To save space, and to facilitate a comparison between the approaches, let us adopt the following conventions:

> X and Y are artworks.
> X precedes Y.
> A and B are artists (authors, . . .).
> X was created by A and Y by B.

1. *An intentionalist approach.* Y alludes to X (or B alludes to X), if and only if B by writing Y intended to make those who contemplate Y think of X.

A definition of this kind, such as has been proposed, for example, by Henri Morier—"A rhetorical figure consisting of saying one thing with the intention of making the reader understand something else by it"[9]—seems too wide, since it covers other stylistic figures as well, for example, irony, and parody.

But apart from objections of that kind, the general weakness of this analysis is that the role of the author's (or artist's) intention appears to be overemphasized; the notion of intention is made to carry a heavy burden. How do we find out what the artist intended? Is he willing to tell us? And can we trust what he tells us? Since there are no restrictions built into the definition, a work of art can apparently allude to anything, and we cannot say that an artist intended to allude to something but failed to do so. Thus the crucial difference between success and failure becomes difficult to explain on this analysis.

2. *The internalist approach.* Y alludes to X (or B alludes to X), if and only if the internal or intrinsic properties of X and Y resemble each other.

The main weakness of this analysis is that any two works of art resembling each other as far as their internal or intrinsic properties are concerned will necessarily allude to each other. This will be so even if the two artists were not familiar with the existence of each other, let alone with each other's works, which certainly seems counterintuitive.

Nor does this analysis account for the direction of allusion: why should Y be said to allude to X rather than the other way around on this account?

3. *The conventionalist approach.* Y alludes to X (or B alludes to X), if and only if Y includes a reference to X.

Some of the problems raised by this analysis have already been discussed.[10] Here I call attention to some further difficulties and elaborate on the points made earlier. As John Searle has pointed out, it is characteristic of referring expressions "that their utterance serves to pick out or identify one 'object' or 'entity' or 'particular' apart from other objects, about which the speaker then goes on to say something, or ask some question."[11]

Allusions differ from referring expressions in the last respect, among others. When an author, for example, alludes to another text, it is not to name or describe it, nor is it to say anything about it or to ask some question about it. Instead, his intention is to enrich the meaning and structure of the present text by alluding to the former (the same holds, *mutatis mutandis*, for the visual arts).

For example, a writer may try to achieve a comical effect or a dialectical tension in the contents of his present text by alluding to similar phrases with a different content, or he may want to make the structure more complex and intriguing by alluding to phrases with similar contents but different form. Whether he will succeed or not in achieving this enrichment or expansion of meaning is, of course, another matter.

Another theoretical difficulty, related to this one, can be stated as follows. Gareth Evans has rightly suggested that the semantic relation of reference between singular terms and objects in the world "is empirically anchored by its connection with the concept of truth."[12] Thus Evans simultaneously and implicitly defines reference and satisfaction in terms of truth.

But it is hard to see how all of this can be applied to allusion. The reason for these difficulties has to do with the point made in the previous paragraph. The author does not allude to another text in order to say something about it or to ask some question about it. The point is not to assert something but to present something for our consideration and aesthetic attention. Hence the question of truth does not arise, at least not in the same way as in standard cases of reference (descriptions, proper names, possessive pronouns followed by a noun, etc.).

Thus, to sum up, the notion of reference is, first, far from clear.[13] Second, the analysis proposed seems to be at odds with ordinary usage: "London" refers to London; it does not allude to London. Third, the analysis blurs the distinction between symbolism and allusion. Fourth, there is also a danger of circularity, if (1) "reference" is qualified by inserting "oblique" or "indirect" in front of reference, as the OED definition of "allusion" suggests, and (2) "oblique or indirect reference" then is explained as the kind of reference that characterizes allusion. To avoid such dangers, "indirect reference" needs to be explained in a way that does not presuppose a prior understanding of "allusion."

4. *The effect approach.* Y alludes to X (or B alludes to X), if and only if beholders contemplating or reading Y as a matter of fact make associations with X.

For example, such an analysis has been proposed by Emile Littré: "A rhetorical figure consisting of saying one thing that makes the reader think of another."[14]

The main weakness of this analysis is that anything any beholder may come to think of, however idiosyncratic, is considered to be of equal importance. Given our ordinary intuitions about allusions, and the way this term has come to be used in criticism, I think it can be argued that this analysis is both too wide and too narrow.

5. *Combinations.* Perhaps the weaknesses of each of the analyses considered separately can be eliminated or reduced if they are combined with each other in one way or another? I have elsewhere suggested an analysis in terms of a combination of some of these approaches.[15] The idea there is simply that "allusion" can be defined with the help of the following clauses:

1. The artist intended to make beholders think of the earlier work by giving his work certain features.
2. As a matter of fact, beholders contemplating his work make associations with that earlier work.
3. These beholders recognize that this is what the artist (among other things) intended to achieve.

Stephanie Ross has discussed this account and suggested a slightly different one, since she finds my last clause—and perhaps also the second one— "too strict."[16] She prefers to combine some of the other approaches mentioned in this section and suggests that one work of art alludes to another (if and?), only if (1) the artist intended to refer to the earlier work, and (2) incorporated into his work an indirect reference to the earlier work. What is new in her analysis is the second clause. But this clause raises some of the problems already mentioned.

For example, what are the criteria of direct and indirect reference? When Lichtenstein alluded to the works of some other artists (an example Ross uses to illustrate what she has in mind), there did not—either before or after Lichtenstein's paintings were created—exist a convention that could serve as the basis of the reference; Lichtenstein's paintings were the first of their kind. So what is meant by "indirect reference"?

If what is meant is only that the artist has created a work with certain features (minimal resemblances, systematic differences, etc.) in order to force readers to make associations with the earlier work, and it is because of these features that those who study the later work make associations with the earlier one, then the differences between our analyses may seem to be very slight.

VIII

For now I would like to stick to some of the basic ideas of my earlier analysis. But I would also like to improve it by making some changes, as well as by making some ideas explicit that were not explicit in my earlier treatment of this problem. Thus I propose to replace the three clauses mentioned earlier with the following intuitive idea, which I elaborate on later, assuming, as before, that normal input and output conditions obtain, that X and Y are works of art, that A and B are artists (authors), that A created X and B created Y, and X precedes Y.

The intuitive idea, given the background outlined earlier, can be stated roughly as follows. To say that an artist or writer alludes to another work of art in one of his own works is to say or imply that he intends those who look at his work to recall the other work and therefore creates his work with features reminiscent of the other work; and because his work has these features, beholders will (or would, if they studied the work under standard conditions) come to think of the earlier work; furthermore, they will recognize that this is what the artist, among other things, wanted them to do.

In this section, then, I propose a more careful and detailed analysis, obviously inspired by Searle, though the differences between my analysis and his analyses of speech-acts like promising and referring should be conspicuous enough.

To begin with, whatever is alluded to must exist (at least in the sense outlined by W. V. Quine: to be is to be the value of a variable).[17] This first necessary condition can be stated as follows:

1. *The existence requirement.* There exists some text (work of art) or part of such a text (work) Y such that the artist or author B is able to supplement his work with an identifying description of (the relevant part of) Y.

An alternative can be obtained by replacing "text (work of art)" with "thought, expressed in a text (work of art)." But I take (1) to be the canonical version of the existence requirement.

Then several intentional clauses are necessary:

2. *The first-order intention requirement.* B intends those who read or look at some part (phrase, motif) of Y in its context to think of the earlier work X.

3. *The second-order intention requirement.* B wants them to recognize that this, among other things, is what he intended.

4. *The intended recognition requirement.* B wants this recognition to be achieved by means of their familiarity with (the style, form, structure, function, meaning, aesthetic, and other features of) X and Y, as well as with the genres and traditions to which they belong.

These clauses will, of course, be objectionable to those to take the hard anti-intentionalist line advocated by Monroe Beardsley and W. K. Wimsatt in their classical essay.[18] But, as we see later, whether these requirements can survive a confrontation with the arguments in that essay depends both on how intentions are construed and on some normative assumptions.

The clause that follows enables us to distinguish between alluding, for example, to a text and calling attention to it in some other way, for example, by quoting or describing it:

5. *The negative requirement.* X and Y are not—entirely or to a considerable extent—identical, one of them is not a proper name of the other, or an instance of the other, nor does one of them describe the other, nor are they synonymous.

This requirement can perhaps be illustrated by the following example: "tube be or not tube be" (an advertisement for the London underground) alludes to (and paraphrases)—like "to see or not to see" (an advertisement for the arrangement center of the hydrofoil company in Copenhagen) or "two beer or not to beer"—Hamlet's famous words in Shakespeare's play: "to be or not to be—that is the question."

These examples all satisfy requirement (5). There is no convention according to which one of these phrases stand for the other. Nor do the rules governing the meaning of the phrases or motifs in question decide the issue here (as in many other kinds of speech-acts). The latter expression is not conventionally associated with the former. It is not identical with it nor does it describe it nor is it a name of it.

The form and structure of the phrases is more important than the meaning of the expressions, as the examples show. But I do not want to say that meanings are altogether irrelevant. If "tube" succeeded by "be" means something different than "tube" preceded by "not"—very unlikely, but not logically impossible—then it would perhaps have been difficult for later expressions to allude to the earlier ones.

The expression "considerable" introduces an element of vagueness in the requirement that is hard to escape. To say that no parts of X and Y must be identical would be too strict, since that would block the possibility that X is an allusion to Y, if and when they have one word in common, like "not" or "to." But if they are identical to a considerable extent, we would not say that one of these expressions alludes to the other but that it is a quotation, perhaps unmarked, of the other.

The fact that the artist (author) has the requisite first- and second-order intentions mentioned earlier is not sufficient. His or her intentions must also be made clear and communicated to the reader or beholder; the reader or beholder must get the point in the way indicated here:

6. *The selected-features requirement.* B creates, or has created, Y with the features F (concerning style, form, structure, function, meaning, aesthetic, and other features), which he believes will make those familiar with the genre and tradition to which X and Y belong think of the earlier work X.

This is a crucial requirement, and it is important to be as specific as possible about these features. But no definitive lists of such specific features should be hoped for. No such proposed list or classification of rhetorical devices will be complete. Poetic and artistic ingenuity will always find new ways of alluding to works of art. The relevant features typically include structural similarity, qualitative similarity, systematic contrasts, paraphrases, metonomy, and perhaps *pars pro toto* in the sense that a quotation or a reproduction of part of one of the works could be included in the other to make those who looked at the later work recall the earlier one.

An author may try to allude to something but fail. Maybe there are clues or signs of allusions in the text, but nobody recognizes them, or readers recognize them but misinterpret them. Thus the author as well as the readers may fail. The same holds, *mutatis mutandis*, for artists and beholders. This possibility has to be taken seriously. The explanation could simply be that the features F are too ambiguous or too vague.

Nevertheless, it is not enough that the previous two conditions, (4) and

(6), both happen to be satisfied; there has also to be a connection between them of a certain kind. We must assume that the fact that condition (6) is satisfied depends causally on the fact that the previous condition (4) is satisfied. Thus:

7. *The first causal requirement.* (6), because (4).

Adapting a point by Evans,[19] we might say that to understand an allusion, the speaker or beholder must discover the right (i.e., intended) interpretation, and must know that it is the right interpretation. Hence the following two conditions suggest themselves:

8. *The effect requirement.* Those who read or look at some part (phrase, motif) of Y will come to think of the earlier work X.

9. *The recognized-intention requirement.* Those who think of Y when they read or look at some part (phrase, motif) of Y, recognize that this, among other things, is what B intended.

An alternative to (8) with certain obvious advantages can be stated as follows:

8*. *The alternative effect requirement.* If well-informed readers or beholders were to study some part (phrase, motif) of Y in its context, they would come to think of the earlier work X.

The perception of similarities between two works of art depends on the background knowledge of the beholders, including their familiarity with artistic and critical practice, as well as on their interests and expectations. But their perception and classification is also affected by the way the works are classified as belonging to this or that genre, what tradition they are taken to exemplify, how they are interpreted, and so forth.

It could very well be that (6) is true and that, because of some idiosyncratic reaction, (8) only happens to be satisfied by chance. To be able to meet certain possible counterexamples, then, we have to make explicit the causal connection between (6) and (8):

10. *Second causal requirement.* (8), because (6).

Alternatively, if (8) is replaced by (8*):

10*. *Second causal requirement* (alternative). (8*) because (6).

IX

We cannot take for granted that "allude" and "allusion" are always by all critics and scholars in all contexts used consistently in the same way or in one sense only. But the requirements stated here provide us with the conceptual tools needed to make some distinctions, which I think may be useful. On the basis of these requirements, I propose the following definitions of three concepts of allusion, assuming, as before, that normal input and output conditions are satisfied:

> B alludes to X in *the weak sense*, if and only if the requirements (1) and (6) are satisfied.

> B alludes to X in *the standard sense*, if and only if the requirements (1) through (7) are all satisfied.

> B alludes to X in *the strong sense*, if and only if all requirements above are satisfied.

A possible objection to the first definition is that it would appear to conflate the concept of allusion with (at least part of) the evidence that could be used to support the claim that the author of a text has alluded to another text. For that reason, I think the second definition deserves to be called a definition of the standard sense.

In my view it is primarily persons that allude ("allusion" in a basic or primary sense), not texts. Texts can, however, be said to allude to other texts in a secondary or parasitic sense, or as a shorthand for a complex relation, involving agents in the sense indicated earlier. Thus the distinctions between the three senses of "allude" should not be conflated with the distinction between allusion in primary and secondary senses.

The definitions outlined here do not exclude that literary critics take an interest in what a text suggests to more or less well-educated readers, regardless of what the author intended. But this should not be called a study of allusions. That would be misleading, given the strong conceptual ties between "allusions" and "intentions" in critical language. Besides, several other terms might be used for such purposes, such as "intertexts," "intertextuality," "intertextual polyphony," "vertical context systems," to mention but a few that have recently been introduced into the theory of literature.

Nor do the definitions here exclude the possibility that "allusion" and the concepts mentioned can in varying degree be applied fruitfully to literature (and works of art) from different periods and belonging to different genres. Perhaps the concept of allusion applies more fruitfully to modern literature than to sixteenth- and seventeenth-century poetry, since contemporary readers were more homogeneous by education, interests, expectations, and so on, in those days than they are today. This, of course, is an empirical question.[20]

X

The difference between success and failure is crucial in this context. The concept of allusion must be defined in such a way that the possibilities of success as well as failure are not blocked on conceptual grounds.

It is tempting to say that surely it must be the work that matters and not the intentions of the author or the reactions of the readers. There can be subtle features in a work that most or all readers miss. It is also tempting, however, to say that the critical examination of the theories of the New Critics and their supporters have indicated clearly that it is very hard to distinguish sharply between "the work itself" and the intentions of the creator and the reactions of the beholder.

How does the reader know what the author intended? First, this depends on how intentions are construed. I assume that intentions are not to be construed as mental states but as dispositions, in the way suggested by Donald Davidson. Second, the key to the answer to the question posed earlier is the phrase "the features F" mentioned in requirement 6. But this phrase needs to be supplemented and clarified.

If intentions are not construed as mental states but as dispositions in a Davidsonian manner, and the work understood as a cultural artifact within a certain tradition, we are entitled to look for signs or indications of authorial intentions. Suppose an author says that he intends to favor analogies but never uses any available opportunity to do so. In that case we may rightly become skeptical about this claim about his intentions.

In many instances we have to admit that the reader does not know what the artist intended or that the allusion is there. The evidence may be ambiguous or inadequate, and in those instances a number of interpretations may all be more or less possible, plausible, convincing, and so forth, given the available evidence. The following factors may be particularly important to consider in such cases of uncertainty:

1. The literary competence of present-day readers (familiarity with tropes, literary traditions and works)
2. Assumptions about contemporary readers (their familiarity with tropes, etc.)
3. Historical and biographical assumptions about the author or artist of the work
4. Assumptions about the genre of the work in question (how it was classified by the author and by readers at different times)

5. Assumptions about the functions of literary criticism and the basic aims of interpretation

Can an author intend anything whatsoever? If a mental-state view of intentions is abandoned in favor of a dispositional view, the answer must be no. Thus, if restrictions are placed on what an author or artist meaningfully can intend, or on what intentions are relevant in this context, the ontological gap between the work and what the author intended is further narrowed down.

Moreover, at this point we may invoke the theory of action. If to create a work is to perform an action, and if intentions are required to distinguish between actions and behavior, the sharp distinction between work and intention is undermined. The assumption is then that literature (and other art forms) in our culture can be understood as cultural artifacts within a certain tradition; and the required restrictions on authors and readers can be based on an analysis of that more or less rule-governed practice.

Among other things, these practices (I am not assuming that there is only one—there may be underground literature and various kinds of cultures and subcultures within this institution) help to define the "contract" between writers and readers, to use Michael Wheeler's apt term.[21] They also help to settle disagreements as to what expectations are "proper."

To be sure, an author can say that he intended to make his readers think of the first lines of, say, the Bhagavad-Gita by writing the following line: "he looked at her, chuckled, and lit a cigarette." But if there is no identifiable similarity, contrast, hidden quotation, metonomy, etc., that connects this line with the beginning of the Bhagavad-Gita, his claim is not to be taken seriously.

But even so, there are, as I have suggested elsewhere,[22] behind the arguments for and against the relevance of the artist's or author's intentions, normative disagreements about which approaches to art and literature are fruitful and worthwhile, what the proper attitude to literature and art should be, what function art and literature ought to have in society, what the proper role of critics and the aims of interpretation are, and so on.

These normative assumptions and the values they are based on are rarely made explicit, and that is why the discussion for and against the intentional fallacy seems so inconclusive. It appears prima facie to be a theoretical dispute over logic and semantics, as the word "fallacy" suggests, but it is a disguised normative dispute.

XI

Why are allusions important? Why bother with them? To trace allusions is not to denigrate works of art or to detract from the originality of their creators. On the contrary, works of art are often enriched by their allusions to each other. In "Tradition and the Individual Talent," T. S. Eliot puts the point very well by saying that "the historical sense involves a perception, not only of the pastness of the past, but of its presence."[23]

NOTES

Acknowledgments: This is an abbreviated and considerably revised version of a paper presented at a meeting of the Pacific Division of the American Society for Aesthetics at Asilomar, California. Jay Bachrach commented on my paper on that occasion. I want to thank those who took part in the discussion, including Jay Bachrach, Noël Carroll, George Dickie, John Fisher, Peter Kivy, and Alan Tormey, for helpful comments.

1. Erwin Panofsky, *The Life and Art of Albrecht Dürer* (Princeton: Princeton University Press, 1967), p. 153.

2. Harold Bloom, *A Map of Misreading* (New York: Oxford University Press, 1975), p. 126.

3. Michael Wheeler, *The Art of Allusion in Victorian Fiction* (New York: Barnes and Noble, 1979), p. 3.

4. Ibid.

5. Gunnar Tidestrom, *Ombord pa Aniara* (Stockholm: Aldus, 1975), p. 62. Martinsson's original text reads: "solsystemet stangde / sitt grindvalv a den renaste kristall" (song 4).

6. As the title of Wittgenstein's *Tractatus Logico-Philosophicus* was chosen by G. E. Moore to allude to the title of one of Spinoza's treatises.

7. See John R. Searle, *Speech Acts* (Cambridge: Cambridge University Press, 1969), p. 57, for a discussion of a rather different set of input and output conditions, characterizing speech acts in ordinary language.

8. Nicholas Wolterstorff, *Works and Worlds of Art* (Oxford: Clarendon, 1980), p. 233.

9. Henri Morier, *Dictionaire de poetique et de rhetorique* (Paris: Press Universitaire de France, 1961), p. 4 (my translation).

10. See section III in this chapter.

11. See Searle, *Speech Acts*, p. 26.

12. Gareth Evans, *The Varieties of Reference* (New York: Oxford University Press; and Oxford: Clarendon, 1982.

13. For a penetrating discussion of its many complexities, see ibid.

14. Emile Littré, *Dictionaire de la langue française* (Paris: Librairie de L. Hachette, 1956), 1:339. (My translation.)

15. Göran Hermerén, *Influence in Art and Literature* (Princeton: Princeton University Press, 1975), pp. 75–77.

16. Stephanie Ross, "Art and Allusion," *Journal of Aesthetics and Art Criticism* 40, no. 1 (Fall 1981): 63–64.

17. Willard Van Orman Quine, *From a Logical Point of View* (Cambridge, Mass.: Harvard University Press, 1953), chap. 1.

18. W. K. Wimsatt, Jr., and Monroe C. Beardsley, "The Intentional Fallacy," first published in the *Sewanee Review* in 1946, reprinted in many anthologies on aesthetics, e.g., in Joseph Margolis, ed., *Philosophy Looks at the Arts: Contemporary Readings in Aesthetics*, 3rd ed. (Philadelphia: Temple University Press, 1987), p. 367ff.

19. Evans, *Varieties of Reference*, p. 310.

20. Cf. Claes Schaar, *The Full Voic'd Quire Below*, Lund Studies in English No. 60 (Lund: Gleerup, 1982), chap. 1.

21. Wheeler, *Art of Allusion*, p. 25.

22. Göran Hermerén, "Intention and Interpretation in Literary Criticism," *New Literary History* 7 (1975–76): 81.

23. T. S. Eliot, "Tradition and the Individual Talent," in *Twentieth-Century Literary Theory*, ed. Vassilis Lambropoulos and David Neal Miller (Albany: State University of New York Press, 1987).

Intention and Interpretation:
A Last Look

13

JERROLD LEVINSON

I

THE NEWLY WRITTEN essays in this book—by
Gary Iseminger, Noël Carroll, Colin Lyas, Michael Krausz, Richard Shusterman, Daniel Nathan, and Göran Hermerén—explore in many ways the issues
surrounding the interpretation of literary texts and the relation of that activity
to the existence and character of an author's intention in writing such texts. It
would not be possible, or particularly desirable, for me to try to summarize
in this space the twists and turns in the debate to which I have been asked to
make a final contribution. What I plan to do instead is briefly spell out what
I take to be the most defensible position on the central question in dispute
between intentionalists and anti-intentionalists and, having done so, engage
selectively with my predecessors in this volume in the light of the perspective
I have arrived at.

The view I defend is strictly neither intentionalism nor anti-intentionalism, as those are usually delineated, but what might be called *hypothetical* (or
constructive) *intentionalism*. Hypothetical intentionalism is logically and importantly different from the *actual* intentionalism that Iseminger (following
Hirsch) and Carroll are ultimately drawn to, while distinct from the sort of
anti-intentionalism of which Nathan (following Beardsley) is a proponent—
though approaching the latter taken at its most comprehensively contextual.[1]

A more detailed situating of my view at the outset in relation to my fellow
contributors in the latter half of this book is of use. My position, a contextualist hypothetical intentionalism, is perhaps closest to that of Nathan, but
it is framed in a way that allows greater rapprochement with the intentionalism favored by Iseminger and Carroll, and that shows what is right-headed
about the intuitions behind such a view. As it turns out, though I ultimately

favor contextualism in regard to *semantic* intentions (and semantic content), I support intentionalism, by contrast, in regard to *categorial*—including art making—intentions, ones that govern not what a work is to mean but how it is to be conceived, approached, classified on a fundamental level (see section VI.). The ontology I recommend is motivated similarly to Iseminger's in that I take a distinction between texts, as sequences of words in a language, and literary works, to be unavoidable, but my notion of the latter is differently worked out (see section VII). I am sympathetic both to Lyas's strictures against an overly mentalistic view of intentions, on which they are too easily detachable from works, and to Carroll's notion that the projecting of literary works has much in common with ordinary, nonliterary attempts at discourse, involving some of the same ends and rewards. But those sympathies fall short of a wholesale embrace of intentionalism regarding literary meaning. And though Hermerén's discussion of allusion makes a strong case for an unqualifiedly intentionalist view of at least that aspect of literary meaning, there is, I think, still room for an alternative hypothetical-intentionalist angle on allusion. Finally, my position is farthest from those of Krausz and Shusterman in that I hold work meaning to be both conceptually bound to at least projectible or attributable authorial meaning and in the ideal limit, unitary, and because I hold the literary work itself to have reasonably circumscribable boundaries and identity conditions.

II

When we ask ourselves, What do literary texts mean, and how do they embody such meaning as they have? I think there are only four models to choose from in answer. One is that such meaning is akin to word-sequence (e.g., sentence) meaning *simpliciter*. Another is that it is akin to the utterer's (author's) meaning on a given occasion. A third assimilates it to the utterance meaning generated on a given occasion in specific circumstances.[2] And a last model pictures it, most liberally, in terms of what may be called ludic meaning.[3]

Word-sequence meaning, roughly, is "dictionary" meaning—the meaning (or, usually, meanings) attachable to a sequence of words taken in the abstract in virtue of the operative syntactic and semantic (including connotative) rules of the specific, time-indexed, language in which those words are taken to occur. *Utterer's meaning* is the meaning an intentional agent (speaker, writer) has in mind or in view to convey by the use of a given verbal vehicle. *Utterance meaning*, in contrast, is the meaning that such a vehicle ends up conveying in its context of utterance—which context includes its being uttered by such-and-such agent. Ludic meaning, finally, comprises any meanings that can be attributed to either a brute text (a word sequence in a language), or a text-as-utterance, in virtue of interpretive play constrained by only the loosest requirements of plausibility, intelligibility, or interest.

Literary meaning cannot be equated simply with untethered word-sequence (or sentence) meaning, because it is crucial to the task of interpretation that the sentences of a literary text be presumed to issue from a single mind,[4] to have a purpose, and to be the vehicle of a specific act of communication, widely construed. We do not treat literary texts the way we would random collections of sentences, such as might be formed in the sands of a beach or spewed out by computer programs. The sentences that make up a literary work, on a primary level, are not merely a collection or assemblage but the body and substance of what we assume to be a unitary act of expression.

Equally clearly, though, literary meaning cannot be equated tout court with utterer's meaning, since that would dissolve the distinction between normal practical linguistic activity—where the paramount object is to communicate what the speaker or writer is thinking or wanting to say—and communication in a literary mode, where the text is held to have a certain amount of autonomy, to be something we interpret, to some extent, for its own sake, and thus not jettisonable in principle if we could get more directly at what the author had in mind to tell us. When a poet vouchsafes us, in plain language, what some enigmatic poem of his might mean, we do not react by then discarding the poem in favor of the offered precis. In ordinary verbal intercourse, what a person means takes precedence over, or overrides, what the person's language as uttered may end up meaning to a suitably grounded interlocutor; this seems not clearly so in the sphere of literary production. Finally, what I have labeled ludic meaning—which is akin to what Arthur Danto posits as the object or outcome of "deep" interpretation[5]—is an inappropriate candidate for at least the fundamental meaning of literary texts, if only because it presupposes such in order to get off the ground.

This leaves only utterance meaning—the meaning a linguistic vehicle has in a given context of presentation or projection, which context arguably includes, in addition to directly observable features of the act of utterance, something of the characteristics of the author who projects the text, something of the text's place in a surrounding oeuvre and culture, and possibly other elements as well. But what does such meaning amount to, for a typically complex work of literature? How do we get at it, and what are we aiming at in seeking it? To these questions, William Tolhurst has given an instructive answer:

> Utterance meaning is best understood as the intention which a member of the intended audience would be most justified in attributing to the author based on the knowledge and attitudes which he possesses in virtue of being a member of the intended audience. Thus utterance meaning is to be construed as that hypothesis of utterer's meaning which is most justified on the basis of those beliefs and attitudes which one possesses qua intended hearer or intended reader.[6]

> In understanding an utterance one constructs a hypothesis as to the intention which that utterance is best viewed as fulfilling.[7]

So utterance meaning is logically distinct from utterer's meaning and at the same time is necessarily related to it conceptually: we arrive at utterance meaning by aiming at utterer's meaning in the most comprehensive and informed manner we can muster as the utterance's intended recipients. Actual utterer's intention, then, is not what is determinative of the meaning of a literary offering (or other linguistic discourse) but such intention as optimally *hypothesized*, given all the resources available to us in the work's internal structure and the relevant surrounding context of creation, in all its legitimately invoked specificity.[8] The core of utterance meaning can be conceived of analytically as our best appropriately informed projection of author's intended meaning from our positions as intended interpreters.

The compromise between intentionalism and anti-intentionalism suggested by Tolhurst's approach is thus that the core of literary meaning, as with any piece of discourse publicly presented, is not the meaning (the many meanings) of the words and sentences taken in abstraction from the author, or precisely of necessity the meaning that the author actually intended to put across, but our best hypothetical attribution of such, formed from the position of intended audience. This latter will tend often (e.g., in successful cases) to coincide with actually intended meaning, but the principled distinction between them remains important, both for seeing clearly what we are about when we strive to pin down with some degree of definiteness the meanings—possibly manifold—of a work of literature and for the light it casts on interpretive disputes in difficult cases.

This is a good point to remark how the idea of a best hypothetical attribution of intention to an author is itself best understood. I have in mind that this be done with a certain duality. Principally, a "best" attribution is one that is epistemically best—that has the most likelihood of being correct, given the total evidence available to one in the position of ideal reader. But secondarily, a "best" attribution of intention to an author might involve, in accord with a principle of critical charity, choosing a construal that makes the work artistically better, where there is room for choice, so long as plausibly ascribed to the author given the full context of writing. In other words, if we can, in a given case, make the author out to have created a cleverer or more striking or more imaginative piece, without violating the image of his work as an artist that is underpinned by the total available textual and contextual evidence, we should perhaps do so. That is then our best projection of intent—"best" in two senses—as informed and sympathetic readers. This does not, however, license our viewing a work under an interpretation on which it comes off well artistically if such is not one we could on good grounds epistemically associate with or impute to the historical author as we in the main grasp him.

Such is the view of literary meaning that guides my reflections throughout this essay. Before proceeding, though, we must address certain problems inherent in Tolhurst's formulation of the view and consider ways of meeting them.

III

The notion of a literary work's meaning, and thus of correct interpretations of it, is properly tied, as I have said, not to actual—even successfully realized—artist's intent,[9] but to our best construction, given the evidence of the work and appropriately possessed background information, of the artist's intent to mean such and such for his or her intended audience. In short this is because literature making (and art making generally) is closely analogous to a speech-act, that is, it is an act of attempted communication in a broad sense, one of an oblique sort. As such, its products—works of literature—should have the sort of meaning that the products or upshots of speech-acts—utterances—centrally have, namely, utterance meaning. And it can further be argued, as Tolhurst has done, that utterance meaning is capturable through the idea of the best contextually informed hypothesis of what a speaker–writer is attempting to communicate to the intended audience.

Tolhurst's proposal, however, was criticized a few years back by Daniel Nathan, on a number of grounds.[10] I first address those I regard as less troubling and then proceed to the one that strikes me as more weighty. Nathan begins by criticizing Tolhurst for having too narrow a notion of word-sequence meaning, one that abstracts unnecessarily from the "connotative characteristics of words."[11] I think this charge is unfounded. Tolhurst could allow all the general, language-wide, time-bound connotations of words to be comprised in word-sequence meaning and yet insist that the full meaning of an utterance in many cases is still determinately different from what the denotative and connotative meanings of the words involved will themselves underwrite and is instead finally fixed by features of the individual, pragmatic context of utterance.

Nathan next holds that Tolhurst's examples, in particular his appeal to Swift's *A Modest Proposal*, depend essentially on ignoring the complete texts of which his extracts are a part. But surely the theoretical point that Tolhurst is after still holds—that there easily could be literary texts that in their completeness justified either an ironic or literal reading, leaving context of utterance aside, but that, given such context, we would judge as clearly either ironic or nonironic. Consider as an example the following, which also illustrates the dependence of utterance meaning on activated context and its independence of speaker's actual meaning.

Emilia is a graduate student in history, whose adviser, Basil Bushwacker, is leaving to take a post at another university. As is well-known among her friends, Emilia harbors ambivalent and resentful feelings toward her rather egoistic and unavailable mentor, though he, fortunately, is oblivious to this. She will, however, continue to require his support in external ways for the near future. After a farewell presentation in his honor, she writes him a short note, whose purpose is to ensure his continued goodwill toward her in the coming years:

> Dear Dr. Bushwacker:
>
> I was delighted to be present at your valedictory event last week; the tributes, although impressive, did not do you justice. We will all be immeasurably sad to lose you, and hope you will find many opportunities to visit the friends and colleagues you leave behind at Wunderwelt U.
>
> Sincerely,
> Emilia Edelweiss

The meaning of the above, as a letter sent (or to be sent) to Dr. B., is roughly one of appreciation, praise, and gentle entreaty. That is the utterance meaning of the text employed in that fashion—it is how Dr. B., or a similarly placed recipient of a letter from a seemingly respectful charge, would naturally take it. Label this Open Letter. On the other hand, as a text circulated (or to be circulated) among the student's circle of friends, with the knowledge they are privy to and rightly bring to bear, the phrases of the text acquire ironic content that they did not possess as part of a letter written openly to the salutee: the "tributes" do not do justice because insufficiently upbraiding, the "sadness" will be immeasurable because minuscule, and so on. The utterance meaning of this entity—label it Private Epistle—is quite different from that of Open Letter. It is one of blame, relief, and excoriation, for that is the authorial intention that would most naturally be projected on the words by Private Epistle's intended or appropriate audience. The texts—the complete texts—of both Open Letter and Private Epistle, however, are absolutely identical.[12]

I come now to Nathan's more worrisome charge. Tolhurst's proposal, he notes, is motivated by the desire to escape from strong intentionalism and its attendant problems, appealing instead only to a hypothesized author's intention. But Tolhurst has failed to notice that his proposal is still anchored in the author's actual intentions, through that intention, namely, that picks out a certain class or kind of reader as charged with the justifiable projection of intended authorial meaning definitive of work meaning. This reference to author's intention, claims Nathan, is both pernicious and ineliminable.

> Tolhurst allows cases where identifying the intended audience is not possible on public grounds, that is, the intended audience is different from the one the author is in fact addressing. . . . Further, given no limits to the narrowness of the intended audience, the author may be speaking a language the meaning of which is known only to himself and his family. . . . Tolhurst claims that the author is not in a privileged position vis-à-vis what he has written, that any member of that audience shares access to that meaning. But the determination of the intended audience is in principle a private matter, hence ultimately so is meaning.[13]

How should a hypothetical intentionalist respond to this? I think there are two options. One is to try to show that an author's intentional identification of an intended *audience* is significantly different from, and less troubling than, an author's intentional determination of the meaning of his text, as endorsed by full-fledged intentionalists. The other is to abandon the notion of an intended audience in favor of that of an *appropriate* audience, where this is not up to authorial determination.

Taking the first tack, we may note that the content of an audience-identifying intention is at least less problematic than the content of a semantic intention, especially one that would govern a complex work of literature as a whole. Dostoyevsky's intended audience in writing *The Brothers Karamazov*, if we could ascertain it, would be something on this order: competent readers of Russian, practiced in narrative fiction, aware of Russian history, familiar with Russian religious traditions, and so on. But Dostoyevsky's comprehensive meaning intention for The Brothers Karamazov has as object something hardly even imaginable apart from the novel itself and an exhaustive interpretation of it. Given this great difference in level between the two, then, it might seem to represent some progress that an analysis would, if not wholly avoiding intentions whose accessibility is in question, at least substitute for one whose scope is rather mind-boggling another that is more down to earth, in the role of anchoring a work's otherwise indeterminate meaning.

Note, next, that the nature of the audience intentionally targeted by an author is not, after all, particularly opaque to us. Consider my partial sketch of the audience at which The Brothers Karamazov was undoubtedly aimed. I consulted no oracle for it, neither did I study Dostoyevsky's diaries or the records left by his physician. I merely considered the novel itself, the demands of comprehension inherent in it, and the novel's context of creation (e.g., nineteenth-century Russia). This observation, however, shifts us toward the second option, that of an appropriate, as opposed to authorially intended, audience, in that it in effect invokes a hypothesization of the intended audience; that is, as that audience we would be most justified in assuming the author was aiming at—where "we" are now understood as just rational judgers possessed of all relevant contextual information. But if this is the pass to which we come, it might be better simply to drop reference to intended audiences, even reasonably hypothesizable intended audiences, and just speak of an audience that is an *appropriate* (or *ideal*) one for a given work, as judged by what it would appear to take to understand such a work properly. Let us pursue that idea.

I suggest we may be guided in identifying an appropriate audience for a given work, whose best projection of authorial intention will, as before, be constitutive of basic work meaning, by certain norms and conventions understood to define the sphere of literary production and reception.[14] Thus, an appropriate reader, for anything presented in the framework of literature, might be profiled generally as one versed in and cognizant of the tradition out of which the work arises, acquainted with the rest of the author's oeuvre, and perhaps familiar as well with the author's public literary and intellectual identity or persona. These are ground rules, as it were, of the literary enterprise, of the implicit contract between writer and reader, and it is not clear that an author can unilaterally abrogate such an understanding in favor of a specified audience whose information or capacities are significantly at variance with those involved in the profile just sketched.

Thus the best response to Nathan's criticism of the residual actual intentionalism in Tolhurst's conception, as embodied in the idea of the author's intended audience, may be to excise that residue and rely instead on a notion of an appropriate reader, where the meaning of that is filled in both by what can be seen, from the work itself, as incontrovertibly required for textual understanding—for example, competence in the language (including dialects) employed and knowledge of the references and allusions embedded in the text—and certain givens of the cultural "language game" in which writer and reader are bound, involving a presumption of shared knowledge of traditions, oeuvres, writerly identities, and the like.[15]

Finally, to emphasize the fact that the central meaning of a literary work should be thought of as akin to that of an utterance in a context, as opposed to either what a text means apart from its quite specific context of issuance or what the author–utterer intends to convey, but to foreground more clearly its written condition and more formal mode of presentation, we could coin the term *literance* for what literary works are. Poems, novels, short stories are literances—texts presented and projected in literary contexts, whose meaning, it is understood by both author and audience, will be a function of and con-. strained by—though in ways neither might clearly predict—the potentialities of the text per se together with the generative matrix provided by its issuing forth from individual A, with public persona B, at time C, against cultural background D, in light of predecessors E, in the shadow of contemporary events F, in relation to the remainder of A's artistic oeuvre G, and so on.

IV

As an illustration of the hypothetical-intentionalist position on interpretation I am advocating, consider Kafka's story, *A Country Doctor*. In this singular fiction the doctor of the title is awakened suddenly at night and summoned to the bedside of a boy suffering from a horrible wound, leaving his house servant at the mercy of his menacing groom. Though the boy is beyond help, the doctor is induced to attempt a curious cure, which involves getting into bed with the patient; the cure is, naturally, futile, and the doctor can scarcely extricate himself from the situation to return to what he fears are only the shambles of home and hearth he left behind just hours before. The relevant background information, or author-specific context of understanding, for an interpretation of this enigmatic narrative would surely include the following: Kafka regularly worked at night; Kafka thought of writing as "medicinal," "therapeutic," "a calling"; Kafka did not separate his writing and his life; Kafka was familiar with Freud's *Interpretation of Dreams*; and the content of Kafka's "A Hunger Artist," written five years after *A Country Doctor*, about a man who starves himself publicly as both an artistic performance and an admission that ordinary food had no appeal for him.

Given that as background, and given the intrinsic matter of the text, one might readily come up with this interpretation: A Country Doctor is a stylized dream report. Its content is basically the conflict between ordinary, sensual life, as represented by the servant girl Rose and the doctor's comfortable home, and one's calling: to heal, edify, spiritually succor. The doctor is in effect an artist, as is, more transparently, the Hunger Artist of Kafka's later tale. He is caught betwixt and between, naked and disoriented, as was Kafka between his literary and his domestic duties and desires. And the sick boy is like the doctor's younger self—through art (Arzt), one primarily tries to heal oneself, and only secondarily others.[16]

Thus our best informed-reader construction of what this specific writer, Kafka, was aiming to convey—was engaged in communicating—in writing A Country Doctor, may be something like the one just given. It makes sense to attribute such a meaning or content to the author as he is available to us—his appropriate, contextually sensitized, readers.

Still, we might just find out—from Kafka's secret diary, say, or a close informant, or even advanced aliens who were scanning Kafka's thought processes at the time—that Kafka's immediate, explicit intent in writing A Country Doctor was in fact to critique rural medical practices, to lampoon their typical unpreparedness and lack of materials, and to expose the deep-seated ignorance of the Czech peasantry. The text could just barely support such a meaning, much as "my car ran out of gas" can just manage to be the vehicle of a meaning in mind involving cabooses and clouds of chlorine.[17] Still, this would not supplant the interpretation just given as what the work, in a reader-accessible, Kafka-specific context, means. Our best construction, in a dual sense,[18] of what Kafka the writer is communicating in A Country Doctor would trump our discovery of what Kafka the person might oddly have been intending to mean on the occasion of penning the story. Admittedly the possibility of divergence between specific actual intent and best hypothesized intent given all appropriate reader data is a fairly thin one, but it is not therefore zero. And theoretically the difference is important for the philosophy of literary criticism.

V

We must briefly confront yet another problem for any hypothetical-intentionalist conception of literary meaning. Let us assume that the core meaning of a literary work is utterance meaning, that is, what a text says in an author-specific context of presentation to an appropriate, or suitably back-grounded, reader. Even if we agree that such meaning is given by a reader's best projection-in-context of what its author intended to mean, this still seems to leave aspects of utterance meaning—of what is said in a work—that go beyond that. There are, it can be fairly held, unenvisaged and not plausibly en-visageable implications, unforeseen and not plausibly foreseeable resonances, hidden significations, and the like, of a given text, which are yet properly comprised in literary meaning as just defined. These can seem part of what is conveyed literarily even while not reasonably attributable to the author as we have hypothesized him on the basis of our relevantly engaged background knowledge.

Three strategies suggest themselves for dealing with unintended mean-ings properly ascribed to a literary work, from the point of view of hypotheti-cal intentionalism. The first is to acknowledge them straightforwardly, but to qualify them as secondary; primary or central literary meaning, it could be held, must still be in line with reasonably projectible intention, even though secondary meanings, ascribable to a work once it is centrally interpreted, need not conform to that standard of projectibility. The second is to pro-pose a broader notion of the author's intended meaning, as hypothesizable by an appropriate reader, one that takes the existence of discoverable but unintended (and not reasonably ascribable) specific meanings in a literary utterance to be reasonably ascribable to the author as a class, or collectively, in virtue of his entry into the literary domain and implicit acceptance of a principle roughly licensing discerning of not explicitly intended, though possible-for-the-author[19] meanings that directly emerge from or are implied by a text centrally interpreted in line with reasonably projected intent, even when such meanings are not individually ascribable to the author as likely to have been meant.[20]

A third strategy, going beyond even a broadened notion of author's in-tended meaning, would be to appeal to what I have elsewhere called perspec-tives justified with respect to a given historically positioned work, although not accessible to its author (and therefore not plausibly projectible by him). Such perspectives might be considered justified, and thus the aspects of the work they revealed part of its literary content, if they can be shown to be rooted, abstractly or embryonically, in the concerns of the historically constructable author.[21]

Since my main concern in this essay is primary or central literary mean-ing, and since I think hypothetical intentionalism gives the best account of that, I will not attempt here definitively to settle this issue of aptly-ascribed-to-work-yet-improbably-ascribable-to-author unintended meanings, but will assume that a treatment along one or another of the lines just sketched would ultimately be adequate.

VI

Though I have distanced myself, following Tolhurst, from Hirschian intentionalism as an account of the meaning of literary works, I nevertheless hold certain actual intentions to bear ineliminably—though indirectly—on such meaning, and on the appreciation and evaluation of works of art generally. What is more, these intentions are ones that remain extrinsic to the works themselves, in the last analysis, in the sense that they are not guaranteed to be implicit in, and extractable from, a work or its observable manner of production, but reside instead in the stances and decisions of a work's maker, themselves perhaps embodied only in behavioral dispositions.

We need to distinguish two kinds of intentions relevant to the production and reception of art: *categorial* intentions, on the one hand, and *semantic* intentions, on the other. An author's intention to mean something in or by a text T (a semantic intention) is one thing, while an author's intention that T be classified, taken, approached in some specific or general way (a categorial intention) is quite another. Categorial intentions involve the maker's framing and positioning of his product vis-à-vis his projected audience; they involve the maker's conception of what he has produced and what it is for, on a rather basic level. The most general of categorial intentions of concern here would be the intention that something be regarded as literature (or art) at all, which obviously enjoins certain modes of approach as opposed to others.

A modern writer might intend a text to project an attitude of reverence to nature, and yet, due to the writer's clumsiness or his mistaken beliefs about the plant kingdom, it not do so; his semantic intention would have failed. But if the writer intends the text *as a poem*—as opposed to a short story, a dramatic monologue, a piece of calligraphic visual art, or a mere diary entry—then that intention is of a different sort and of a different order, and virtually cannot fail as long as the text in question at least allows of being taken, among other things, as a poem. And it is clear that whatever meaning the text-as-work ends up possessing, this will not be independent of whether it is properly construed as in one category or genre or medium rather than another, that is, whether it is to be read as a poem or scanned as a design or imagined as a passage to be acted, or treated—by averting our eyes—as a private confession with no envisioned relation to an audience whatsoever.[22] Semantic intentions, like that of our unfortunate writer, do not determine meaning, but categorial intentions, such as concern a literature maker's basic conception of what is made, do in general determine how a text is to be conceptualized and approached on a fundamental level and thus indirectly affect what it will resultingly say or express. Categorial intentions serve to orient a reader vis-à-vis a text at a very basic level, and without knowledge of them one is powerless even to begin to sort out its meanings, if any it has, by casting about for readings that could most reasonably be attributed to its contextually situated maker.

VII

In Chapter 8, Colin Lyas has persuasively sketched a neo-Wittgensteinian account of literary intentions, according to which they, like intentions in other spheres, are embodied in and through the concrete acts and situations they govern and are inseparable from them.[23] But I think there is a real question whether this account will do for all sorts of artistic intentions, and categorial intentions toward texts or objects susceptible of being conceptually regarded in various ways invoked above are a case in point. It is just not clear that all artistic intentions are displayed in or through a work itself, or even the act of producing it. Lyas's strictures seem to me to apply fairly vigorously to semantic intentions, but much less so to categorial ones; the former may not have embodiment in a work, so to speak, but only in the vicinity of it.[24]

But intentions are intentions, one might reply, whether semantic or categorial, so what ultimately is the difference? A rationale for treating them differently seems to be called for. In short, it is this. A categorial intention, unlike a semantic one, is literally part of making or creating the artwork in question. When a person finishes applying oils to a rectangular surface, or molding clay into a certain shape and firing it, or writing sentences consecutively in a notebook, or inscribing an index card with numbers and symbols, he has not yet made a painting, or a sculpture, or a poem, or a piece of conceptual art unless at some point in the process he decides and registers (at least to himself) that the first is a painting (not merely a hole covering), the second a sculpture (not just a doorstop), the third a poem (not a grocery list), and the fourth a conceptual piece (not the mere doodle it appears to be). Since categorial intentions are inherently part of artmaking, and since artists must be allowed to constitute their works as they wish, to make them whatever (within natural and logical limits) they want them to be, if not to make them mean, by fiat, whatever they want them to mean, categorial intentions must be recognized to have a status different from semantic ones.[25]

Contra Lyas, not all intentions relevant to appreciation of a work of literature can be effectively located internal to the work or its process of production. Those that relate to what the author is trying to communicate in writing a certain way perhaps can, by and large. But certainly not those that relate to how the text is to be taken as a whole, at a ground-floor level. Such intentions will generally reside outside the text per se or its observable conditions of genesis, since a given text, however produced, could be projected in several different ways—as fiction or as nonfiction, as an instance of traditional (i.e., purely verbal) or concrete (i.e., partly graphic) poetry—by the same author, and the fact of such projection might be grounded only in the hypothetical behavior of the author, or in ancillary indications (e.g., writers' diaries, program notes, interviews) beyond the boundaries of the work and the action of creating it, properly speaking.

Furthermore, even where semantic intentions are concerned, I think the intimacy that Lyas posits between them and the publically determinable meaning of texts is somewhat in excess of what is warranted. Even if an intention to mean such and such by a text may be more nearly analyzed in terms of the observed product and circumstances than an intention that a text be conceptualized or taken in a certain manner, there is still, I think, an irreducible psychological remainder to such intention not always inherent in the text's outward face and full context of presentation. In discussing utterances—and by implication, literances—Lyas rightly observes that part of the meaning of such is constituted by the force, or illocutionary thrust, of what is uttered. Going on to observe that a given utterance does not end up having a particular force in virtue of facts about the speaker's will, Lyas notes that this might suggest that "reference to intention is not required when we are dealing with questions about the force of an utterance." But, despite appearances, this is, he claims, not so:

> What is true is that whether or not an utterance has a clear force is not decided by asking the speaker what force he or she wanted it to have. For all that, force sometimes is made clear by the production of an utterance in a certain context. When it is made clear, then what is made clear is an intention on the part of the speaker to do something in speaking—for example, to give a warning, threat, or promise. Hence to refer to the force of an utterance is to refer to its

speaker's intention, even though what that force is need not be determined by asking the speaker what that intention was.[26]

The problem here is that utterer's meaning and utterance meaning are once again in danger of being collapsed into one another. When the force of an utterance is clear, from its lexical content, the context in which it issues, and any relevantly engaged information about the speaker as a public player in a given speech community, then that is an element of the utterance's meaning and that, as we have seen, can be identified with the most plausibly ascribed intention to the utterer to do such and such in speaking. But this is still not the same as the actual, concrete intention of the speaker, unless one is waxing verficationist, since this last may, even in such cases, reside in aspects of the situation outside those public indications that fix utterance meaning, and force in particular. So even though I might grant that a speaker's or writer's semantic intentions are often transparently evident in the meaningful utterance or literance that results, this still seems to me a matter of inference, however natural and automatic. There is always some possibility of divergence; the inference is always defeasible. The most plausibly ascribable intention in context from an audience's point of view may turn out to be mistaken.[27] Utterance meaning, in brief, is never constitutive of utterer's meaning, however good a guide it is to it in most circumstances.

VIII

Gary Iseminger, following Hirsch, has produced a clear and elegant argument that he has labelled, tentatively, "the intentional demonstration," that is, a demonstration that actual intentionalism in literary interpretation is correct.[28] Part of me would like to accede in this "demonstration" in that I concur with two of its three premises and agree with much of the argument's motivation, particularly the desire to distinguish texts (or, for clarity, "brute" texts) from literary works and the idea that what makes a text into a poem, and in part the poem that it is, is an intention resident outside the text as such. Unfortunately, I have come not to believe in its conclusion, namely, the coincidence of literary meaning and authorially intended meaning. The culprit, naturally, is the third premise, which holds that if just one of two opposed interpretations of the opening stanza from Gerard Manley Hopkins's "Henry Purcell," each of which is compatible with its brute text (word sequence in English circa 1880), is true, then the true one is the one that conforms to the meaning intended by Hopkins. The justification for this, of course, is that if the stanza's (and by extension, the poem's) meaning is to be determinate, so as at least to license either a given interpretive statement or its negation in regard to it, then such determinacy can only be reasonably supplied by the lines meaning what the poet actually intended them to mean in writing them. And it is by identifying the poem in part with actually willed or intended meanings that the poem can be distinguished from the brute text, which is potentially ingredient in other, distinct poetic works.

It will be no surprise at this point why I find this brief for premise 3 insufficiently compelling. The determinacy in question, I would maintain, can just as easily and reasonably come from an audience's best contextually informed hypothesis of authorial intention in a given passage, all things considered. So in the case at hand, in particular, if one takes into account Hopkins's unusual metrical and grammatical practices in other poems, his known religious views and sympathies (it is significant that, though born into the Anglican church, he converted to Catholicism in 1866 and subsequently entered the priesthood), his documented appreciation for Purcell's music, and the demands of coherence with the remainder of the poem, it turns out that the informed reader's best projection of what Hopkins was intending to convey in the opening stanza will make it determinately the case that the wish for past good fortune in spiritual matters, rather than anything exclusive of that, is what is expressed.[29] In addition to securing determinacy as represented by premise 2, such optimally hypothesized semantic intentions, together with concomitant actual categorial intentions, are more than enough to distinguish the poem from the text per se, and from other potential poems employing the same text, penned by poets other than Hopkins, or Hopkins himself at a different historical or cultural juncture, or even a more counterfactual Hopkins arrived at by altering aspects of the situation in which "Henry Purcell" was in fact indited.

Furthermore, not only is specific-context-based hypothetical intentionalism equally as efficacious in underpinning minimal determinacy of meaning and in constituting a poem from a mere text, but it seems to me to have two signal advantages over actual intentionalism in this matter. One is that it preserves the intuitive difference between what ends up being *said* (or conveyed) in a complex discourse situation, whether literary or nonliterary, and what some agent was *trying* (or aiming) *to say*, that is, what someone—not some work—meant.[30] The second, closely related, is that it acknowledges the special interests, and attendant constraints, of the practice or activity of *literary* communication, according to which works—provided they are interpreted with maximal attention to relevant author-specific context and thus really as the works of so and so—are ultimately more important than, and distinct from, the individuals who author them and those individuals' inner lives; works of literature thus retain, in the last analysis, a certain autonomy from the actual mental processes of their creators during composition, at least as far as resultant meaning is concerned. It is this small but crucial dimension of distinctness between agent's meaning and work's meaning—even when the latter is understood as roughly an optimal reader's best projection of the former from the text-in-full-context—which is obliterated by actual intentionalism, but safeguarded by the hypothetical variety.

It is interesting to note that, in principle, different literary works turn out to be ambiguous on hypothetical intentionalism [HI] than on actual intentionalism [AI], though it is not obvious that more turn out ambiguous on the former than the latter. Instances when there is no optimally projectible intention for a given passage, but when a clear authorial intention exists (though beyond the reach of an individual in ideal reader position) will be ambiguous on HI but unambiguous on AI, whereas instances when a contextually informed ideal reader can arrive at a best attributable intention, though no such clear authorial intention exists or existed, will be ambiguous on AI but unambiguous on HI. Of special note would be cases where there are two divergent though equally defensible projections, all things considered, of authorial intent, that is, two "good" projections possible, which would indicate a work with an inherently dual, or disjunctive, meaning. In such instances we see again that the meaning of a work according to HI can outstrip its meaning according to AI: let the author have in actuality only one of the two "optimally" projectible intentions just posited.

I now turn to the specific ontology that Iseminger recommends as part and parcel of the actual intentionalism he favors. This is an ontology, as noted, to which I am broadly sympathetic, taking its *raison d'être* as it does from the obvious nonidentity between literary works and the brute texts out of which, in a sense, they are composed. My sympathy, however, does not run to complete agreement, for two reasons. One is that I think there are some unintuitive consequences of Iseminger's particular proposal. The other is that I have my own previously developed and similarly motivated ontological proposal for type artworks, which I think answers better to the critical and experiential data.

Iseminger offers the following, which he labels the Revised Identity Thesis: "A (typical) literary work is a textually embodied conceptual structure, whose conceptual component is (identical to) the structure—compatible with its text—which its author intended (meant) in composing it."[31]

In other words, seeing clearly that brute texts (i.e., word sequences in a language) are not enough to individuate poems (i.e., works of literature with specific meanings and qualities rooted in their authors' identities and lifeworlds), Iseminger arrives at the plausible suggestion that a poem is the sum or complex of the text and the specific literary content of which it is the vehicle, that is, a set of thoughts or ideas. A literary work is in effect an ordered pair of a text (verbal structure) and a meaning (conceptual structure). Though there are, in an abstract way, texts without authors, there are no literary works without authors, for only by being used to carry a given meaning does a text become transformed into a work of literature.

My first qualm about this suggestion is perceptual. You can read a poem—that being a central mode of access to such—but can you read a conceptual structure, which constitutes part of the poem on Iseminger's proposal? Can you scan, recite, count the number of lines in, or grasp the rhyme scheme of a conceptual structure—even a textually embodied one? From being fundamentally a verbal object, a poem becomes on Iseminger's formula fundamentally a conceptual one—or at least as much a conceptual object as a verbal one. But we have just seen that this is a mistake. We must instead retain the idea that a poem is at base a structure of words, so that the fundamental activities proper to poems still make sense, while somehow acknowledging that the poem is not the brute text—the word-sequence simpliciter—out of all connection to the particular author and act of writing. My own preference is to regard a poem as a *text-as-indicated-in-a-context*, which as a result has a certain meaning or conceptual content without being such—even in part.[32] It acquires this content through its being indicated or projected by an author A with artistically relevant characteristics R in literary context C, not necessarily through what the writer intends it to mean. What determines the content it has—rather than is—is, again, the best hypothesis of authorial meaning arrivable at by audiences fully cognizant of A, C, and R.

My principal objection to Iseminger's proposal is thus its distorting the basic kind of thing a poem is. Here, though, is another objection. On Iseminger's proposal, a given individual on a given day could write two poems, in the same genre, by writing down the same eight-line text twice, alternating inscriptions of each sentence, but thinking (intending) different construals with each inscription, so yielding distinct conceptual structures. But this seems wildly implausible. If poems with identical texts are distinct, it must be differences in the context of generation, and thus appropriate later context of understanding, that differentiate them.[33] A difference in provenance or projection, not just fleeting authorial construal, must ground artistic difference among identical structures.

A person might be able to mean different things in ordinary discourse, by saying the same words over twice within the space of a few minutes, in virtue of his inner states during those utterings, but the nature of the literary "language game" does not, I would claim, allow for identical texts issuing from the same person at the same time to count as different in meaning—at least not in virtue of the writer's concurrent semantic intendings. It is instead by having a differential categorial intention, not by meaning or conceiving different things during penning, that the one text might (just barely) generate a different poem than the other. And for such subtly nuanced categorial intentions to be effective, even for the artist, the poem seemingly would have to avail himself of some internal individuating device, for example, different titles or different dates appended to the two texts.

One last objection, which cuts in the opposite direction from the preceding: on Iseminger's proposal, two people with different literary identities and backgrounds would yet write the same poem if they produced the same text and had the same meaning in mind. But there are reasons to think there would be artistic differences between such poems (e.g., in virtue of different relations, resonances, with other works of their respective authors), thus confounding the supposition of their identity.[34]

IX

This is a good juncture at which to observe that distinguishing between texts and literary works in the manner that I suggest pretty much douses—whereas that favored by Iseminger only fans the flames of—the problem that so concerns Michael Krausz (following Margolis), namely, that of the elusive identity of literary works, which seem to change as one goes from one interpretation of them to the next.[35] The poem, the object of interpretation on Krausz's conception, varies as interpretations vary. For example, with Wordsworth's familiar lyric, there is Bateson's "A Slumber," and then there is Brooks's "A Slumber." These objects of interpretation, not having what Krausz calls "Leibnizian self-identity," have yet sufficient overlap for critical purposes (e.g., comparison, mutual confrontation), what is then labeled "unicity."

But these are unnecessary complications, a product both of constructivist metaphysical inclinations and the decision, shared with Iseminger, to see a literary work on the level of ontology as partly its meaning, or content under an interpretation. This is to confuse a property, or aspect, of the thing with the thing itself. Instead, there is no difficulty whatsoever with saying that there is just one poem "A Slumber . . . , "Henry Purcell," etc.), though there are perhaps numerous interpretations or readings of it—as long as we recognize that the poem is not, of course, the brute text that it comprises, but rather that text poetically projected in a specific context anchored to a particular person, time, and place. That anchoring, together with the text's complete orthography, is enough to fix a literary work's identity for all critical intents and purposes, and so there is no need to bring meanings, conceptual complexes, or interpretive guises into it. A poem, as I suggest we ontologically construe it, will, to be sure, *generate* meanings and conceptual structures under interpretation, correct or incorrect, multiple or singular, but the poem itself is not to be *identified*, even partially, with such meanings, concepts, thoughts, or views.

There is one further issue on which I must stand with Iseminger, Nathan, Lyas, and Carroll, as against Krausz, who echoes Margolis: the question of the status and truth of (at least some) interpretive remarks. I think it incontrovertible that the ordinary construal of such remarks makes them out to be (1) statements about a work, which purport to give its meaning or point to its proper understanding, which statements (2) can be clearly true or false.[36] One way to firmly establish the second point, it seems to me, if the first be granted, is to focus on *negative* interpretive statements, ones that indicate content indirectly, by exclusion or denial of what patently does not belong to it. For example, "Hamlet does not hesitate because he is waiting to see if he has won the Danish National Lottery," "Antonioni's *Red Desert* fails to embody or project a cheerful, carefree view of life," "Stevens's *The Emperor of Ice Cream* is not about the frozen dessert industry." Surely no one, no matter what interpretive uncertainties he or she might have in mind, could question the truth of statements such as these, which, if not very adventurous, are most certainly interpretive.[37]

X

A main thrust of Noël Carroll's engaging essay[38] is to undercut opposition to intentionalism that derives from the belief that the context of literary discourse is significantly different from that of ordinary conversation so that the intentionalism that is an exceedingly natural perspective in the latter case is not appropriate in the former. I am in partial agreement with that thrust, since I would hold, with Carroll, that a rather more absolute disjunction between the two contexts than is warranted is a characteristic of a number of recent influential theories of literary meaning, for example, Beardsleyan "New Criticism" and Barthesian "death-of-author-ism." But, *contra* Carroll, I think there are residual differences between the contexts and the rules and procedures of decipherment that hold sway in them. One difference, it seems to me, between literary and conversational situations is that utterer's meaning is virtually *all important* in the latter, while the meaning of the vehicle itself, if opposed to the former, counts for virtually nothing. I agree that when an author proffers a text as literature to a literary audience, just as when he or she speaks to others in the ordinary setting, he or she is entering a public language game, a communicative arena, but suggest that it is one with different aims and understandings than apply in normal, one-on-one (or even many-on-many) conversational settings. Although in informative discourse we rightly look for intended meaning first, foremost, and hindmost, in literary art we are licensed, if I am right, to consider what meanings the verbal text before us, viewed in context, could be being used to convey and then to form, if we can, in accord with the practice of literary communication to which both author and reader have implicitly subscribed, our best hypothesis of what it is being used to convey, ultimately identifying that with the meaning of the work. What distinguishes our forming that hypothesis in regard to a literary work, as opposed to a piece of conversation, is that we do so for its own sake, the contextually embedded vehicle of meaning in literature being indispensable, not something to be bypassed in favor of more direct access to personal meaning when or if that is available.

So here I would agree with Shusterman,[39] as against Carroll, that literary and practical linguistic communication *are* to be distinguished: Carroll errs in denying or minimizing any difference in the operative conditions and criteria of the two. But I am very far from anchoring such distinctness, as Shusterman does, by ascribing historically unconstrained and reader-driven interpretability to the former. We may admit various modes of literary interpretation, answering to interests other than those of truth, expression, and communication, but still hold it possible to locate among them what I have called basic interpretation, and to characterize in a fairly stable manner what that must orient itself toward. Only in relation to the results of basic, author-and-history respecting, interpretation, can such further modes of interpretation have a proper foothold and warrant. Shusterman claims that even if textual meaning (what Iseminger and I would call work meaning) is, as Knapp and Michaels (and Hirsch and Juhl) insist, ineluctably intentional, there is no reason to think it must always be authors' intentions that are at issue.[40] Textual meaning is inseparable from intention, Shusterman allows, but perhaps readers' intentions are as relevant to determining, or contributing to, textual meaning as those of authors. This enfranchising of readers' intentions (purposes, perspectives), unconstrained by the goal of hypothetically reconstructing best authorial intention, is a good illustration of what I earlier labeled the ludic model of interpretation taken as paramount. By contrast, a virtue of hypothetical intentionalism stands out clearly, which is to mediate between a position, actual intentionalism, which gives just a little too much to authors as persons, and a ludic position such as that of Barthes or Derrida or Rorty or Shusterman, which gives altogether too much to readers and threatens to undermine the motivations of authors for upholding their end of the implicit literary contract.[41] Lest I be misunderstood, let me remark that I regard ludic interpretation, about which I have no more to say in this essay, as potentially an exciting and rewarding exercise in its own right, and a harmless one—as long as it does not displace the primary project of discerning fundamental, authorially anchored, if not authorially determined, literary meaning.

But to return to Carroll's essay, there is much I find congenial in it. Carroll rightly observes that, having tentatively accepted the basic relevance of authorial intention, one can avoid being driven back into anti-intentionalism by the problem of aberrant authorial pronouncements, for these need not be taken at face value: the finished work will often make incredible certain stated intents. And Carroll generally agrees with Lyas, sensibly enough, that the intentions most relevant to literary (or cinematic) works are ones that are largely evident in the works themselves, including both successful and failed intentions, and that these should not be conceived after the fashion of private mental episodes, but instead in neo-Wittgensteinian fashion, as fully embodied in behavior and its products.

It is the next step in the dialectic that worries me:

> Insofar as the intention is identified as the purposive structure of the work, this intention is the focus of our interest in and attention to the artwork . . . tracking the intention—the purposive structure of the work—is the very point of appreciation . . . the more attractive, neo-Wittgensteinian view of intention not only makes authorial intention relevant to the interpretation of artworks, but implies that in interpreting an artwork, we are attempting to determine the author's intentions.[42]

I am strongly inclined to concur with what is said here—but only if transposed into the key of hypothetical intentionalism, or if taken, charitably, as having a sense compatible with that already. The discernible purposive structure of the work can only be identified with the author's intention, I would say, if by this last one really means an optimal construction of authorial intention from the viewpoint of an ideal reader, imbued with the sorts of background information sketched earlier. For, Wittgenstein or no Wittgenstein, it is still possible for an author's semantic intentions in regard to a work, in whole or in part, not to be fully embodied in that work plus its ideal-reader accessible context of production.[43] And though it is true that "in interpreting an artwork we are attempting to determine the author's intentions," the (actual) author's intentions function here mainly as a heuristic goal, and success in this attempt is to be measured, not by correctly arriving at that actual intention, which may still, despite Lyas's and Carroll's confident internalism, be grounded in matters external to the total literary context, but by the process of constructing (projecting, hypothesizing) a most plausible authorial intention, in the light of both the text and the literature-germane circumstances of its issuance, having come to an end or achieved reflective equilibrium.

Perhaps Carroll's most striking example of an artwork whose correct interpretation putatively requires us to advert to the author's actual intentions, even though we can, by ignoring such intentions, arrive at an interpretation that makes the work more rewarding aesthetically, concerns a grade B (or C) science-fiction movie of 1959, Edward Wood's *Plan 9 from Outer Space*. Carroll claims that Wood's film, which contains narrative incoherence and editing discontinuities, is not properly seen as "boldly and provocatively transgressing Hollywood codes" (as *Village Voice* film critic J. Hoberman has suggested) because Wood did not have the intentions in filmmaking that avant-gardists of the 1970s or 1980s had, with whom Wood is being ranged by this suggestion. I certainly agree with Carroll in rejecting Hoberman's interpretation as a correct one—as opposed to a practical recommendation for dealing with schlock most enjoyably—but am not convinced that Wood's *actual* semantic intentions need be called to account. For can we not say that such expressive intent as Hoberman ascribes to Wood is simply not our best *hypothesis* of such intent, given all appropriate internal and external evidence (e.g., Wood's solid track record of earlier hack films)? Indeed, if we read him closely, this is precisely what Carroll does say:

> All the evidence indicates that Edward Wood did not have the same intentions to subvert the Hollywood style of filmmaking that contemporary avant-gardists have. Indeed, given the venue Wood trafficked in, it seems that the best hypothesis about his intentions is that he was attempting to imitate the Hollywood style of filmmaking in the cheapest way possible. Given what we know of Edward Wood and the B-film world in which he practiced his trade, it is implausible to attribute to him the intention of attempting to subvert the Hollywood codes of filmmaking.[44]

Thus, hypotheticized authorial (or, in this case, directorial) intent is perfectly adequate to handle the case of Wood's movie, that is, to avoid attributing avant-garde meaning and merit to it. Though we take aim at directorial intent, in our hypothetical construction of cinematic meaning, this doesn't entail that a director's actual semantic intent, whether plausibly hypothesizable or not, is determinant of such meaning.[45]

XI

Carroll musters other considerations, however, which he labels "ontological," in arguing against Barthes's and Beardsley's extreme anti-intentionalisms. Barthes claims that when language is divorced from normal communicative purposes and narrated "intransitively," as in literature, the author and his intentions immediately become irrelevant, and the reader is instead freed "to explore the text in all its intertextual associations."[46] Carroll's reply to this is astutely skeptical: "I am not sure that once language is used 'intransitively,' the author becomes irrelevant, since identifying such a use would appear to depend on fixing the author's intention to work in certain genres or forms, namely, those that function intransitively. That is, how will the interpreter know that the writing in question is of the right sort to be read in a writerly fashion without adverting to authorial intentions?"[47]

This is exactly on the mark, but the point to note is that the real authorial intentions, which it is crucial to get right here, are categorial intentions, not semantic (expressive, symbolic) ones.

In another of his observations in this vein Carroll says, in the light particularly of work in film, dance, and painting as well as literature, that since in art we are often interested in doings, we must also be interested in intentions, since an action is only the action it is in virtue of the intention that informs it. But I would suggest that where the "doings" in question are semantic, symbolic, or expressive (as opposed to ones of creating, framing, projecting), it is open to us to ascribe such "doings" to the work directly, and only indirectly to the artist, in virtue of his "doings"—his performance of actions—of that other sort. And that would mean that as far as art was concerned, our interest in what has been done would take us only so far as the actual categorial intentions of artists, allowing ideally hypothesizable semantic intentions sway in fixing what, if anything, has been meant.

This brings me, finally, to a suggestion Carroll makes in the course of his discussion of Beardsley's claim that literature always involves the representation of illocutionary actions, for example, stating, questioning, relating, discoursing, haranguing, and never the actual performance of such (e.g., by the author). After observing, fairly enough, that not all literature is, in the first instance, fictional, Carroll goes on to propose that there is no justification, even where literary fiction is concerned, for universally positing an implied speaker or narrator distinct from the author, thus insulating the stating, questioning, etc., that often seems to be going on from the actual individual whose blood, sweat, and tears appears to have gone into the book. Carroll makes his strongest case for this in connection with what might be labeled essayistic or didactic novels, such as Tolstoy's *War and Peace*, Mann's *Magic Mountain*, and Proust's *A la recherche de temps perdus*. He says, of the discursive portions of such novels, for example the discourse on whales in Melville's *Moby Dick*, that "though housed in fictions, where they undeniably perform a literary function, these are also essays whose authors produced them in order to make assertions. In interpreting these interludes, one needs to approach them as one would any other form of cognitive discourse."[48]

Though I recognize the motivation for wanting to connect the views expressed in literary works with the authors of those works, I think it cannot be done as easily as Carroll would like, even in the case of such quasi essays. This is because the "nonfiction" parts of an essentially fictional work must, on pain of incoherence, first be attributed to an implied speaker or narrator of the sort Beardsley (following Wayne Booth) invokes. I will try to explain why. The narrator of a novel is fundamentally someone whom we agree to pretend is telling us about people and events that we know are fictions. That is to say, we know that, by and large, the people of the narrator's "world" do not (really) exist and the events of that "world" did not (really) happen. The narrator is, therefore, a particular sort of fictional character himself, who is in "contact" with things out of our ken and who "believes" in things we do not; he or she cannot be taken to be a real individual expressing real beliefs. But the essayish portions of something like Melville's *Moby Dick* or Mann's *Magic Mountain* are understood to issue from the same persona, the same voice as is relating the narrative of (fictional) people and events; there are cross-references, allusions, similarities of style, explicit self-identifications, etc. These essayish portions must, then, be the direct utterances of the (fictional) narrator of the novel's (fictional) occurrences. They cannot, logically, be unmediated pronouncements of the real person of the author—Thomas Mann, say—since Mann, unlike his narrator, is not someone who believes in Hans Castorp and Claudia Chauchat, and who reports that the two had an encounter at a Swiss sanatorium. This is not to deny that we are often entitled, in virtue of our more comprehensive grasp of the whole context of literary communication involved, to infer, in given cases, that the author is virtually speaking, sometimes preaching, to readers in his own person via that of the narrator. But the narrator remains, in a traditional, non-self-deconstructive novel (which includes any we have mentioned) as the immediate locus of all ostensibly direct pronouncements.

Making the narrative and essayistic portions out to have different sources in The Magic Mountain, War and Peace or Moby Dick threatens the artistic integrity of these ambitious works—they become neither fiction nor nonfiction.[49] Only if the fictional premise is in place, however transparently, throughout, is it possible to interpret such novels intelligibly and favorably, for without such an assumption, the minimal unity of voice or narrational identity necessary to construe the texts as wholes disappears.

So this attempt to establish semantic intentionalism, at least for the essayistic portions of novels, seems to me not to go through in the way Carroll suggests. And if not here, one may rightly ask, then where?

XII

Carroll's and Nathan's essays in this volume are the ones with which I find myself most in agreement; the position I favor is located somewhere in the logical space between the two. Where I disagree with Carroll is in insisting explicitly that the most defensible intentionalism is of the hypothetical or constructive variety—consider this a "leftist" version of intentionalism. Where I disagree with Nathan,[50] in contrast, is in suggesting that the most defensible anti-intentionalism—of which hypothetical intentionalism could, equally well, be seen as a "far rightist" version—must acknowledge a readerly context of textual reception considerably broader, more replete than that which Nathan is prepared to contemplate.

Nathan grants that a literary text, to be interpreted properly, must be understood to be in a language in a relatively rich sense: one tied to the usage of a particular time and place, with all connotative and associative aspects intact.[51] When the language of the text is so understood, and when one takes care to consider the complete text involved, says Nathan, one is in an adequate position to assign to such a text its best sense, including whether it is ironical or metaphorical. In this way, he claims, is vindicated "the sufficiency of public conventions of usage to resolve questions of meaning."[52]

But I think it is clear that if this rather thin notion of a text's public context suffices in some cases to allow discrimination of its literary content, there are many cases in which it will not—many cases in which confining one's projection of work meaning to what can be grounded in the text and the specific public language it is written in will not accord with what entrenched critical opinion or considered judgment would rather take this content to be.

Nathan's notion of context is simply too narrow to do the job—the job of allowing a work's full content to emerge—because it is not an *author-specific* context. Two writers writing the same texts in the same public language at a given time and place may still end up saying different things, in virtue of their national identities, what they have done in the world, what circles they belong to, what their other works are like, etc., all of which are relevantly brought to bear by potential readers, and which then qualify, in subtle ways, what the full utterance is that each writer is making in employing the text in question—in literating it, so to speak, from out of who he or she is. Nathan relatedly fails to see that specific information about an author's other works, his general stance in civic life, and so on—and not just what is given in the text or its observable manner of presentation—can serve to modify or cancel what he labels "background default assumptions"[53] for construing some stretch of discourse in the usual public language fashion.

Consider something as simple and as timely as the judgment that a given newspaper column (or story or poem) is or is not racist (sexist, ageist, anti-Semitic, etc.). It seems we do not—and properly do not—form such judgments only from the language of the text itself and its current connotative resonances. Instead, nothing is more common than to consider the gender, vintage, and ethnic identity of the author, his or her public persona, his or her track record in previous writings or in the political sphere more generally, and any peculiar beliefs or trademark opinions that have become part of the author's known worldview. What is more, such writers *expect* readers to take this into account as a background frame for assessing the force and import of what is actually said. When William Buckley writes something, it means one thing; when Richard Cohen or William Raspberry or Judy Mann or Dorothy Gilliam write the very same "thing"—and at roughly the same place and time, it can mean something else.[54] This is not to say one cannot express a view or attitude in print contrary to what might be expected for one or another of one's "identification groups" or even one's own specific past self, but this will require careful decisions as to how and what to write so as to accomplish that; at the least, an author who neglects to consider the background set of the informed reader in respect to where the author is publically "coming from," as the current phrase has it, is sure not to communicate effectively what he or she wishes to say. I should stress that though my illustration refers to journalistic writers of nonfiction, the moral clearly applies, more indirectly, to writers of literary fiction.

The following, at least, are plausibly elements in relevant author-specific interpretive contexts: the author's ancillary theoretical pronouncements; the rest of the author's corpus; the work of those of the author's contemporaries of whom he was aware; the social movements or political developments of the time that had a demonstrable impact on the author; and the author's participation in, or identification with, artistic movements. The real issue, to my mind, is not whether any of this is relevant, as a New Critic might wonder—I think it incontestably is—but what the limits of relevant author-specific contextuality are.[55] How individualized a context can an author, in his own mind, be effectively writing out of, and how extensive a grasp of such context can an author—particularly a literary one—legitimately expect of even an ideal reader? I do not have a principled answer to this, but it is where I believe future discussion should focus. Where Nathan and I would agree is that excluded from such context, at least, is any fact about the author's actual mental state or attitude during composition, in particular what I have called his semantic intentions for a text.

Nathan observes fairly that "the actual author must always intend . . . that [a work's] meaning be borne in a sufficiently public fashion that he need not personally accompany it to explain the meaning he placed there. Actual authors intend to create a work that can stand on its own, to send their work off complete, capable of being understood by its audience."[56] My response to this is a qualified affirmative: Yes, but arguably only when such audiences bear in mind the author's specific nature, oeuvre, background, intellectual breeding ground, and so on. The work, if any good, will stand on its own, without the author on hand to explain regularly what he meant, but only if taken as the work of that specific author, with all that entails.

Literary meaning is generated out of knowledge shared between an author and his or her readers, but there is no reason to take it that the author must rely on communicating only on the basis of shared knowledge of the world and language generally, rather than the author's "own," more individualized, world and language, which an ideal reader will apprise himself of, to an appropriate extent. This need not—and more, must not—require of the reader "inside" knowledge, for example, that which may be in the possession only of family members, private secretaries, and clairvoyants—as much as publically accessible knowledge of the author's distinctive cultural identity and situation. For that, in part, is what enables the creation and communication of aesthetic vehicles with richer, more finely nuanced contents than if we preclude any possibility of readers coming to authors with more than common knowledge of world and language in their interpretive kits. Why should authors be forced to present themselves on the literary stage only as Everymen, stripped of their individual identities and pasts behind a kind of critical "veil of ignorance"? Why should we accept only the more etiolated or generalized contents their writings will attain if we insist in taking them in that way?

XIII

A few thoughts, finally, concerning allusion, of which Göran Hermerén has provided an admirable analysis in his essay.[57] As Hermerén quite sensibly submits, to allude is to perform an action, actions are performed by agents, and so the existence and identity of an allusion, a sophisticated action of referring, would seem to be bound up with a concrete intention on some agent's part.[58] Thus, if there are allusions in a work of literature, and if these are part of its meaning in a broad sense, then meaning will apparently depend directly, in part, on certain (semantic) intentions of the author.

The phenomenon of allusion clearly poses about the hardest case for any kind of thoroughgoing nonintentionalism regarding the meaning of literary works. And since, viewed from one angle—Carroll's and Iseminger's, rather than Nathan's—that is what I am defending, some accommodation with allusion, if possible, is in order.

I think if we distinguish between (1) allusion as a property of an author or an author's act in creating a work and (2) allusion as a property of a work, then there is at least one sense of the latter that is not dependent on or tied to the former—that is, the actual author's act of alluding—but only to a reasonably projected such act, whether or not realized in actuality. What I am suggesting is that work allusion (as opposed to artist allusion) can be understood to operate contextually—where the notion of context is a highly artist-specific one—and as not requiring an artist's will or knowledge to secure the reference involved.

The allusive reference of one work to another can be seen as independent, if not of the concrete context in which the work is generated and put forward, at least of the actual act of referring, if any there be, on the artist's part. And that is where the work is, taken in context, *most reasonably construed* to have been a vehicle of allusion on the creator's part.

Consider a title of a work that would be taken as a manifest allusion, given full knowledge of author and style, yet was not so intended or thought of by author. I think we might say the work alludes to this earlier thing even if the author was not alluding in so titling it, because that is a defensible projection of intent on the author by an appropriately informed audience. Clearly, in any event, such a work will be construed by the most well-informed of auditors—in fact, particularly by them—as if the author were alluding, in the robust sense. So it seems not inapt to label this aspect of a work, which such readers would be responding to, its allusiveness.

A concrete example: One section in Bruce Duffy's recent remarkable novel *The World as I Found It*,[59] about the lives, ideas, and interactions, romanticized to be sure, of Ludwig Wittgenstein, Bertrand Russell, and G. E. Moore, carries the heading "A Modest Proposal." The section deals with Russell's mental preparations for, and actual propositioning of, a beautiful young Belgian teacher who has just come to work at the school he has set up in the English countryside, and follows directly a section whose focus is the destructive antics of a misfit of a pupil recently deposited at the school, whom Russell and his wife are at wit's end to get rid of. Thus, given such an internal context, and assuming in addition an Irish extraction for the author, it seems unavoidable that the heading in question be taken as an allusion to Swift's famous essay on the potato famine in Ireland and the naturalness of ameliorating it by consuming and hence doing away with excess children. As such, the heading neatly ties together the two sections in question, describing with a touch of litotes the substance of the section to which it is affixed, just as, in its allusive aspect, it makes explicit the sort of drastic solution to the problem of unwanted urchins that it is hinted Russell in his extremity may have been driven to contemplate, if only idly.

The point to make now is that we would still insist on retaining the attribution of allusion or allusiveness, on some level, even if it were determined that Duffy himself was, improbably, ignorant of Swift's essay and had come up with his section heading only as a chiding label for Russell's rather immodest priapic ambitions—and thus that he, Duffy, was not literally alluding to Swift at all. And that is because we would still have every reason, as competent readers, to attribute such an intention and action to Duffy, given the internal evidence of his novel and the external evidence of his public position as an educated, twentieth-century Anglophone author.

XIV

Throughout this essay, one of my leading concerns has been the issue of the potential gap between (1) what an author intended to convey in writing his or her text and (2) an ideal reader's best construction or hypothesis of that intention, given ample knowledge of the author's and text's relevantly engaged diachronic and synchronic context. The gap narrows to zero if we take it that (2) in effect constitutes (1), just as warranted assertibility, according to some philosophers, is equivalent to or substitutable for truth. But I resist such a vanishing of the gap because what we would most reasonably ascribe, even with all relevant knowledge as intended readers in hand, may not be what is the case, in matters of psychology and semantics—or in any others.[60]

Note that even on a neo-Wittgensteinian view of intention such as Lyas and Carroll favor, it is possible for actual intention, and best hypothetical intention from the point of view of an ideal reader, to diverge, even leaving such factors as authorial incompetence or misguidedness, usually invoked in this connection, to one side. In such instances as I have in mind an author's actual intention would be embedded in the world, but in aspects of the complete situation of the author's life and activity not open to an appropriate reader for the work and thus playing no proper part in the reader's imputation of a best semantic intention for the author in regard to the given text.

Thus, we arrive at neither intentionalism nor anti-intentionalism, but at the form of nonintentionalism I call hypothetical intentionalism. Anti-intentionalism is right in thinking actual intention is not strictly determinative or criterial of a work's basic meaning, but intentionalism is right, first, insofar as our notion of the meaning of an artwork is one that makes essential reference to the artist's intentions, as plausibly projectible by an informed audience, and second, insofar as, in many instances ("successful ones"), artistic meaning and author's actual concrete intent happily coincide.

Knapp and Michaels have thrown down as a slogan that "there is no intentionless meaning".[61] I would concur, where literature is concerned, but not for the extreme intentionalist reasons they offer. Instead, it is because for something to be a literary work, rather than a set of meaningless shapes or even an abstract word sequence in a concrete language, is for it to be intended for a kind of reception whose character is given by the tradition and history of literating—for it to be created and conceived with such possible reception in mind. But the indissolubility of literature from categorial intentions of that kind does not entail that there is and can be no meaning in a literary work other than what the author in fact intended it to mean. We are in the last analysis entitled and empowered to rationally reconstruct an author as meaning, in a work, something different from what he or she did, in private and in truth, mean, as long as we have put ourselves in the best position for receiving the utterance of this particular, historically and culturally embedded, author.

NOTES

1. My view on these matters derives, in large part, from the theory of interpretation sketched by William Tolhurst, "On What a Text Is and How It Means," *British Journal of Aesthetics* 19 (1979), though I suggest refinements to, and extensions of, what he there proposes. In addition, the view I favor resonates with that found in Alexander Nehamas, "The Postulated Author: Critical Monism as a Regulative Ideal," *Critical Inquiry* 8 (1981)—at least on one reading of that essay.

2. The distinction of word-sequence meaning, utterer's meaning, and utterance meaning is clearly set out in Tolhurst, "On What a Text Is." It is also usefully reviewed in Jack Meiland, "The Meanings of a Text," *British Journal of Aesthetics* 21 (1981).

3. From the Latin for "play" or "game."

4. Or several working in tandem, as with coauthored works.

5. Arthur Danto, "Deep Interpretation," *Journal of Philosophy* 78 (1987).

6. Tolhurst, "On What a Text Is," p. 11. I previously favorably invoked Tolhurst's ideas on literary interpretation in "Artworks and the Future," reprinted in Jerrold Levinson, *Music, Art, and Metaphysics* (Ithaca, N.Y.: Cornell University Press, 1990).

7. Tolhurst, "On What a Text Is," p. 13; emphasis added.

8. As we see later, this is really the crux of the issue as I conceive it: what is the scope of specific author-based contextual factors in the genesis of a literary work that are legitimately appealed to in constructing our best hypothesis of intended meaning? The answer to this, I suggest, lies somewhere between narrowing such scope, on the one hand, to nothing more than the language and century of composition, and widening it, on the other hand, so far as to encompass the expressed intentions of the author to mean such and such as recorded in external sources (e.g., private diaries, taped interviews). As players in the literary language game, readers are expected and entitled to take into account much more than the former, while stopping short of the latter. The question is where exactly, along this continuum, to stop.

9. Tying literary meaning to successfully realized authorial intent is central to Annette Barnes's theory of interpretation in her book *On Interpretation* (Oxford: Basil Blackwell, 1988). I think such a strategy is problematic because there is no way of cashing out what such success amounts to without an independent notion of what a work means or when it is being correctly understood.

10. Daniel O. Nathan, "Irony and the Artist's Intentions," *British Journal of Aesthetics* 23 (1982).

11. Ibid., p. 248.

12. It is almost, but not quite, the case that the utterance meaning of Private

Epistle is equatable with the utterer's meaning of its predecessor, Open Letter. Although the student undoubtedly had the ironic content in mind while penning Open Letter, she does not intend to convey that to her aimed-at audience—that is, Dr. Bushwacker.

13. Ibid., p. 250.

14. The note of sympathy here with Fish's notion of interpretive communities is intended but does not extend so far as to embrace the idea that it is the evolving consensus of such communities that fixes, through preferred strategies of interpretation, the meanings of works. Instead, such communities serve only to embody and exemplify the kinds of background assumptions and knowledge relevant to attempting to ascertain literary meanings generally.

15. The degree of knowledge, however, is not expected to be the same between authors and readers. Obviously, in most cases, an author will be in "possession" of his own oeuvre, tradition, and public persona to a much higher degree than the average well-disposed appropriate reader.

16. The substance of this interpretation owes to Walter Sokel, Franz Kafka (New York: Columbia University Press, 1966).

17. I have substituted chlorine for the argon of Hirsch's original example because the latter, being invisible, is narratively less apt.

18. See note 8.

19. I mean by this phrase to exclude such things as anachronistic meanings. An anachronistic meaning is one that is not just unlikely for an informed reader to attribute to a given author, it is one the author could not, in a strong sense, have meant. I mean to suggest also a stronger condition, namely, that such meanings, though unintended, would not be ones that would clearly be repudiated by the author of a text whose primary meaning is such as we have justifiably projected in context.

20. Hirsch's attempt to address this problem by appeal to the notion of an intentional horizon is in the spirit of this second strategy.

21. I proposed such a strategy in "Artworks and the Future," as a way of dealing with the possible oedipal content of Hamlet from a Freudian perspective, despite the impossibility of Shakespeare's assuming any such point of view.

22. The idea behind this discussion, of course, can be traced at least to Northrop Frye's notion of the "radical of presentation." A later development of the importance of genre or kind classifications in understanding art is Kendall Walton's well-known "Categories of Art," Philosophical Review 79 (1970).

23. See Chapter 8.

24. I am granting that they must have embodiment somewhere in the total situation but am prepared to say that in some cases this may be only in an author's

behavioral dispositions to respond to queries, or perhaps even only in the obtaining of certain states in the author's head.

25. Support for this view of categorial intentions can be found in remarks of Richard Wollheim on the artist's work in his "Minimal Art," *Arts Magazine*, January 1965; and in Timothy Binkley, "Piece: Contra Aesthetics," *Journal of Aesthetics and Art Criticism* 35 (1977). See also my "Defining Art Historically" and "Refining Art Historically," in Levinson, *Music, Art, and Metaphysics*.

26. Chapter 8, p. 145.

27. And not, I might add, because the ghost-scanner has detected some private episode—an option that Wittgensteinians would scare one into thinking was the only alternative here.

28. See Chapter 6.

29. If there is, as in the present instance, a clear most-plausibly-ascribed-by-the-contextually-informed authorial semantic intention, then the true interpretive claim is one that accords with that (e.g., 1A). If there is not such, then the true interpretive claim is one that denies the preceding (or any univocal) ascription of content (e.g., 1B).

30. Iseminger seems to me to cloud these waters a bit when, in discussing the employment of a given sentence-type to say varying things, he states that "where a given type can be used to say more than one thing, *which one . . . among the possibilities it is being used to say* [my emphasis] on a given occasion is a function of . . . the *intention of the user*" (p. 86). The problem is that the phrase in italics is equivocal between "what is attempting to be said (by the speaker)" and "what ends up being said (by the speaker)," that is, between utterer's meaning and utterance meaning. The former is clearly a function of user's intention, but the latter may be only a function of intention reasonably projected on the user by a hearer sensitive to the relevant full context.

31. See Chapter 6, p. 92.

32. For more on this conception, see "What a Musical Work Is," "Autographic and Allographic Art Revisited," and "Titles," in Levinson, *Music, Art, and Metaphysics*.

33. Of course I have in mind here Borges's much-discussed "Pierre Menard, Author of the Quixote," in which the seventeenth-century Spaniard Cervantes and the nineteenth-century Frenchman Menard end up producing distinct literary works that are, however, identical in text.

34. See the essays cited in note 32 for support of this point.

35. See "Intention and Interpretation: Hirsch and Margolis," Chapter 9 in this volume.

36. This thesis is amply defended by Barnes in *On Interpretation*.

37. Iseminger's (1B), of course, is an interpretive statement of this kind, but its truth or falsity is not as patent as that of my examples.

38. See Chapter 7.

39. See Chapter 10, where the point is made in the course of a critique of Knapp and Michaels.

40. Ibid., pp. 169–70.

41. By contrast, one recent influential continental view of interpretation, Jauss's Reception theory, seems on my limited knowledge of it to aim at the kind of balance between author and reader that hypothetical intentionalism represents.

42. See Chapter 7, p. 101.

43. This is not, as I have cautioned earlier (note 27), to deny that such intentions must be embodied somewhere in the physical situation of the author and his lived world, but only to insist that they may in some (unfortunate) cases be embodied in ways that are not open to discovery even by appropriate readers of the publically available work.

44. See Chapter 7, pp. 119–20; emphases added.

45. Carroll comes closest to displaying his intentionalism as really of the hypothetical type defended in this essay, in his note 46, with which I find nothing to disagree.

46. See Chapter 7, p. 111.

47. Ibid.; emphasis added.

48. Ibid., p. 107.

49. And not, I might add, in the less problematic way of the "New Journalism" narratives of Capote, Mailer, or Wolfe.

50. See Chapter 11.

51. Nathan also appeals to observable utterance features, e.g., gesture, tone of voice, for their role in giving sense to otherwise less determinate utterances, but there cannot be, on his account, anything analogous to this with written texts, whose conditions of actual emission are not part of the public face of literature, but are instead closed to view in the author's study. See ibid.

52. Ibid., p. 184.

53. For example, widely known facts about the world, such as that alligators do not standardly wear shoes, which help to make a statement like "we sell alligator shoes" unambiguous in meaning. See ibid, p. 194.

54. These are columnists, some of them nationally syndicated, who appear regularly in the *Washington Post*. Their public identities are, respectively and minimally: WASP male conservative; Jewish male liberal; black male moderate; white female liberal; black female liberal.

55. See note 8.

56. See Chapter 11, p. 198.

57. See Chapter 12.

58. I am leaving out many complexities and qualifications in Hermerén's review of the topic. Here, though, is a relatively concise statement of what Hermerén apparently would endorse: "To say that an artist or writer alludes to another work of art in one of his own works is to say or imply that he intends those who look at his work to recall the other work and therefore creates his work with features reminiscent of the other work; and because his work has these features, beholders will . . . come to think of the earlier work; furthermore, they will recognize that this is what the artist, among other things, wanted them to do." Ibid., p. 212.

59. Bruce Duffy, *The World as I Found It* (New York: Ticknor & Fields, 1987).

60. Once again, "all interpretation-relevant knowledge" cannot go so far as to include the author's actual meaning intent, or else (2) always would coincide with (1).

61. See Chapter 4.

Bibliography

THIS BIBLIOGRAPHY IS NOT RESTRICTED to works cited in the essays in this volume. It aims to include also the main writings by Anglo-American philosophers since the appearance of E. D. Hirsch, Jr., *Validity in Interpretation* (1967), on the topic of the relations between authorial intention and critical interpretation, along with selected writings on this topic by literary critics and by philosophers in the continental tradition, and selected writings in metaphysics, the philosophy of mind, and the philosophy of language that bear directly on it.

Aagaard-Mogensen, Lars, and Luk De Vos. *Text, Literature, and Aesthetics: In Honor of Monroe C. Beardsley.* Amsterdam: Rodopi, 1986.

Abbott, Claude Colleer, ed. *The Letters of Gerard Manley Hopkins to Robert Bridges.* London: Oxford University Press, 1935.

Aiken, Henry. "The Aesthetic Relevance of Artists' Intentions." *Journal of Philosophy* 52 (1955).

Alexander, Thomas M. *John Dewey's Theory of Art, Experience, and Nature: The Horizons of Feeling.* Albany: State University of New York, 1987.

Anscombe, G.E.M. *Intention.* Oxford: Blackwell, 1959; Ithaca, N.Y.: Cornell University Press, 1963.

Armstrong, Paul. "The Conflict of Interpretations and the Limits of Pluralism." *Proceedings of the Modern Language Association* 98 (1983).

——. "The Multiple Existence of a Literary Work." *Journal of Aesthetics and Art Criticism* 44 (1986).

Austin, J. L. *How to Do Things with Words.* Oxford: Oxford University Press, 1962.

Bagwell, J. Timothy. *American Formalism and the Problem of Interpretation.* Houston: Rice University Press, 1986.

Barnes, Annette. "Half an Hour before Breakfast." *Journal of Aesthetics and Art Criticism* 34 (1976).

——. "Is There a Doctrine to This Landscape?" *Journal of Aesthetic Education* 23 (1989).

————. *On Interpretation*. Oxford: Basil Blackwell, 1988.

Barthes, Roland. "The Death of the Author." In Roland Barthes, *Image–Music–Text*. New York: Hill and Wang, 1977.

————. *The Pleasures of the Text*. New York: Hill and Wang, 1975.

————. "From Work to Text." In *Textual Strategies: Perspectives in Post-Structuralist Criticism*, edited by Josue V. Harari. Ithaca, N.Y.: Cornell University Press, 1979.

Bateson, F. W. *English Poetry: A Critical Introduction*. London: Longmans, Green, 1950.

Beardsley, Monroe C. "An Aesthetic Definition of Art." In *What Is Art?* edited by Hugh Curtler. New York: Haven, 1984.

————. *Aesthetics*. New York: Harcourt, Brace and World, 1958.

————. "Fiction as Representation." *Synthese* 46 (1981).

————. "Intending." In *Values and Morals*, edited by Alvin I. Goldman and Jaegwon Kim. Dordrecht: Reidel, 1978.

————. "Intentions and Interpretations: A Fallacy Revived." In *The Aesthetic Point of View*, edited by Michael J. Wreen and Donald M. Callen. Ithaca, N.Y.: Cornell University Press, 1982.

————. "The Limits of Critical Interpretation." In *Art and Philosophy*, edited by Sidney Hook. New York: New York University Press, 1966.

————. "On the Creation of Art." In *Aesthetic Inquiry*, edited by Monroe C. Beardsley and Herbert M. Schueller. Belmont, Calif.: Dickenson, 1967.

————. "The Philosophy of Literature." In *Aesthetics: A Critical Anthology*, edited by George Dickie and Richard J. Sclafani. New York: St. Martin's Press, 1977.

————. *The Possibility of Criticism*. Detroit: Wayne State University Press, 1970.

Bernstein, Richard. "Pragmatism, Pluralism, and the Healing of Wounds." *Proceedings and Addresses of the American Philosophical Association* 63 (1989).

Binkley, Timothy. "Piece: Contra Aesthetics." *Journal of Aesthetics and Art Criticism* 35 (1977).

Black, Max. "How Metaphors Work: A Reply to Donald Davidson." In *On Metaphor*, edited by Sheldon Sacks. Chicago: University of Chicago Press, 1979.

Bloom, Harold. *A Map of Misreading*. New York: Oxford University Press, 1975.

Booth, Wayne. "Metaphor as Rhetoric." In *On Metaphor*, edited by Sheldon Sacks. Chicago: University of Chicago Press, 1979.

————. *The Rhetoric of Fiction*. Chicago: University of Chicago Press, 1961.

Brooks, Cleanth. "Irony as a Principle of Structure." In *Literary Opinion in America*, edited by M. D. Zabel. 2d ed. New York: Harper, 1951.

————. "Literary Criticism: Marvell's 'Horatian Ode.'" In *Explication as Criticism*, edited by W. K. Wimsatt, Jr. New York: Columbia University Press, 1963.

Butler, Christopher. "Saving the Reader." In *Future Literary Theory*, edited by Ralph Cohen. New York: Routledge, 1989.

Carroll, Lewis. *The Annotated Alice*, edited by Martin Gardner. Cleveland and New York: The World Publishing Company, 1963.

———. *Through the Looking Glass.* In *The Complete Works of Lewis Carroll.* New York: Vintage, 1976.

Carroll, Noël. "Trois propositions pour une critique de la danse contemporaine." In *La Danse au defi*, edited by Michele Febvre. Montreal: Editions Parachute, 1987.

Cascardi, Anthony, ed. *Literature and the Question of Philosophy.* Baltimore: Johns Hopkins University Press, 1987.

Casey, John. *The Language of Criticism.* London: Methuen, 1966.

Cassirer, Ernst. *The Philosophy of Symbolic Forms.* Vol. 1, *Language*, trans. Ralph Manheim. New Haven: Yale University Press, 1953.

Cavell, Stanley. "Aesthetic Problems of Modern Philosophy." In Stanley Cavell, *Must We Mean What We Say?* New York: Scribner's, 1969; Cambridge: Cambridge University Press, 1976.

———. "A Matter of Meaning It." In Cavell, *Must We Mean What We Say?*

———. "Music Discomposed." In Cavell, *Must We Mean What We Say?*

Child, Arthur. *Interpretation: A General Theory.* Berkeley: University of California Press, 1965.

Cioffi, Frank. "Intention and Interpretation in Criticism." *Proceedings of the Aristotelian Society* 64 (1963–64).

Close, A. J. "Don Quixote and the 'Intentionalist Fallacy.'" In *On Literary Intention: Critical Essays*, edited by David Newton-de Molina. Edinburgh: Edinburgh University Press, 1976.

Connolly, John M. "Gadamer and the Author's Authority: A Language-Game Approach." *Journal of Aesthetics and Art Criticism* 44 (1986).

Cross, Wilbur. "Machine Miltons." *New York Times Magazine*, December 4, 1966.

Culler, Jonathan. "Issues in Contemporary American Critical Debate." In *American Criticism in the Post-Structuralist Age*, edited by Ira Konigsberg. Ann Arbor: University of Michigan Press, 1981.

———. *Structuralist Poetics.* Ithaca, N.Y.: Cornell University Press, 1975.

Dannebertg, Lutz, and Hans-Harald Muller. "On Justifying the Choice of Interpretive Theories." *Journal of Aesthetics and Art Criticism* 43 (1984).

Danto, Arthur. "Deep Interpretation." *Journal of Philosophy* 78 (1987).

———. *The Transfiguration of the Commonplace.* Cambridge, Mass.: Harvard University Press, 1981.

Dauenhauer, Bernard. "Authors, Audiences, and Texts." *Human Studies* 5 (1982).

Davidson, Donald. "A Nice Derangement of Epitaphs." In *Truth and Interpretation*, edited by E. Lepore. Oxford: Blackwell, 1986.

———. "Truth and Meaning." *Synthese* 17 (1967).

———. "What Metaphors Mean." In *Inquiries into Truth and Interpretation*. Oxford: Blackwell, 1984.

Davies, Stephen. "True Interpretation." *Philosophy and Literature* 12 (1988).

Davis, Walter A. *The Act of Interpretation: A Critique of Literary Reason*. Chicago: University of Chicago Press, 1978.

Dennett, Daniel. *Elbow Room*. Cambridge, Mass.: MIT Press, 1984.

Derrida, Jacques. "Signature Event Context." *Glyph* 1 (1977): 172–97.

Dewey, John. *Art as Experience*. Carbondale, Ill.: Southern Illinois University Press, 1987.

———. "The Development of American Pragmatism." In *Pragmatism: The Classical Writings*, edited by H. S. Thayer. Indianapolis: Bobbs-Merrill, 1982.

———. "The Practical Character of Reality." In *Pragmatism: The Classical Writings*, edited by H. S. Thayer. Indianapolis: Bobbs-Merrill, 1982.

Dickie, George. *Aesthetics: An Introduction*. Indianapolis: Pegasus, 1971.

———. "Meaning and Intention." *Genre* 1 (1968).

———. Review of E. D. Hirsch, Jr., *Validity in Interpretation*. *Journal of Aesthetics and Art Criticism* 26 (1968).

Dutton, Denis. "Plausibility and Aesthetic Interpretation." *Canadian Journal of Philosophy* 7 (1977).

———. "Why Intentionalism Won't Go Away." In *Literature and the Question of Philosophy*, edited by Anthony Cascardi. Baltimore: Johns Hopkins University Press, 1987.

Eaton, Marcia. "Good and Correct Interpretations of Literature." *Journal of Aesthetics and Art Criticism* 29 (1970–71).

———. "The Truth Value of Literary Statements." *British Journal of Aesthetics* 12 (1972).

Eco, Umberto. *The Open Work*. Cambridge, Mass.: Harvard University Press, 1989.

Eldridge, Richard. "Deconstruction and Its Alternatives." *Man and World* 18 (1985).

Eliot, T. S. *On Poetry and Poets*. New York: Farrar, Straus and Cudahy, 1957.

———. "Tradition and the Individual Talent." In *Twentieth-Century Literary Theory*, edited by Vassilis Lambropoulos and David Neal Miller. Albany: State University of New York Press, 1987.

Ellis, John M. *The Theory of Literary Criticism: A Logical Analysis*. Berkeley: University of California Press, 1974.

———. "What Does It Mean to Say That All Interpretation Is Misinterpretation?" *Revue Internationale de Philosophie* 41 (1987).

Empson, William. *Seven Types of Ambiguity*. New York: Meridian, 1955.

Evans, Gareth. "Can There Be Vague Objects?" *Analysis* 38 (1978).

———. *The Varieties of Reference*. New York: Oxford University Press; Oxford: Clarendon, 1982.

Feagin, Susan L. "Incompatible Interpretations of Art." *Philosophy and Literature* 6 (1982).

———. "On Defining and Interpreting Art Intentionalistically." *British Journal of Aesthetics* 22 (1982).

Feyerabend, Paul. *Against Method*. London: NLB; Atlantic Highlands, N.J.: Humanities Press, 1975.

Fish, Stanley. "Change." *South Atlantic Quarterly* 86 (1987).

———. *Is There a Text in This Class?* Cambridge, Mass.: Harvard University Press, 1980.

———. "No Bias, No Merit: The Case Against Blind Submission." *Proceedings of the Modern Language Association* 103 (1988).

———. "Profession Despise Thyself: Fear and Self-Loathing in Literary Studies." *Critical Inquiry* 10 (1983).

———. "Working on the Chain Gang: Interpretation in the Law and in Literary Criticism." *Critical Inquiry* 9 (1982).

Fodor, J. A., and J. J. Katz. *The Structure of Language*. Englewood Cliffs, N.J.: Prentice Hall, 1964.

Foucault, Michel. "What Is an Author?" In *The Foucault Reader*, edited by Paul Rabinow and translated by Josue V. Harari. New York: Pantheon, 1984.

Gadamer, Hans-Georg. *Truth and Method*. New York: Continuum, 1975.

Gass, William. *On Being Blue: A Philosophical Inquiry*. Boston: Godine, 1976.

Geiger, Don. *The Dramatic Impulse in Modern Poetics*. Baton Rouge: Louisiana State University Press, 1967.

Graff, Gerald. *Professing Literature: An Institutional History*. Chicago: University of Chicago Press, 1987.

Grice, H. P. "Meaning." *Philosophical Review* 66 (1957).

———. *Studies in the Way of Words*. Cambridge, Mass.: Harvard University Press, 1989.

———. "Utterer's Meaning and Intentions." *Philosophical Review* 78 (1969).

———. "Utterer's Meaning, Sentence-Meaning, and Word-Meaning." *Foundations of Language* 4 (1968).

Hampshire, Stuart. "Types of Interpretation." In *Art and Philosophy*, edited by Sidney Hook. New York: New York University Press, 1966.

Hancher, Michael. "Humpty Dumpty and Verbal Meaning." *Journal of Aesthetics and Art Criticism* 40 (1981).

———. "Three Kinds of Intention." *Modern Language Notes* 87 (1972).

Hare, R. M. *Moral Thinking*. Oxford: Clarendon Press, 1981.

Harman, Gilbert. "Moral Relativism Defended." *Philosophical Review* 84 (1975).

Harris, Wendell V. *Interpretive Acts: In Search of Meaning*. Oxford: Oxford University Press, 1988.

Heath, James M., and Michael Payne, eds. *Text, Interpretation, Theory*. Vol. 29 of *Bucknell Review*, 1981.

Heidegger, Martin. *Unterwegs zur Sprache*. Pfullingen: Neske, 1959.

Hempel, Carl. *Aspects of Scientific Explanation*. New York: Free Press, 1965.

Henze, Donald. "Is the Work of Art a Construct?" *Journal of Philosophy* 52 (1955).

———. "The Work of Art." *Journal of Philosophy* 54 (1957).

Hermerén, Göran. *Influence in Art and Literature*. Princeton: Princeton University Press, 1975.

———. "Intention and Interpretation in Literary Criticism." *New Literary History* 7 (1975–76).

———. "Interpretation: Types and Criteria." *Grazer Philosophische Studien* 19 (1983).

———. "Standards of Interpretation." *Proceedings of the Sixth International Congress of Aesthetics*. Uppsala, Sweden, 1972.

Hernadi, Paul, ed. *What Is Criticism?* Bloomington: Indiana University Press, 1981.

Hirsch, E. D., Jr. *The Aims of Interpretation*. Chicago: University of Chicago Press, 1976.

———. "On Justifying Interpretive Norms." *Journal of Aesthetics and Art Criticism* 43 (1984).

———. *Validity in Interpretation*. New Haven: Yale University Press, 1967.

Hoberman, J. "Bad Movies." *Film Comment*, July–August 1980.

———. "Vulgar Modernism." *Artforum*, February 1982.

Hofstader, Albert. "On the Interpretation of Works of Art." In *The Concept of Style*, edited by Berel Lang. Philadelphia: University of Pennsylvania Press, 1979.

Hough, Graham. "An Eighth Type of Ambiguity." In *On Literary Intention: Critical Essays*, edited by David Newton-de Molina. Edinburgh: Edinburgh University Press, 1976.

Hoy, David Cozzens. *The Critical Circle: Literature, History, and Philosophical Hermeneutics*. Berkeley: University of California Press, 1978.

Hume, David. *A Treatise of Human Nature*. London: Dent, 1911.

Hungerland, I. C. "The Concept of Intention in Art Criticism." *Journal of Philosophy* 52 (1955).

Hynes, Samuel. "Whitman, Pound, and the Prose Tradition." In *The Presence of Walt Whitman*, English Institute Papers, edited by R.W.B. Lewis. New York: Columbia University Press, 1962.

Ingarden, Roman. *The Cognition of the Literary Work of Art*. Evanston, Ill.: Northwestern University Press, 1973.

———. *The Literary Work of Art*. Evanston, Ill.: Northwestern University Press, 1973.

Iseminger, Gary. "Constituting the Aesthetic Object." *Studia Estetyczne*, forthcoming.

————. "A Revised Identity Thesis." In *Text, Literature, and Aesthetics: In Honour of Monroe C. Beardsley*, edited by Lars Aagaard-Mogensen and Luk De Vos. Amsterdam: Rodopi, 1986.

————. "Roman Ingarden and the Aesthetic Object." *Philosophy and Phenomenological Research*, 33 (1973).

Isenberg, Arnold. "Some Problems of Interpretation." In *Aesthetics and the Theory of Criticism: Selected Essays of Arnold Isenberg*, edited by William Callaghan et al. Chicago: University of Chicago Press, 1973.

Iser, Wolfgang. *The Implied Reader*. Baltimore: Johns Hopkins University Press, 1974.

James, William. *Pragmatism and Other Essays*. New York: Simon and Schuster, 1963.

————. *The Principles of Psychology*. New York: Dover, 1950.

Jarvie, I. C. "The Objectivity of Criticism in the Arts." *Ratio* 9 (1967).

————. "Understanding and Explanation in Sociology and Social Anthropology." In *Explanation in the Behavioural Sciences*, edited by Robert Borger and Frank Cioffi. Cambridge: Cambridge University Press, 1970.

Jones, Peter. *Philosophy and the Novel*. Oxford: Oxford University Press, 1975.

Juhl, P. D. "The Appeal to the Text: What Are We Appealing To?" *Journal of Aesthetics and Art Criticism* 36 (1978).

————. *Interpretation: An Essay in the Philosophy of Literary Criticism*. Princeton: Princeton University Press, 1980.

Kemp, John. "The Work of Art and the Artist's Intentions." *British Journal of Aesthetics* 4 (1964).

Kermode, Frank. Review of Jan Kott's *Shakespeare, Our Contemporary. New York Review of Books*, September 24, 1964.

Kierkegaard, Søren. *Concluding Unscientific Postscript*. Princeton: Princeton University Press, 1941.

Kittay, Eva Feder. *Metaphor*. Oxford: Oxford University Press, 1987.

Knapp, Stephen, and Walter Benn Michaels. "Against Theory." In *Against Theory: Literary Studies and the New Pragmatism*, edited by W.J.T. Mitchell. Chicago: University of Chicago Press, 1985.

————. "Against Theory 2: Hermeneutics and Deconstruction." *Critical Inquiry* 14 (1987).

Krausz, Michael, ed. *Relativism: Interpretation and Confrontation*. Notre Dame: Notre Dame University Press, 1989.

Kripke, Saul. *Wittgenstein on Rules and Private Language*. Cambridge, Mass.: Harvard University Press, 1982.

Kuhn, Thomas. *The Structure of Scientific Revolutions*. Chicago: University of Chicago Press, 1970.

Kuhns, Richard. "Criticism and the Problem of Intention." *Journal of Philosophy* 57 (1960).

Lang, Berel. "The Intentional Fallacy Revisited." *British Journal of Aesthetics* 14 (1974).

Leavis, F. R. *The Common Pursuit*. Harmondsworth: Penguin Books, 1962.

Leddy, Thomas. "Robust Relativism Rejected." *Journal of Aesthetics and Art Criticism* 42 (1984).

Levinson, Jerrold. *Music, Art, and Metaphysics*. Ithaca, N.Y.: Cornell University Press, 1990.

———. "Philosophy as an Art." *Journal of Aesthetic Education*, forthcoming.

———. "What a Musical Work Is." *Journal of Philosophy* 77 (1980).

Littré, Emile. *Dictionaire de la langue française*. Vol. 1. Paris: Librairie de L. Hachette, 1956.

Lohner, Edgar. "The Intrinsic Method: Some Reconsiderations." In *The Disciplines of Criticism*, edited by Peter Demetz et al. New Haven: Yale University Press, 1968.

Lukes, Stephen. "Relativism: Cognitive and Moral." *Proceedings of the Aristotelian Society*, supplementary vol. 48 (1974).

Lyas, Colin. "Anything Goes: The Intentional Fallacy Revisited." *British Journal of Aesthetics* 23 (1983).

———. "Personal Qualities and the Intentional Fallacy." In *Philosophy and the Arts: Royal Institute of Philosophy Lectures*. Vol. 6. New York: St. Martin's Press, 1973.

McGinn, Colin. *Wittgenstein on Meaning*. Oxford: Blackwell, 1984.

Margalit, Avishai. "The 'Intentional Fallacy' Fallacy." *Iyyun* 27 (1976–77).

Margolis, Joseph. "Aesthetic Interests and Aesthetic Qualities." Introduction to part 1 of *Philosophy Looks at the Arts: Contemporary Readings in Aesthetics*. 3d ed. Philadelphia: Temple University Press, 1987.

———. *Art and Philosophy: Conceptual Issues in Aesthetics*. Atlantic Highlands, N.J.: Humanities Press, 1980.

———. *The Language of Art and Art Criticism*. Detroit: Wayne State University Press, 1965.

———. "Moral Cognitivism." *Ethics* 85 (1975).

———. *The New Puzzle of Interpretation*. Chicago: University of Chicago Press, 1992.

———. "Reinterpreting Interpretation." *Journal of Aesthetics and Art Criticism* 47 (1989).

———. "The Truth about Relativism." In *Relativism: Interpretation and Confrontation*, edited by Michael Krausz. Notre Dame: University of Notre Dame Press, 1989.

———. *The Truth about Relativism*. Oxford: Blackwell, 1991.

———. "Works of Art Are Physically Embodied and Culturally Emergent Entities." *British Journal of Aesthetics* 14 (1974).

Matthews, Robert J. "Describing and Interpreting Works of Art." *Journal of Aesthetics and Art Criticism* 36 (1977).

Meiland, Jack W. "Interpretation as a Cognitive Discipline." *Philosophy and Literature* 2 (1978).

——— . "The Meanings of a Text." *British Journal of Aesthetics* 21 (1981).

Mohanty, J. N. "Communication, Interpretation and Intention." *Journal of Indian Council of Philosophical Research* 2 (1984).

Morier, Henri. *Dictionaire de poetique et de rhetorique.* Paris: Press Universitaire de France, 1961.

Mothersill, Mary. *Beauty Restored.* Oxford: Oxford University Press, 1984.

Nathan, Daniel O. "Categories and Intentions." *Journal of Aesthetics and Art Criticism* 31 (1973).

——— . "Irony and the Artist's Intentions." *British Journal of Aesthetics* 23 (1982).

Nehamas, Alexander. "The Postulated Author: Critical Monism as a Regulative Ideal." *Critical Inquiry* 8 (1981).

——— . "What an Author Is." *Journal of Philosophy* 83 (1986).

Newton-de Molina, David, ed. *On Literary Intention: Critical Essays.* Edinburgh: Edinburgh University Press, 1976.

Novitz, David. "Towards a Robust Relativism." *Journal of Aesthetics and Art Criticism* 41 (1982).

Nowell-Smith, P. H. "Acts and Locutions." In *Art, Mind, and Religion,* edited by W. H. Capitan and D. D. Merrill. Pittsburgh: University of Pittsburgh Press, 1965.

Nozick, Robert. *Anarchy, State, and Utopia.* New York: Basic Books, 1974.

Ohmann, Richard. "Speech, Action and Style." In *Literary Style: A Symposium,* edited by Seymour Chatman. London: Oxford University Press, 1971.

——— . "Speech Acts and the Definition of Literature." *Philosophy and Rhetoric* 4 (1971).

Olsen, Stein Haugom. "Authorial Intention." *British Journal of Aesthetics* 13 (1973).

——— . *The End of Literary Theory.* Cambridge: Cambridge University Press, 1987.

——— . "Interpretation and Intention." *British Journal of Aesthetics* 17 (1977).

——— . *The Structure of Literary Understanding.* Cambridge: Cambridge University Press, 1978.

Palmer, Richard E. *Hermeneutics: Interpretation Theory in Schleiermacher, Dilthey, Heidegger, and Gadamer.* Evanston, Ill.: Northwestern University Press, 1969.

Pappas, Nickolas. "Authorship and Authority." *Journal of Aesthetics and Art Criticism* 47 (1989).

Peirce, Charles Sanders. "Abduction and Induction." In *The Philosophy of Peirce: Selected Writings,* edited by Justus Buchler. New York: Harcourt, Brace, 1940.

Pepper, Stephen. *The Work of Art.* Bloomington: Indiana University Press, 1955.

Perry, John Oliver. *Approaches to the Poem.* San Francisco: Chandler, 1965.

Pettersson, Torsten. "Incompatible Interpretations of Literature." *Journal of Aesthetics and Art Criticism* 45 (1986).

Pettit, Phillip. "The Possibility of Aesthetic Realism." In *Pleasure, Preference and Value*, edited by Eva Schaper. Cambridge: Cambridge University Press, 1983.

Pick, John, ed. *A Hopkins Reader*. New York: Oxford University Press, 1953.

Polanyi, Michael. *Personal Knowledge*. Chicago: University of Chicago Press, 1962.

Quine, Willard Van Orman. *From a Logical Point of View*. Cambridge, Mass.: Harvard University Press, 1953.

——— . *Word and Object*. Cambridge, Mass.: Harvard University Press, 1960.

Radford, Colin, and Sally Minogue. *The Nature of Criticism*. Brighton: Harvester Press, 1981.

Ray, William. *Literary Meaning: From Phenomenology to Deconstruction*. Oxford: Basil Blackwell, 1984.

Redpath, Theodore. "The Meaning of a Poem." In *British Philosophy in the Mid-Century*, edited by C. A. Mace. London: Macmillan, 1957.

Reichert, John. "Description and Interpretation in Literary Criticism." *Journal of Aesthetics and Art Criticism* 28 (1969).

——— . *Making Sense of Literature*. Chicago: University of Chicago Press, 1978.

Richards, I. A. *The Philosophy of Rhetoric*. 1936; reprinted, New York: Oxford University Press, 1965.

Ricoeur, Paul. *Interpretation Theory: Discourse and the Surplus of Meaning*. Fort Worth: Texas Christian University Press, 1976.

——— . "On Interpretation." In *Philosophy in France Today*, edited by Alan Montefiore. Cambridge: Cambridge University Press, 1983.

Roma, Emilio. "The Scope of the Intentional Fallacy." *The Monist* 50 (1966).

Rorty, Richard. *Consequences of Pragmatism*. Minneapolis: University of Minnesota Press, 1982.

——— . *Contingency, Irony, and Solidarity*. Cambridge: Cambridge University Press, 1989.

——— . "Philosophy without Principles." In *Against Theory: Literary Studies and the New Pragmatism*, edited by W.J.T. Mitchell. Chicago: University of Chicago Press, 1985.

——— . "Texts and Lumps." *New Literary History* 17 (1985).

Roskill, Mark. "On the Artist's Privileged Status." *Philosophy* 54 (1979).

——— . "On the 'Intention' and 'Meaning' of Works of Art." *British Journal of Aesthetics* 17 (1977).

Ross, Stephanie. "Art and Allusion." *Journal of Aesthetics and Art Criticism* 40 (1981).

Russell, Bertrand. "On Denoting." In *Readings in Philosophical Analysis*, edited by Herbert Feigl and Wilfrid Sellars. New York: Appleton-Century-Crofts, 1949.

Ryle, Gilbert. *The Concept of Mind*. New York: Barnes and Noble, 1949.

Sacks, Sheldon. *On Metaphor*. Chicago: University of Chicago Press, 1979.

Sartre, Jean-Paul. *What Is Literature?* London: Methuen, 1950.

Saville, Anthony. "The Place of Intention in the Concept of Art." *Proceedings of the Aristotelian Society* 69 (1968–69).

Schaar, Claes. *The Full Voic'd Quire Below*. Lund Studies in English No. 60. Lund: Gleerup, 1982.

Schaper, Eva. "Interpreting Art." *Proceedings of the Aristotelian Society*, supplementary vol. 56 (1981).

Schiffer, Stephen. *Meaning*. Oxford: Clarendon Press, 1972.

Scruton, Roger. *Art and Imagination*. London: Methuen, 1974.

——— . "Public Text and Common Reader." In Roger Scruton, *The Aesthetic Understanding*. London: Methuen, 1983.

Searle, John R. "The Logical Status of Fictional Discourse." *New Literary History* 6 (1974).

——— . "Metaphor." In *Metaphor and Thought*, edited by Andrew Ortony. Cambridge: Cambridge University Press, 1979.

——— . "Reiterating the Differences: A Reply to Derrida." *Glyph* 1 (1977).

——— . *Speech Acts: An Essay in the Philosophy of Language*. Cambridge: Cambridge University Press, 1969.

Sharpe, Robert A. "Interpreting Art." *Proceedings of the Aristotelian Society*, supplementary vol. 56 (1981).

Shusterman, Richard. "Analytic Aesthetics, Literary Theory, and Deconstruction." *The Monist* 69 (1986).

——— . "Analytic and Pragmatist Aesthetics." *Proceedings of the XI International Congress of Aesthetics*, forthcoming.

——— . "Croce on Interpretation: Deconstruction and Pragmatism." *New Literary History* 20 (1988).

——— . "Four Problems in Aesthetics." *International Philosophical Quarterly* 22 (1982).

——— . "Interpretation, Intention and Truth." *Journal of Aesthetics and Art Criticism* 46 (1988).

——— . "The Logic of Interpretation." *Philosophical Quarterly* 28 (1978).

——— . *The Object of Literary Criticism*. Atlantic Highlands, N.J.: Humanities Press, 1984.

——— . *Pragmatist Aesthetics: Living Beauty, Rethinking Art*. Oxford: Blackwell, 1992.

——— . *T. S. Eliot and the Philosophy of Criticism*. New York: Columbia University Press, 1988.

Sircello, Guy. "Expressive Qualities of Ordinary Language." *Mind* 76 (1967).

Sirridge, Mary. "Artistic Intention and Critical Prerogative." *British Journal of Aesthetics* 18 (1978).

Skinner, Quentin. "Motives, Intentions, and the Interpretation of Texts." *New Literary History* 7 (1975).

Smith, Barbara Herrnstein. *On the Margins of Discourse: The Relation of Literature to Language.* Chicago: University of Chicago Press, 1978.

———. "Poetry as Fiction." In *New Directions in Literary History*, edited by Ralph Cohen. Baltimore: Johns Hopkins University Press, 1974.

Smith, Barry D. "Distanciation and Textual Interpretation." *Laval Theologique et Philosophique* 43 (1987).

Sokel, Walter. *Franz Kafka.* New York: Columbia University Press, 1966.

Sparshott, F. E. *The Concept of Criticism.* Oxford: Clarendon Press, 1967.

Stern, Laurent. "Facts and Interpretation." Address to the Pacific Division meetings of the American Philosophical Association, Spring 1988.

———. "On Interpreting." *Journal of Aesthetics and Art Criticism* 39 (1980).

Stevenson, Charles L. "Interpretation and Evaluation in Aesthetics." In *Philosophical Analysis*, edited by Max Black. Ithaca, N.Y.: Cornell University Press, 1950.

———. "On the Reasons That Can Be Given for the Interpretation of a Poem." In *Philosophy Looks at the Arts*, edited by Joseph Margolis. New York: Scribner's, 1962.

Stout, Jeffrey. "The Relativity of Interpretation." *The Monist* 69 (1986).

Strawson, Peter F. "Intention and Convention in Speech Acts." *Philosophical Review* 73 (1964).

Strelka, Joseph P. *Literary Criticism and Philosophy.* University Park: Pennsylvania State University Press, 1983.

Tarski, Alfred. "The Semantic Conception of Truth and the Foundations of Semantics." *Philosophy and Phenomenological Research* 4 (1944).

Taylor, Charles. *Philosophy and the Human Sciences.* Cambridge: Cambridge University Press, 1985.

Tidestrom, Gunnar. *Ombord pa Aniara.* Stockholm: Aldus, 1975.

Tillyard, E.M.W., and C. S. Lewis. *The Personal Heresy: A Controversy.* London: Oxford University Press, 1939.

Tolhurst, William. "On What a Text Is and How It Means." *British Journal of Aesthetics* 19 (1979).

Tolhurst, William, and Samuel C. Wheeler. "On Textual Individuation." *Philosophical Studies* 35 (1979).

Tomasevskij, Boris. "Literature and Biography." In *Twentieth-Century Literary Theory*, edited by Vassilis Lambropoulos and David Neal Miller. Albany: State University Press of New York, 1987.

Trigg, Roger. *Reason and Commitment.* Cambridge: Cambridge University Press, 1973.

Wain, John, F. W. Bateson, and W. W. Robson. " 'Intention' and Blake's *Jerusalem.*" *Essays in Criticism* 2 (1952).

Walton, Kendall. "Categories of Art." *Philosophical Review* 79 (1970).

———. "Style and the Products and Processes of Art." In *The Concept of Style*, edited by Berel Lang. Philadelphia: University of Pennsylvania Press, 1979.

Watson, Stephen. "Aesthetics and the Foundation of Interpretation." *Journal of Aesthetics and Art Criticism* 45 (1986).

Wellek, Rene. *Concepts of Criticism*. New Haven: Yale University Press, 1965.

Wellek, Rene, and Austin Warren. *Theory of Literature*. New York: Harcourt, Brace, 1956.

Wheeler, Michael. *The Art of Allusion in Victorian Fiction*. New York: Barnes and Noble, 1979.

Wilsmore, S. J. "The Literary Work Is Not Its Text." *Philosophy and Literature* 11 (1987).

Wimsatt, W. K., Jr. "Genesis: A Fallacy Revisited." In *On Literary Intention*, edited by D. Newton-de Molina. Edinburgh: University of Edinburgh Press, 1976.

———. *The Verbal Icon: Studies in the Meaning of Poetry*. Lexington: University Press of Kentucky, 1954.

Wimsatt, W. K., Jr., and Monroe C. Beardsley, "Intention." In *Dictionary of World Literature*, edited by J. T. Shipley. New York: Philosophical Library, 1943.

———. "The Intentional Fallacy." *Sewanee Review* 54 (1946).

Winch, Peter. *The Idea of a Social Science*. London: Routledge and Kegan Paul, 1958.

———. "Understanding and Explanation in Sociology and Anthropology." In *Explanation in the Behavioural Sciences*, edited by Robert Borger and Frank Cioffi. Cambridge: Cambridge University Press, 1970.

Wittgenstein, Ludwig. *Lectures and Conversations on Aesthetics, Psychology, and Religious Belief*, edited by Cyril Barrett. Oxford: Blackwell, 1966.

———. *Philosophical Investigations*, New York: Macmillan, 1953.

———. *Tractatus Logico-Philosophicus*. London: Routledge and Kegan Paul, 1966.

Wollheim, Richard. "Criticism as Retrieval." In Richard Wollheim, *Art and Its Objects*. 2d ed. Cambridge: Cambridge University Press, 1980.

———. "Minimal Art." *Arts Magazine*, January 1965.

———. *Painting as an Art*. Princeton: Princeton University Press, 1987.

Wolterstorff, Nicholas. *Works and Worlds of Art*. Oxford: Clarendon, 1980.

Zemach, Eddy. "Interpretation, the Sun, and the Moon." *Revue Internationale de Philosophie*, no. 162–63 (1987).

Ziff, Paul. "On H. P. Grice's Account of Meaning." *Analysis* 28 (1967).

———. "What Is Said." In *Semantics of Natural Language*, edited by Donald Davidson and Gilbert Harman. Dordrecht: Reidel, 1972.

Notes on Contributors

The late MONROE C. BEARDSLEY taught for many years at Swarthmore College and at Temple University. His writings were of seminal importance for postwar philosophical aesthetics in the United States. His books include *Aesthetics* (1958), *Aesthetics from Classical Greece to the Present: A Short History* (1966), *The Possibility of Criticism* (1970), from which the selection in this volume is taken, and *The Aesthetic Point of View* (1982).

NOËL CARROLL teaches philosophy at the University of Wisconsin-Madison. His papers in aesthetics have appeared in the *Journal of Aesthetics and Art Criticism*, and he has recently published two books on the aesthetics of film, *Mystifying Movies* (1988) and *Philosophical Problems of Classical Film Theory* (1988), as well as *The Philosophy of Horror; or, Paradoxes of the Heart* (1990).

GÖRAN HERMERÉN teaches at Lund University, Lund, Sweden. His books include *Representation and Meaning in the Arts* (1969), *Influence in Art and Literature* (1975), *Aspects of Aesthetics* (1984), and *The Nature of Aesthetic Qualities* (1988).

E. D. HIRSCH, JR., teaches English at the University of Virginia. His books include *Validity in Interpretation* (1967), whose argument forms the basis of this book, *The Aims of Interpretation* (1976), and the widely discussed *Cultural Literacy* (1987).

GARY ISEMINGER teaches at Carleton College. His papers in aesthetics have appeared in such journals as *Analysis*, the *Journal of Aesthetics and Art Criticism*, and the *British Journal of Aesthetics*.

STEVEN KNAPP teaches English at the University of California, Berkeley. He is the author of *Personification and the Sublime: Milton to Coleridge* (1985) and, with Walter Benn Michaels, of the widely discussed title essay in the collection *Against Theory: Literary Studies and the New Pragmatism* (1985), edited by W.J.T. Mitchell, which is the basis for the selection in this volume.

MICHAEL KRAUSZ teaches at Bryn Mawr College. His articles in aesthetics have appeared in such journals as the *Journal of Aesthetics and Art Criticism*. He is editor of *The Concept of Creativity in Science and Art* (1980), coeditor, with Jack W. Meiland, of *Relativism: Cognitive and Moral* (1982), and editor of *Relativism: Interpretation and Confrontation* (1989). His book *Rightness and Reasons: Interpretation in Cultural Practices* will appear soon.

JERROLD LEVINSON teaches at the University of Maryland. He is the author of *Music, Art, and Metaphysics* (1990), and his articles in aesthetics have appeared in such journals as the *British Journal of Aesthetics*, the *Journal of Aesthetics and Art Criticism*, *Philosophical Studies*, and the *Journal of Philosophy*.

COLIN LYAS teaches at the University of Lancaster, Lancaster, England. His articles in aesthetics have appeared in such journals as *Philosophy*, the *Journal of Philosophy*, *Proceedings of the Aristotelian Society*, and the *British Journal of Aesthetics*. He has published a new translation of Benedetto Croce's *Estetica* under the title *The Aesthetic as the Science of Expression and of the Linguistic in General* (1992).

JOSEPH MARGOLIS teaches at Temple University. Among his many publications in virtually all areas of philosophy are one of the first anthologies of aesthetics in the analytic tradition, *Philosophy Looks at the Arts* (1962; revised ed., 1978; 3d ed., 1987), *The Language of Art and Art Criticism* (1965), *Art and Philosophy* (1980), from which the selection included in this volume is taken, and *The New Puzzle of Interpretation* (1992).

WALTER BENN MICHAELS teaches English at Johns Hopkins University. He is the author of *The Gold Standard and the Logic of Naturalism* (1987) and coauthor, with Steven Knapp, of the widely discussed title essay in the collection *Against Theory: Literary Studies and the New Pragmatism* (1985), edited by W.J.T. Mitchell, which is the basis for the selection in this volume.

DANIEL O. NATHAN teaches philosophy at Texas Tech University. His articles in aesthetics have appeared in such journals as the *British Journal of Aesthetics*, the *Journal of Aesthetics and Art Criticism*, and *Philosophy and Literature*.

RICHARD SHUSTERMAN teaches at Temple University. His articles in aesthetics have appeared in such journals as the *Journal of Aesthetics and Art Criticism*, the *British Journal of Aesthetics*, and the *Philosophical Quarterly*. His books include *The Object of Literary Criticism* (1984), *T. S. Eliot and the Philosophy of Criticism* (1988), and *Pragmatist Aesthetics: Living Beauty, Rethinking Art* (1992).

Index of Names